T. S. ELIOT AND
THE POETICS OF
LITERARY HISTORY

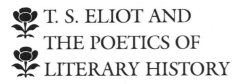

T. S. ELIOT AND THE POETICS OF LITERARY HISTORY

Gregory S. Jay

LOUISIANA STATE UNIVERSITY PRESS

BATON ROUGE AND LONDON

Copyright © 1983 by Louisiana State University Press
All rights reserved
Manufactured in the United States of America
Designer: Joanna Hill
Typeface: Linotron Galliard
Typesetter: G&S Typesetters, Inc.
Printer: Thomson-Shore
Binder: John Dekker

LIBRARY OF CONGRESS CATALOGING IN PUBLICATION DATA

Jay, Gregory S.
    T. S. Eliot and the poetics of literary history.

    Includes bibliographical references and index.
    1. Eliot, T. S. (Thomas Stearns), 1888–1965—Criticism and interpretation.
2. Poetics. 3. Poetry—History and criticism.   4. Influence (Literary,
artistic, etc.).   I. Eliot, T. S. (Thomas Stearns), 1888–1965.   II. Title.
PS3509.L43Z6848 1983   821'.912   83-748
ISBN 0-8071-1099-X

Excerpts from *Selected Essays, Murder in the Cathedral, Collected Poems: 1909–1962, Four Quartets,* and *The Waste Land: A Facsimile and Transcript of the Original Drafts*, all by T. S. Eliot, are reprinted by permission of Harcourt Brace Jovanovich, Inc.; copyright 1932, 1935, 1936, 1950, by Harcourt Brace Jovanovich, Inc.; copyright 1943, 1960, 1963, 1964, by T. S. Eliot; copyright 1971, 1978, by Esme Valerie Eliot; copyright © 1971 by Valerie Eliot. Excerpts from *The Family Reunion* are reprinted from T. S. Eliot, *The Complete Poems and Plays: 1909–1950* by permission of Harcourt Brace Jovanovich, Inc.; copyright 1934, 1935, 1936, 1952 by Harcourt Brace & World, Inc.; 1930, 1939, 1943, 1950, 1958, 1962 by T. S. Eliot; 1971 by Valerie Esme Eliot.
Acknowledgment is made to Farrar, Straus and Giroux, Inc., for permission to quote from the following books by T. S. Eliot: from *On Poetry and Poets*, copyright © 1943, 1945, 1951, 1954, 1956, 1957 by T. S. Eliot; from *To Criticize the Critic*, copyright © 1965 by Valerie Eliot; from *Knowledge and Experience in the Philosophy of F. H. Bradley*, copyright © 1964 by T. S. Eliot; from *Poems Written in Early Youth*, copyright © 1967 by Valerie Eliot. Additional acknowledgments appear on pages ix and x.

Publication of this book has been assisted by a grant from the Andrew W. Mellon Foundation.

FOR MARTHA

CONTENTS

ACKNOWLEDGMENTS

The seeds of this study were planted some six years ago during a sum-mer seminar on modernism conducted by Herbert Schneidau, whose encouragement and criticism helped guide the project in its early stages. At the State University of New York at Buffalo, Neil Schmitz acted as principal advisor and became a treasured friend. I am especially grateful to him for sharing with me his knowledge of American literature. James Bunn, Richard Fly, and Henry Sussman also contributed valuable comments on the book's first draft. Others now removed to warmer climates taught me much about critical theory, though they cannot be held responsible for the use I have made of it in the ensuing years. No one earned my appreciation more, how-ever, than Mitchell Breitwieser. His friendship during those years was a con-stant source of intellectual and personal enrichment.

At the University of Alabama, David L. Miller read the manuscript with exacting care, pointing out numerous places for improvement in style and substance. The Department of English was most supportive during the proj-ect's completion, and I want particularly to thank in this regard Claudia Johnson, Philip Beidler, and Hank Lazer. Grants and fellowships from the College of Arts and Sciences and the Office of Academic Affairs allowed me the time to finish my research and revisions. Fred Hagan, Angie Duncan, Karen Nelson, and Kathy Oviatt cheerfully aided in the preparation of the manuscript.

Joseph Riddel took the time to read a late draft and make many helpful suggestions on matters bibliographical, interpretative, and theoretical.

This book, so concerned with what we inherit from the past, is ultimately a tribute to my own family and to the values they have handed on to me. My parents, Lester and Midge Jay, and my brothers, Paul and Criss, deserve an expression of gratitude from me I scarcely know how to begin. So I offer this book in partial recompense for their love, their wit, their patience, and their faith.

Excerpts are reprinted by permission of Faber and Faber Ltd from *Collected Poems, 1909–1962* by T. S. Eliot, *Poems Written in Early Youth* by T. S. Eliot, *Murder in the Cathedral* and *The Family Reunion* by T. S. Eliot, and *Selected Essays, On Poetry and Poets, To Criticize the Critic, The Use of Philosophy and the Use of Criticism,* and *Knowledge and Experience in the Philosophy of F. H. Brad-*

ley by T. S. Eliot. Extracts from the original drafts of *The Waste Land* and from T. S. Eliot's uncollected letters are reprinted by permission of Mrs. Valerie Eliot and Faber and Faber Ltd from *The Waste Land: A Facsimile and Transcript of the Original Drafts Including the Annotations of Ezra Pound* edited by Valerie Eliot and from *The Composition of the "Four Quartets"* by Helen Gardner.

Excerpts are quoted from T. S. Eliot's notebooks in the Henry W. and Albert A. Berg Collection, New York Public Library, Astor, Lenox, and Tilden Foundations with permission of the library and Mrs. T. S. Eliot; from Michel Foucault, *The Order of Things: An Archaeology of the Human Sciences,* trans. Alan Sheridan-Smith, copyright 1970 with permission of Pantheon Books, a Division of Random House, Inc. Portions of this study were previously published as "Eliot's Poetics and the Fisher King," *Yeats/Eliot Review,* VII (June, 1982), 28–35, and "Ecstasy's Script: Emotion and Deconstruction in *Four Quartets,*" *New Orleans Review,* IX (Spring, 1982), 65–76.

A NOTE ON ABBREVIATIONS AND EDITIONS

1. Works by T. S. Eliot

There is no complete collected edition of Eliot's prose. Many important essays and reviews remain scattered and in need of compilation. Eight volumes of criticism are widely known. Citations from individual volumes are given according to the abbreviations listed below. Eliot quotations from periodicals, pamphlets, interviews, introductions, and anthologies have been footnoted. The guide to this maze is Donald Gallup's indispensable *T. S. Eliot: A Bibliography* (Rev. ed.; New York, 1969). There is no definitive edition of Eliot's poetry or plays. Minor discrepancies persist throughout all available versions. Passages from the widely circulated works thus appear without reference to edition. On the question of textual variants see A. D. Moody's appendix to his *Thomas Stearns Eliot: Poet* (Cambridge, England, 1979) and Helen Gardner's *The Composition of "Four Quartets"* (New York, 1978). Excerpts from the published manuscripts of *The Waste Land* are cited by the abbreviation given below. Quotations from *Four Quartets* are cited according to the abbreviations for the individual poems given below.

ASG *After Strange Gods: A Primer of Modern Heresy.* London, 1934.
BN "Burnt Norton."
CC *To Criticize the Critic.* New York, 1965.
DS "The Dry Salvages."
EC "East Coker."
ICS "The Idea of a Christian Society." In *Christianity and Culture.* New York, 1968.
KE *Knowledge and Experience in the Philosophy of F. H. Bradley.* New York, 1964.
LG "Little Gidding."
OPP *On Poetry and Poets.* New York, 1961.
PWY *Poems Written in Early Youth.* New York, 1967.
SE *Selected Essays.* New edition. New York, 1950.
SP *Selected Prose of T. S. Eliot.* Edited by Frank Kermode. New York, 1975.
SW *The Sacred Wood.* London, 1960.
UPUC *The Use of Poetry and the Use of Criticism.* London, 1964.
WLFS *The Waste Land: A Facsimile and Transcript of the Original Drafts.* Edited by Valerie Eliot. New York, 1971.

2.   Other Frequent Citations

All quotations from the writings of Sigmund Freud refer to *The Standard Edition of the Complete Psychological Works* (24 vols.; London, 1953–74), abbreviated as *Works* in the footnotes and followed by volume and page numbers. Quotations from the works of Dante, Milton, Shelley, Tennyson, and Whitman are taken from the following editions and appear unannotated in this study with the exception of lengthy prose excerpts or editorial commentary.

Dante. *The Divine Comedy*. Translated, with commentary, by Charles S. Singleton. 6 vols. Princeton, 1977.

Milton, John. *Milton's Complete Poetry and Prose*. Edited by Merrit Y. Hughes. New York, 1957.

Shelley, Percy Bysshe. *Shelley's Poetry and Prose*. Edited by Donald H. Reiman and Sharon B. Powers. New York, 1977.

Tennyson, Alfred. *Tennyson's Poetry*. Edited by Robert W. Hill, Jr. New York, 1971.

Whitman, Walt. *Leaves of Grass*. Edited by Sculley Bradley and Harold W. Blodgett, New York, 1973.

T. S. ELIOT AND
THE POETICS OF
LITERARY HISTORY

OPENING FIGURES

The Naming of Cats is a difficult matter,
  It isn't just one of your holiday games;
You may think at first I'm as mad as a hatter
When I tell you, a cat must have THREE DIFFERENT NAMES . . .

But above and beyond there's still one name left over,
  And that is the name that you never will guess;
The name that no human research can discover—
  But THE CAT HIMSELF KNOWS, *and will never confess.*

"The Naming Of Cats"

Literary criticism is a kind of naming. From out of a wealth of different events and expressions the critic fashions an identity for the poet or novelist or text, nominating certain qualities as essential, others as peripheral. The names that we bestow, moreover, take their meaning from the surrounding context of critical language as well as from the particulars of the writer's work. To call an author "great" or "self-conscious" or "American" canonizes a part or moment of the career within an interpretative framework tied to the critic's contemporary setting. No act of criticism can help proceeding from its historical conditions, its ideological premises, and its author's personal investments. Only an absolutist would then conclude that criticism has nothing to offer us in the way of knowledge. On the contrary, the naming that we produce in our readings of others can be seen as exemplary of human knowing in general: if the truths so spoken are inflected by their relations to history or subjectivity, then the richness and significance of such truths increase, despite the loss of some metaphysical center of objectivity. Human understanding, as a naming that interprets, has given itself a measuring image in Adam's perfect nomenclature for the beasts of Paradise. Literary criticism inhabits a postlapsarian world where we resist any final name, though we draw ourselves on in the hopes that our appellations may have a lasting role in shaping what others know and do.

Writers and critics alike are attracted to the idea of the "Deep and inscrutable singular Name" Old Possum conjures and to the fiction that "THE CAT HIMSELF KNOWS, and will never confess." I suspect that the figure of this Name, like any apparition of the logos, recedes by design toward the horizon of meaning and does so in direct proportion to our attempts to grasp its shadowy substance. The fabulation of this Name (and of those appearing in Eliot's criticism, such as Dante, Yeats, Tradition, Maturity) calls upon us to continue positing and discarding our knowing nomenclatures. Eliot's mask (or masque) suggests a silent or reserved Truth (*Ash Wednesday*'s "silent Word," the "still point" of "Burnt Norton") ever beyond our words, and it is a play that considerably assists his own rhetoric of authority. These performances, however, distract our attention from the oblique ways that writing produces and confesses life's secrets, which we so often would prefer to leave unspoken or unheard. The fabulation of such a "logocentric" or mystical Name cannot avoid leaving the traces of another story, of other names and identities whose acknowledgment would disrupt the unity or signifying economy of the "proper" Name. Upon analysis the "singular Name" of Old Possum appears as an effect, not a hidden cause. It is the momentarily canonized or transfigured version of the "one name left over," that odd remaining term whose resistance to a logocentric economy of assured denomination inspires poetic or critical rewording. The very estrangement of this other name points toward the limitation of the Name and conceptual structure that previously governed and toward a future in which yet another word will undo this briefly recovered nominative. Naming, knowing, and criticism work through this process. They open the inherited figures of meaning, carry the figures of knowing across time's scenes and into other frames of reference, and in doing so both break and enrich everything inscribed. "To become renewed, transfigured, in another pattern" (LG, III).

T. S. Eliot has been called a lot of different names by his readers. He himself quite notoriously invented an array of contradictory poses to baffle his critics and in the process to mediate and express his own "dissociation of sensibility." Charmed by Old Possum's disappearing act, Hugh Kenner called Eliot the Invisible Poet, the "impersonal" cat who alone knows the joke he has put over on his audience. Given the choice, most readers would probably prefer Kenner's Oscar Wildeish version of Eliot to the Reactionary Moralist of *After Strange Gods*, as they have preferred the E. P. of *The Pound Era* to the false prophet Ezra of the Rome broadcasts. But, brilliantly portrayed though it is, Kenner's Eliot has not yet prevailed against the image of the Christian and the traditionalist. The privilege of this guise, of course, stems from Eliot's own endorsements of it and from its persuasive canonization by critics like Helen Gardner. Despite Kenner's ingenuity, it is impossible to read

Eliot's critical, religious, moral, or political statements as pure vaudeville. The weight of evidence seems surely to support Gardner and such recent refiners of her thesis as Lyndall Gordon. The ascendancy of this latter portrait over Kenner's finds its ironic confirmation in the steep decline of Eliot's popularity over the last two decades.

Yet, we need not choose between Old Possum and Saint Thomas. While no amount of interpretation will change the odious and insufferable passages in Eliot's work, the task of explaining their coherence with his best writing continues, as does the correlative challenge of finding a theoretical approach for disclosing the silenced logic behind the manifest content. Kenner's instinct to suspect Eliot of subtle rhetorical manipulations of stance can fruitfully be adapted to an investigation of the conceptual structures that produce the summary statements made by both Eliot and his critics. This involves, however, putting aside Kenner's attractive lightheartedness, which suggests that the disparity between Eliot's secret self and his public pronouncements was essentially comical. I think that the matter is more complicated and that a *theory* of these discontinuities in Eliot's writing must replace the insightful impressionism of Kenner's pioneering rebuttal to the canonizers.

I have attempted to provide such a theory by directing attention to the predominant practice of figuration in Eliot's writing. Whether in poems, plays, or essays the structure of Eliot's thought turns upon an active alteration of previous figures, including that of the poet himself. Refiguration and transfiguration appear to be the best analytical terms for naming the way poetic or critical identities take shape in Eliot's work. The distance that divides the unheard Word from the babble of different voices is a systematic opening that in fact enables both poles of the apparent dichotomy to exist. The figures of Eliot presented by his critics must be subjected to an analysis that attends to the conflicts within apparently singular names and meanings. Such attention traces the modes of literary production that give us the seeming coherence of identities—in lives, in texts, in critical reputations. In the very helpful formulation of Barbara Johnson, criticism calls names into question by asking how judgments convert a difference *within* into a difference *between*.[1] This conversion experience turns up frequently in Eliot's polemics, such as those on classicism and Romanticism and tradition and the individual talent. So to Kenner's irreverent attitude I would add a deconstructive theory in order to account for the relation between conflicting figures in Eliot, a procedure that helps avoid choosing up sides. When Eliot consistently expresses a preference for Dante over Shakespeare or shatters the con-

1 Barbara Johnson, *The Critical Difference* (Baltimore, 1980), 105.

ventions of the elegy in *The Waste Land* or exiles himself from America, he engages in acts of criticism whose meanings lie less in the antinomies than in the motives and methods of their mutual interpretation.

This book, then, responds to the state of transition evident both in Eliot studies and in literary theory. In terms of its theoretical scope, Eliot criticism has generally lagged behind the scholarship on other modernist poets and even seems in some quarters determined to use Eliot as a protective shield against those whom E. D. Hirsch calls the "cognitive atheists" of contemporary literary theory.[2] I am convinced, however, that Eliot studies will benefit from an antithetical encounter with modern speculative criticism. It was inevitable that the "methods" of literary theory be applied to a writer of Eliot's stature, as a number of critics have already done. But it is not my intention to impose a model on Eliot's method. I begin rather with the observation that many of the issues now debated in theoretical circles—influence, originality, authority, genealogy, repetition, difference, structure—are the very problems that generate Eliot's poetics. The use of kinship metaphors in regard to poetic genesis, for example, recurs with monotonous regularity in Eliot's prose. And where would theorists of intertextuality and *écriture* find more puzzling cases than *The Waste Land* or "Little Gidding"? The readings of Eliot's prose and poetry that follow aim, through a close scrutiny of his figurations, to suggest his precedent place: how he shares the interests of our day, how he is a major precursor of contemporary theory and poetry in ways neither he nor his progeny might comfortably imagine.

The wealth of Eliot criticism is intimidating, as Robert H. Canary's invaluable *T. S. Eliot: The Poet and His Critics* so comprehensively shows. Still, there have been few imaginative leaps beyond the views of F. O. Matthiessen, Gardner, and Kenner. In his lifetime Eliot indirectly exercised a powerful check upon his critics and interpreters. A deft manipulator of the authority, partly appropriated and partly bestowed, that he wielded, Eliot set the tone for his readers. Even his opponents spent most of their time fighting him on his own terms, reacting to a set of rather overpublicized doctrines and dogmas that obscured much of the meaning of his work. Sympathizers were similarly handicapped. Candid discussion of Eliot's sexual subject matter was severely limited by his presence, as were "personal" interpretations of his poems. Critical practice followed the so-called New Criticism, whose re-

---

2 Hirsch's theological barb is approvingly cited by Edward Lobb in the polemical conclusion to his *T. S. Eliot and the Romantic Critical Tradition* (London, 1981), 144. In choosing Harold Bloom as his target, Lobb ironically repeats Bloom's own blindness to the complexity of influence in Eliot. Aside from the summary of Eliot's unpublished Clark Lectures in the first chapter, Lobb's book adds little to our understanding of Eliot and Romanticism.

strictions on the scope of interpretative focus found misleading support in some of Eliot's more infamous strictures. The narrow direction taken by Eliot criticism served his defenses well, for it led readers away from a too close inspection of the emotional crises and philosophical dilemmas that were often as hidden from his own conscious attention as from that of his audience. As in the case of Poe and "The Philosophy of Composition," Eliot's stress on impersonality and technique formed a rhetoric of denial that obscured the human problems at stake in his work.

There are important exceptions to the foregoing generalizations, as my own footnotes will show. Valuable revisions of our notions about Eliot are in progress. Two particular and related developments bear especially on the pages to follow. These are the wholesale rethinking of Eliot's relation to the Romantic tradition (including the Victorians) and the renewed study of the personal dimension in Eliot's work. The first has followed the general rehabilitation of Romanticism that explicitly reacted against Eliot and the New Criticism. Here the best work has been that of C. K. Stead, Frank Kermode, A. Walton Litz, Robert Langbaum, and George Bornstein. The second dates back to Matthiessen's ground-breaking study and continues in the work of Bernard Bergonzi, Kenner, Langbaum, Graham Hough, and Gordon. Both of these currents in Eliot studies have drawn support from the now published manuscripts of *The Waste Land* and *Four Quartets* and from what little material in other unpublished manuscripts has been allowed into the light.

These trends in Eliot studies intersect major areas of investigation in contemporary literary theory. The reevaluation of Romanticism includes the contributions of Harold Bloom, Geoffrey Hartman, and Paul de Man, critics whose theories of literary history and poetic voice have aided the present study. The new readings of Romanticism necessitate a reinterpretation of Eliot's quarrel with the Romantics and thus of the significance of that debate in any understanding of his writings. We are now in a better position to analyze the complex ambivalence in his polemics and to read the echoing voices of the Romantics in his texts. The result is a different perception of Eliot's thinking about the origins and powers of poetic writing and a different view of his connections to contemporary theories of Romanticism and literary criticism.

Eliot's dispute with Romanticism often turned on the question of "personality" in poetry. A theoretical ambivalence about the role of subjectivity in literary creation plays a large part in determining the direction of his career. For many years Eliot's early formula for "impersonality" reigned in critical circles despite his own severe modifications of it. Today a relevant parallel may be found in controversies over the function of the authorial subject, a figure very difficult to name in texts such as *The Waste Land, Ulysses,* or Pound's *Cantos.* Since the days of the "intentional fallacy" we have witnessed the rise of structuralist models that demote the author to the status of a discursive or textual "effect." Poststructuralist and deconstructive readings seem similarly to announce the "death of the author" or "the end of man" as the inevitable inheritance of "postmodernism." Yet the "decentering" of the self is not the same as its erasure. Literature and criticism demonstrate the insistence of the subject in textuality, though not as its supreme ruler. The repetitive return of the repressed personal dimension in Eliot's writing may shed some light on the subject's return in contemporary criticism. Jacques Derrida, always sensitive to the entanglements within oppositions such as personality / impersonality, writes: "Somewhere here, beyond the mythology of the signature, beyond the authorial theology, the biographical desire has been inscribed in the text. The mark which it has left behind, irreducible though it may be, is just as irreducibly plural."[3] To read the plurality of subjectivity in a text requires an interpretative art that presumes affinities between textuality and personality, or between the structures of writing and those of human being. My struggle to make coherent sense of Eliot's writings led to the conclusion that his ideas about the Eliot family, America, and sexuality were inseparable from his conceptions of poetic influence, literary innovation, and authorial identity. This assertion does not entail biographical reductionism, but rather an analysis of the overdetermination of figures in Eliot's work.

The most useful aids to an approach of this type come from psychoanalysis, especially as it has been articulated of late by critics who have adapted the new French versions of Freud. Behind this movement floats the inscrutable Jacques Lacan, who announced the "return to Freud" by reminding us that "the unconscious is structured in the most radical way like a language." I say reminded us, for it was in 1940 that Lionel Trilling argued that "the mind, as Freud sees it, is in the greater part of its tendency exactly a poetry making organ. . . . It was left to Freud to discover how, in a scientific age, we still feel and think in figurative formations, and to create, what psychoanalysis is, a science of tropes, of metaphor and its variants, synecdoche and metonymy."[4] Psychoanalytic interpretation, however, does differ from other kinds of semiology or hermeneutics in this focus on subjectivity and sexuality. The relevance of the latter to a study of Eliot's poetry hardly needs

---

3 Jacques Derrida, *Spurs: Nietzsche's Styles,* trans. Barbara Harlow (Chicago, 1979), 105.
4 Jacques Lacan, *Ecrits: A Selection,* trans. Alan Sheridan (New York, 1977), 234; Lionel Trilling, "Freud and Literature," in *The Liberal Imagination* (Garden City, N.Y., 1953), 10–60.

justification any longer, and the extension of psychoanalysis beyond the banalities of libidinal determinism has largely answered the charges made against its application in literary studies. Eliot's poems do spend a great deal of energy representing sterility, impotence, castration, misogyny, adultery, sensuous martyrdom, and ecstatic union. Taken beyond a biographical reading, the structures of these figures become issues in politics, religion, poetics, and philosophy.

It should be clear after this review of my critical itinerary that at least some of the limitations of this book are intentional. It does not present an exhaustive commentary on Eliot's life or work or even pretend to discuss all his "major" poems and essays, tasks completed recently in the work of A. D. Moody. In focusing on Eliot's poetics, my aim is to show how writing operates in Eliot. The theory of transfiguration emerges from consideration of selected examples and can be tested on other passages by readers so inspired. I have tried to discuss enough of Eliot's verse and criticism to substantiate my interpretations in detail and to retain a sense of the career as it develops. If I have dwelled on certain texts at seemingly inordinate length, it reflects my bias toward what Eliot himself called the "lemon-squeezer school of criticism" (OPP, 125). But it was the modernism of Eliot, Joyce, Pound, and Stevens—not structural linguistics—that first showed many readers the importance of attending carefully to the extravagance and treachery of language. We are now accustomed to rigorously close readings of the poems and ought to scrutinize the prose with the same interpretative regard.

Looking back over the manuscript, I see, like any writer, endless possibilities for improvement. In particular there remains the question of Eliot's politics, of the ideology of modernism in general, a subject too large and too difficult for me to undertake now.[5] Nor have I dealt at length with Eliot's theory and practice in drama, especially in the years after *Four Quartets*. My focus on some of Eliot's poetic precursors may seem oddly narrow as well, since it touches so lightly on the proclaimed influence of the French symbolists and deals with the Metaphysicals through Eliot's essays on Shakespeare. In this I have had a purpose, for I think we have often let Eliot lead us astray on such questions. A major argument in the following chapters, successful or not, holds that Eliot's critical essays employ a rhetoric of condensation, displacement, projection, and identification in their accounts of the literary past. Eliot's poetics become a modernist tropology of self-fashioning, so that his choice and portrayal of past masters demands a critical sorting out of mani-

5 For a provocative study on this subject, see Fredric Jameson, *Fables of Aggression: Wyndham Lewis, the Modernist as Fascist* (Berkeley, 1979).

fest from latent content. The book takes shape from an interpretation of what this rhetoric, in verse and prose, can tell us about a writer and his meanings.

Though I find the insights of psychoanalysis useful in examining this rhetoric and other aspects of Eliot's writings, it is by no means the only perspective employed. Eliot's own broad range of interests and allusions can send any critic into studies of philosophy, philology, theology, anthropology, and a dozen other disciplines. Here again the syncretic texts of contemporary theory in the fields of the "human sciences" have aided my discussion of Eliot's larger concerns. Many passages in the present study thus range beyond explication of the text at hand and into the more general problems Eliot raises or encounters. Hence this book's double life: as a reading of Eliot and as a work in critical theory. The hope of this duplicity is not for some transmogrification of Eliot into a prophet of poststructuralism, but rather for the salvation of him from the sleep of canonization or dismissal. I do not wish to make Eliot better or worse, more or less agreeable, but better understood and therefore more interesting. The process should not leave the theories themselves untouched either, for the text should revise the theory as the theory revises the text. Each transfigures the other and is altered in fulfillment.

PART ONE

THE LABOR OF INHERITANCE

Under a juniper-tree the bones sang, scattered and shining
We are glad to be scattered, we did little good to each other,
Under a tree in the cool of the day, with the blessing of sand,
Forgetting themselves and each other, united
In the quiet of the desert. This is the land which ye
Shall divide by lot. And neither division nor unity
Matters. This is the land. We have our inheritance.

Ash Wednesday

CHAPTER I

PREFIGURATIONS
An American Genealogy

Our age is retrospective. It builds the sepulchres of the fathers. It writes biographies, histories, and criticism. The foregoing generations beheld God and nature face to face; we, through their eyes. Why should not we also enjoy an original relation to the universe? Why should not we have a poetry and philosophy of insight and not of tradition, and a religion by revelation to us, and not the history of theirs? Embosomed for a season in nature, whose floods of life stream around and through us, and invite us by the powers they supply, to action proportioned to nature, why should we grope among the dry bones of the past, or put the living generation into masquerade out of its faded wardrobe? The sun shines to-day also. There is more wool and flax in the fields. There are new lands, new men, new thoughts. Let us demand our own works and laws and worship.

Emerson, Nature

Writing entails inheritance. Late in his career, when asked what connection his poetry had to the American past, T. S. Eliot replied that "in its sources, in its emotional springs, it comes from America."[1] While Eliot often seemed to have renounced his American patrimony, he continued to write in response to its contradictions and dilemmas. Even his exile was part of an American tradition, his work as much an interpretation of home as was that of Henry James. In order to understand himself, to compose himself, to channel his "emotional springs," Eliot literally displaced his American dilemmas into foreign contexts. While his primary concerns play variations on persistent themes in Western culture, their peculiar inflection in his work owes much to the strange relation of the American offspring to that parent civiliza-

1 Interview by Donald Hall (1959), reprinted in George Plimpton (ed.), *Writers at Work: The "Paris Review" Interviews, Second Series* (New York, 1965), 110. Of the many fine studies urging the importance of Eliot's American roots, see especially F. O. Matthiessen, *The Achievement of T. S. Eliot* (3rd ed., rev.; New York, 1959), and his *American Renaissance* (New York, 1941), 351–70; Herbert Howarth, *Notes on Some Figures Behind T. S. Eliot* (Boston, 1964); Ferner Nuhn, *The Wind Blew from the East: A Study in the Orientation of American Culture* (New York, 1942), 195–255; and Lyndall Gordon, *Eliot's Early Years* (New York, 1977).

tion. The American identity begins, with the Puritans and Founding Fathers, in self-conscious attempts to make a difference and so anticipates problems that become critical elsewhere in other ways. Emerson's influential manifesto exemplifies this process and foreshadows the major preoccupations of Eliot's poetics. It is not simply that Eliot rejects Emerson's stance against "tradition," for that stance itself is inseparable from a concomitant appeal to higher authorities. Eliot takes up another position *within* the dilemma he has internalized, positing his difference from Emerson (or America or Protestantism or Romanticism) by articulating what Emerson repressed and by repressing what Emerson articulated.

In Emerson, the argument between history and nature, Europe and America, or tradition and the individual talent is never quite settled, though he often seems to declare victory for a higher synthesis. The form the antagonism takes, which makes possible its analysis, is what I shall call genealogy.[2] In the usual sense, genealogy denotes a family history and so organizes our temporal creations into a lineage of names, properties, relations, and destinies. So conceived, it would be another "logocentric" discourse or writing.[3] One need not be an expert in anthropology or cultural history to recognize how genealogical metaphors have structured values in politics, society, and religion. Sophocles, Shakespeare, and the nineteenth-century English novel would be tutorial enough. Responding to the promiscuity of nature, genealogy narrates an order of proper identities or meanings. The role of nature (human and otherwise) in genealogy, however, usually upsets the family's

2 See Michel Foucault, "Nietzsche, Genealogy, History," in *Language, Counter-Memory, Practice*, trans. Donald F. Bouchard and Sherry Simon (Ithaca, 1977), 139–64; and Jacques Derrida, *Of Grammatology*, trans. Gayatri Spivak (Baltimore, 1976), 101–40. "It is now known," writes Derrida, "thanks to unquestionable and abundant information, that the birth of writing (in the colloquial sense) was nearly everywhere and most often linked to genealogical anxiety" (124). See also Eric J. Sundquist, *Home as Found: Authority and Genealogy in Nineteenth-Century American Literature* (Baltimore, 1979).

3 For my purposes, I shall construe Jacques Derrida's "logocentrism" as a name for our habit of thinking in metaphysical structures whose centers are "transcendental signifieds," such as the Word, the Phallus, or the Father. These absolutes appear to both create a structure from the outside and participate in its functions. Deconstruction cites this anomaly in arguing that the Center is not an Origin, but itself the product of a structured interpretation of differences it retrospectively claims to govern. Logocentrism translates differences within experience into a difference between opposing identities that are then arranged in a hierarchy. The Center exerts its authority through the exclusion of an Other whose trace can never be fully elided. The logocentric production of meaning obeys what Derrida calls a "restricted" economy of thought, whereas textuality or *écriture* operates as a "general" economy of signification that does not subordinate the meanings of differences to a metaphysical unity. See Derrida, *Of Grammatology*, 49, and his essay "From Restricted to General Economy: A Hegelianism Without Reserve," in *Writing and Difference*, trans. Alan Bass (Chicago, 1978), 251–77.

plans, for natural desires are notoriously disobedient of the parental or cultural logos. Nature may be called the "other" that genealogy attempts to make into history and significance. It might also be said that in nature we find the "emotional springs" where writing originates and where, for that very reason, writing can never be.

Ideally and etymologically, genealogy ought to provide the logos of the genesis and should trace the history of emergent new things according to a stable law. Thus, the term seems an apt one for literary criticism and has been so used, at least conceptually, since writing began. The word and its theoretical import become even more interesting, and useful for criticism, when understood as an oxymoron. Much depends on one's definitions of *genesis* and *logos*. Can a logos speak, comprehend, or control the system that produced it? Or does the logos retrospectively imagine its genesis, create itself by inventing its origin? What is at stake will emerge more clearly, I hope, in the pages to follow. Here it is sufficient to suggest that in the gap between genesis and logos lies nature and that genealogy narrates the crossings of that gap. Adulteries and bastards are thrown ceremoniously into that abyss to enable the crossing toward propriety, as genealogy defends against the play (as in the play within a machine that indicates a fault in the mechanism) of nature and desire. The recurrent errancy of unauthorized offspring and relations initiates the work of genealogy as a belated writing. Understood from the standpoint of its deconstruction by nature, genealogy is an incessant act of reinscription. The unresolvable dialectic between nature and any interpretative logos takes the form, in time, of genealogy. It names not only a logocentrism, then, but an ongoing critical activity of arrangement, naming, and evaluation. And a genealogical inquiry may solicit the other, as well as exclude it, looking for the skeletons in every metaphysical or textual closet. As a critical method in the pages to follow, genealogy means charting, between writers or texts, those often unauthorized relationships that nonetheless belong to the literary lineage of an essay or poem. The disruption of a literary history or of any conceptual economy by its own acts of genesis may well be due to the nature of language, as many have argued. I am inclined, though, to see the most interesting occasions of decentering in those moments when the authorial subject, with his natures and desires, is inserted into the logocentric machine.[4] Genealogy traces these occasions, as well as the textual constitutions of nature and desire, and so becomes a primary strategy in the con-

4 I refer here to an old crux, lately reformulated in the debate between those who would read the rhetoric of tropes in a text as linguistic phenomena and those who advocate a psychical interpretation of textuality. See, for example, Paul de Man, *Allegories of Reading: Figural Language in Rousseau, Nietzsche, Rilke, and Proust* (New Haven, 1979), 288–301; Harold

struction of literary histories. The interplay between these four terms—nature, history, genealogy, and writing—characterizes both the content of Eliot's American inheritance and the structure he must use to invest it in other (*i.e.* European) places.

When Emerson begins the introduction to *Nature* by lamenting the mediated vision of his age, the metaphor he chooses is genealogical. In "biographies, histories, and criticism," the present generation erects funerary monuments in a literary version of ancestor worship. The myth is a familiar one. In the beginning was the Father, author of true creations through "an original relation to the universe." This envied knowledge once occurred in the instant of perception, subject and object one in the no-time of "insight." Now writing has usurped the place of vision in the primal scene and so marked the intervention of time and death between life and representation. Emerson offers no explanation for this catastrophe; nor does he provide any clarification of the status (historical? mythological? literary? theological?) of these "fathers." What he does put forward is an alternative scene: "Embosomed for a season in nature," the new writer enters a relation that will reverse time, undo history, and return him to an original knowledge of the source. The figures of nature in Emerson are what Harold Bloom calls "lies against time."[5] They retrospectively entail—that is, both involve and restrict—what writing inherits.

This entailment may be seen in the way that Emerson's "new thoughts" repeat the former catastrophe. That sundering from originality can be read allegorically, depending on one's theoretical disposition, as 1) the anxiety of influence, the new writer's overwhelming sense of inferiority and imitation, or 2) the loss of absolute presence that accompanies the fall into language, after which signifying words can never recapture the Signified Word. Such readings have the advantage of being structural and thus of avoiding the naïve realism that would credit Emerson's lament (or any of its thousands of previous and subsequent incarnations) with historical validity. They have the disadvantage, though, of obscuring how the Word of the Father is produced by such structures, how it is an effect, and not a cause, of a conceptual economy it can never fully govern. The worst catastrophe would be to do without the figure of an original catastrophe, for this would preclude the whole

---

Bloom, *Wallace Stevens: The Poems of Our Climate* (Ithaca, 1977), 385–402; and Geoffrey H. Hartman, *Saving the Text: Literature/Derrida/Philosophy* (Baltimore, 1981), 118–57.

5 Of Bloom's many essays on Emerson, see in particular "Emerson and Whitman: The American Sublime," in *Poetry and Repression* (New Haven, 1976), 235–66, and "Emerson: The American Religion," in *Agon: Towards a Theory of Revisionism* (New York, 1982),

movement of thought towards truth defined as the missing thing to be re-stored. The Word of the Father, as a function and not an essence, may be emptied and filled repeatedly, in one revision after another, without ever dis-placing the parental logos. This is just what happens in Emerson, where the attempt to replace genealogy and history with nature follows a genealogical path and returns the being of nature to the Father.

The passage develops an opposition between two series of figures. On the one hand, visionary metaphors imply the possibility of an immediate ap-prehension of truth; on the other hand, "sepulchres" and other writings re-mind us of the mediations of time, distance, and loss in the work of knowing. Following a long tradition, Emerson argues that writing corrupts vision. Yet the imagery is complex: the phrase "we, through their eyes" turns prior texts and present readings into acts of vision. The difference between vision and the mediations of language collapses. To see is to read, and writing is a kind of vision. Emerson counts on a "new" writing, grounded in nature, to re-store our sight, but another look shows that nature, too, participates in the differences it would resolve. As an antidote to the belatedness of culture, na-ture would liberate us from history and genealogy through unmediated ac-cess to the transcendental origin of knowledge. This invocation of nature builds the sepulchers of the fathers in a rebellious sense: it puts the dead in their places, "murders" the authorities of the past. As a rhetorical figure, Emerson's "The sun shines to-day also" blazes out to blind past visions, de-stroy Father Time, and substitute the eternal recurrence of the origin for the fatality of genealogy. As an antagonist to sepulchral writing, this "sun" is a son, hoping to replace prior forms of knowing with the originality of an in-dividual talent.

Genealogical strife, then, structures the emergence of nature as a trope against time. *Nature* will continue the tradition by reading "nature" as a "text" and not a presence. Correspondingly, the meaning of this text will be an authorized one, as Emerson declares in his section entitled "Language": "Spirit is the Creator. Spirit has life in itself. And man in all ages and coun-tries embodies it in his language, as the FATHER."[6] Emerson's exorcism of paternal influences remains within the paradox of genealogy (and of writ-ing). The dethroning of a father seems always to necessitate the nomination of a supplementary logos. One can never be that "father," origin of oneself, since self-reliance depends upon identification, or a speculative relationship, with the inherited function of the father as self-begetter. The recourse to na-ture only generates more history, while history's impositions fail to control

6 Stephen E. Whicher (ed.), *Selections from Ralph Waldo Emerson* (Boston, 1957), 32.

the desires of powerful natures. The result is creation, dissemination, and genealogy.

The contradictions within Emerson's declaration of independence help explain what Eliot meant by "that sense of the past which is peculiarly American." He was writing of Hawthorne's "grip on the past," his "acute historical sense," in contrast to James's "sense of the sense."[7] Only later did he clarify the distinction. James had "*acquired*, though not inherited, something of the American tradition. He was not a descendent of the witch-hangers."[8] (This distinction should be kept in mind when we examine Eliot's public endorsement of acquired over inherited tradition.) The reference to the sins of the fathers and their acts of repression equates the "sense of the past" with what Freud called the "sense of guilt."[9] As opposed to remorse, guilt represents fear of the conscience, or internalized father figure, which punishes desires as well as acts. The sons of New England inherit a conscience whose violent punishment of evil testifies, as Hawthorne showed, to the power of blackness within themselves. Eliot's distrust of "the inner voice, which breathes the eternal message of vanity, fear, and lust" continues the divided mentality of the persecutors of Anne Hutchinson (SE, 16). Emerson tried to bury that brand of Calvinism with the religion of *Nature*, his own primer of modern heresy, only to substitute sublimation for repression, one father for another, losing nature again in writing its philosophy. Reversing Emerson (and Whitman), Eliot returns to building the various incarnations of the logos through nature's negation, denouncing in his moments of extreme crisis the heresy of loving human or created things. What Eliot calls the "New England genius" is haunted by a guilty genealogy of morals, a series of orders that author themselves by what they exclude.

"It would be possible," writes Joseph N. Riddel, "to write a 'history' of American poetics in terms of 'beginnings,' or better, in terms of the changing sense of beginning. . . . Our Adamic poets have, at every turn, had to try to begin again, to supply and resupply a succession of privileged centers as old ones were demystified and disappeared: the Puritans' wrathful God for the Anglican Word; the Deist's Reason for the Puritan God; the Transcendental Spirit for Deity; self for Self. Finally . . . the dominant Idea became the idea of deprivation and dispossession."[10] Eliot's construction of authorizing for-

<hr>

7 "The Hawthorne Aspect," *Little Review*, IV (August, 1918), 50.

8 Quoted by Stephen Spender in "Remembering Eliot," in Allen Tate (ed.), *T. S. Eliot: The Man and His Work* (New York, 1966), 56. See also CC, 52. Eliot's ancestor Andrew Elliott sat on the jury for one of the cases, along with Judge Hathorne, and later recanted.

9 Freud, *Civilization and Its Discontents*, in *Works*, XXI, 123–39.

10 Joseph N. Riddel, *The Inverted Bell: Modernism and the Counterpoetics of William Carlos Williams* (Baton Rouge, 1974), 44–46.

eign traditions to legitimate his break with America follows this pattern and has its roots in the figural and typological thought of Puritan New England. The Puritan fathers vindicated their exile from the Old World with biblical metaphors that inscribed their experiment in a timeless, divine historiography that turned their estrangement into a return to the Promised Land. A genealogical succession was established to link the children of Israel with those of the Massachusetts Bay colony. Typological exegesis joined Old Testament ideas of patriarchy and Reformation concepts of theology to invent an ingenious mode for sanctifying the errancy of American ways. Contemporary figures, such as John Winthrop, were invested with the authority of Moses and Nehemiah, thus obscuring the radical separation of Puritanism from the traditional institutions of Christianity. This tactic soon had reformers like Solomon Stoddard (1643–1729) arguing that "it may possibly be a fault and an aggravation of a fault to depart from the ways of our fathers; but it may also be a virtue and an eminent act of obedience to depart from them in some things."[11] Already it is apparent that an Oedipal economy is at work here: the words of the fathers are up for grabs, and their interpretation is a guilty necessity.

Emerson follows Stoddard in challenging ancestor worship, but his calls for self-reliance demonstrate a basic paradox in the American sense of the past as it shapes the perception of culture. The American writer of the nineteenth century comes to look upon his inheritance as at once too imposing and too insubstantial. For post-Puritan Bostonians (to whom Eliot feels the most telling and uncomfortable kinship) the weight of history prompts a defensive portrayal of America's emptiness. A minor genre of texts on this theme emerges, with contributions by Irving, Cooper, Hawthorne, James, and many others. This litany bewailing America's lack of civilization serves usefully to mitigate the real influence of the American locale and the guilty sense of the past. Proponents of the thesis of America's vacuity most frequently resort to ambivalent comparisons with Europe—ambivalent because even as they help free the writer from native anxieties, these juxtapositions record America's derivation from the Old World. The academic *summa* in this line was Barrett Wendell's *A Literary History of America* (1900), cited by Eliot (who attended Harvard during Wendell's years there) in his 1919 review on American literature. "Their world was thin," Eliot wrote of the culture of his nineteenth-century forebears, "it was not corrupt enough. Worst of all it was secondhand; it was not original and self-dependent—it was a shadow."[12]

11 Sacvan Bercovitch, *The Puritan Origins of the American Self* (New Haven, 1975); Solomon Stoddard, "Concerning Ancestors," in Perry Miller (ed.), *The American Puritans: Their Prose and Poetry* (New York, 1956), 222.

12 "American Literature," *Athenaeum*, No. 4643 (25 April 1919), 237.

American latecomers, then, find themselves working under the shadows cast by past structures of thought on both sides of the Atlantic.

If we are to believe Hawthorne or Henry Adams, nineteenth-century New England had more than its share of corruption. In contrast to Emerson's use of natural rhetoric as a vehicle for transcending time (an effort later educated by fate and experience), Hawthorne followed the Puritans in looking to history for revelation. Despite Emerson's best efforts, the transparent eyeball keeps glimpsing the insufferable lineage of its descent. In Hawthorne's tales this retrospection willfully follows the history of the New England mind into dark woods. Hawthorne opens *The Scarlet Letter* with an "autobiographical" tale of groping among the signs of the past, sifting through documents and manuscripts strewn like waste in a "forgotten corner" of the "Custom-House." In that uncataloged library of time's fragmentary remembrances he discovers the character his writing will transfigure.

> Glancing at such matters with the saddened, weary, half-reluctant interest which we bestow on the corpse of dead activity,—and exerting my fancy, sluggish with little use, to raise up from these dry bones an image of the old town's brighter aspect, when India was a new region, and only Salem knew the way thither,—I chanced to lay my hand on a small package, carefully done up in a piece of ancient yellow parchment. This envelope had the air of an official record of some period long past, when clerks engrossed their stiff and formal chirography on more substantial matters than at present.[13]

Ezekiel's vision of the valley of dry bones, which seems to have exerted a strong hold on the New England soul, offers a type of the resurrection and an allegory of the power of inspiration to revive what time bestows. Emerson, even more radically than the Shelley of "Ode to the West Wind," leaps beyond fallen things to identify with the Spirit breathing through them. Hawthorne, like Poe, intuits that Spirit may have an unconscious or even be a daemon tricked out in divine resemblances. Hawthorne's use of historical fragments does not, despite his self-denigrating portrait as a clerk dealing in lesser matters than his fathers, aim to recapture the lost truth of the past. Rather, he uses the past's bequests against its impositions on the present and adopts a critical stance toward what he inherits. Retrieved from a heap of broken images, the sign of the scarlet letter will not be the Word, but like history and nature, a polysemous text. In the multiple interpretations of the letter as it is read by the novel's dramatis personae, Hawthorne discloses the

---

13 Nathaniel Hawthorne," *The Scarlet Letter*, ed. Sculley Bradley *et al.* (2nd ed.; New York, 1978), 26.

nature of those who read, and that is the truth of the letter. The recovery of the past is an act of desire and so is never literal.

The "sense of the past" in Hawthorne, declared Eliot, "exercised itself in a grip on the past itself."[14] Hawthorne's aggressive grasp of history, his temerity in opening it to the interpretations of his own time, belies his self-deprecations before the figures of his "steeple-crowned" progenitors. He reads the past with a soul haunted by ancestral images, yet among those spirits is the Protestant inner voice that urges him to condemn the authorities if they are evil. When Puritanism becomes an inherited nature in Hawthorne's generation, it lies open to the judgment of a different history. The guilt pervading Hawthorne's fictions reflects the author's desire to strangle "that first ancestor, invested by family tradition with a dim and dusky grandeur." This guilt can hardly be missing in a writer who so intensely imagines his authority through family metaphors. In *The House of the Seven Gables*, an entire chapter revolves about the dead figure of Judge Pyncheon, his corpse at the center of family history. The narrator's account is nearly hysterical. His excitement is manic and macabre; his feelings are a mixture of terror and relief. He resembles the uncanny murderers in Poe's tales who compulsively confess, in tones of glee and horror, their no-longer-secret crimes. The ambivalence in Hawthorne is rendered with gentler, subtler tones, but it responds to a similar catastrophe. However stifling to futurity, the father figure occupied a place of authority that guaranteed the structure of the family logos (usurped though it was). Once an ideal of genealogy controlled the transmission of values through time. The revelation of sins at the origin, compounded by the judge's repetition of the past in his own death, introduces us to far less stable notions of genealogy or writing. In representing the deconstruction of these edifices from the inside, Hawthorne steals their strength, gains his own power from a ghost, and thus writes a history of New England's unnatural authorities.

Eliot endorses Henry James's praise for the "deeper psychology" of Hawthorne, which involved becoming a "receptive medium" for "feeling" the relationship between characters and between people and place, rather than presenting a situation "deliberately constructed" in a manner Eliot attributes to English and French novelists.[15] In other words, Hawthorne suffers history, receives and redistributes it, portraying the engagement of history in the personal or psychological, and vice versa. It is in this deeper psychology of feeling the past that nature returns to disturb history's orders. Hester

14 "The Hawthorne Aspect," 50.
15. *Ibid.*

Prynne's nature clashes violently with New England's historical self-portrait. Arthur Dimmesdale's representative consciousness proves unable to cope with the irruptions of his own buried life as Hester recalls them. Dimmesdale is one in a succession of failed American lovers who soon will include Henry James's bachelor visionaries and Eliot's impotent Prufrock. For each, consummate action in the present is overshadowed by a sense that time has already precluded creation and that to force the moment to its crisis would be to risk generating new identities outside any authorized structure or economy of meaning. In this scenario, nature's displacement of history does not provide a new stable ground, but an opening into the unconscious, where human nature is a case history.

Yet, just as history's restrictions elicit the liberating tropes of nature, the antinomianism of the natural calls forth the corrective of historical knowledge. For post-Emersonian Americans like James and Henry Adams, the lesson of Hawthorne helped inspire a countering tradition in which classical and European models were substituted for the eternal verities of Puritanism or transcendentalism. The Emersonian defense against inheritance is reversed, so that the nature of Americans is now read through the borrowed eyes of Europe. The ancestry of American moderns like Eliot and Pound was thus doubly entailed. On the one hand, a subjective Romantic vision of nature offered to make writing new by entombing history and silencing its ghosts. On the other hand, the nineteenth century sought in history's voices the objective, timeless laws that would save culture from a future of anarchy. So in Eliot's "Cousin Nancy," the uncertain strides of "all the modern dances" are performed under the gaze of "Matthew and Waldo, guardians of the faith, / The army of unalterable law." (The latter phrase was borrowed, appropriately, from George Meredith's elegy for originality, "Lucifer in Starlight.") This bizarre alliance of Arnold and Emerson against modernity pictures the measures of a new poetry judged by the sepulchral icons of the Victorian and Unitarian legacies. Called only by their first names, these forefathers are reduced to a couple of priggish boys. Like the corpse of Judge Pyncheon, however, they continue to dominate the imagination of the present and to determine its alternatives to the past's "unalterable law."

In fact, Eliot's ridicule is directed at the eviscerated canonizations of Matthew and Waldo in the parlors of Saint Louis and Boston, while Arnold and Emerson continue as formidable mentors. Even in this early satire they are doubly employed as targets and exemplars. Eliot ambivalently depicts his own ambition through these images of the poet as philosopher and social prophet, but it is toward Arnold that the young Eliot turns for a way to culture beyond American anarchy. This adoption of Arnold as precursor pre-

cipitates numerous disparaging criticisms of him, highlighted in the arrangement he chose for *The Sacred Wood*. We might think of the quarrel as one
between the internalized touchstones of Eliot's Emerson and Eliot's Arnold.
There is, said Eliot in 1918, "a dignity, about Emerson for example, which
persists after we have perceived the taint of commonness about some English
contemporary, as for instance the more intelligent, better educated, more
alert Matthew Arnold." But this dignity and uncommonness may explain the
opinion of 1919 that "the essays of Emerson are already an encumbrance."[16]
Eliot's "emotional springs" included the powerful tributary of Emerson's
natural sublime, which he rechanneled through methods like Arnold's literary historicism. Arnold's use of the past aids the project Eliot inherits from
Hawthorne, James, and Adams. The American debate over past and present
gets translated into the more emotionally distant terms of English and European literary history. From his New England lineage Eliot inherits a profoundly divided attitude toward nature and his own body, a severe habit of
examining his soul's worth, a keen need for a philosophy of history, and a
Protestant theory of language—a theory that denies to human words the
idolatrous power to speak the Word, though it secretly desires this power at
every turn. Eliot's conversion to Anglo-Catholicism takes the place of a return to the Puritan and Protestant world that shaped him. His "spiritual autobiography," as Lyndall Gordon calls it, has deeper roots in the genealogy
of John Winthrop, Cotton Mather, Jonathan Edwards, Emerson, and Hawthorne than in the assumed parentage of Donne or Lancelot Andrewes.
Eliot, too, chooses his canon of "representative men"—the critics, poets, and
saints who become the figural exemplars or typological antecedents through
whom the individual talent imagines his own identity. Such figures are seen
as inhabitants of the intersection of time and the timeless, as historical incarnations of an eternal pattern. Eliot's pantheon forms a history of timeless
moments whose function is to transfigure the pandemonium of feelings in
his American nature.

The increasing focus on psychological catastrophes in nineteenth-century
American literature indicates the crack in the figural, historical, and theological philosophies that brought order to bear upon the American wilderness.
Brockden Brown's Wieland, Poe's Usher, Hawthorne's Clifford Pyncheon,
Melville's Pierre, James's Winterbourne, and Henry Adams' "Henry Adams"
are among the many whose minds are torn by the rival claims of nature and
culture. More disastrously (and here one might insert the relevance of psychoanalysis), it is the inseparability of our natures and our histories, their

16 *Ibid.*, 48; "American Literature," 237.

common genealogies, that undoes these characters. It is the "undeviating transmission, from sire to son, of the patrimony with the name" that brings on Roderick Usher's anxiety of influence, his "morbid acuteness of the senses" that is "a constitutional and a family evil." His soul is identified with that tradition and with the mansion that shares the genealogical appellation "House of Usher." It is a site or sight that inspires "an unredeemed dreariness of thought which no goading of the imagination could torture into aught of the sublime," as if in rejoinder to the early Emerson. "How shall a man escape from his ancestors," wonders Emerson in a later essay, "or draw off from his veins the black drop which he drew from his father's or his mother's life?"[17] The portraits of agonized artistic self-consciousness in such texts show how consciousness appears as an effect only in time, through memory, and thus in history and inheritance. To know oneself is already to historicize nature, to discover that self-knowledge can never be its own origin. If history is the silenced supplement that nevertheless enables the consciousness of nature in Emerson, the reverse seems true in Hawthorne and in Poe. Memories follow the logic of feeling and the course of present desires. We remember with ourselves and cannot separate our natures from what we represent as history. The work of memory weaves the personal into the fabric of the impersonal, so that the past too becomes a case history, the product of condensation, displacement, identification, and projection.

A striking example of this process occurs in the typescript draft for "Gerontion." Having already alluded to Henry Adams' discovery of a depravity in May, Eliot wrote:

> After such knowledge, what forgiveness? Think now
> Nature has many cunning passages, contrived corridors
> And issues, deceives with whispering ambitions,
> Guides us by vanities.

"Nature" is crossed out in the typescript and "History" inserted in the margin. The substitution could be an emblem of the transition from Romanticism to modernism, from a metaphorics of nature to one of culture. The revision does not signal so much a clean break as another oscillation in an ongoing philosophical debate. An obsession with the meanings of history was a chief legacy of the nineteenth century. The failure of secular history or nature to sustain a logos lies behind Eliot's decision to supplement history and nature with literary, religious, and political logocentrisms. The echo of

17 Edgar Allan Poe, *Tales and Sketches, 1831–1842* (Cambridge, 1978), 399, 402–403, 397. Vol. II of *Collected Works of Edgar Allan Poe*, ed. Thomas O. Mabbott; Whicher (ed.), "Fate" in *Selections from Emerson*, 333.

Adams confirms this, for no American wrote so passionately and ironically of the chaos left by the ruins of previous schemas of natural or historical order. Adams' research in science and historiography yielded the same bitter lesson as did the irrational deaths of his sister and his wife. The world was a playground of powers, history a succession of organized forces, and nature (including human nature) a conflict of influences that unsettled all composure.[18]

Eliot's echo of Adams has often been commented on. (He reviewed *The Education of Henry Adams* in 1919, the year he completed "Gerontion.") The revision, however, suggests that to Eliot's interest in Adams' bleak view of history should be added the kinship he feels to this other New Englander's disturbed experience of "sensual, animal, elemental" life. The Adams connection helps explain the use of "she" as a pronoun for "history" in "Gerontion," and the subsequent sexual puns in "cunning passages," "whispering ambitions," "supple confusions," and "reconsidered passions." We might also look to the most powerfully personal chapter in the *Education*, "Chaos," in which the accidental death of Adams' sister occasions a "violent emotion" toward "Nature's gesture—her attitude towards life," which seems "an insanity of force" that resounds to destroy any belief in society's "pantomime" or God's benevolence: "God might be, as the Church said, a Substance, but He could not be a Person." Mont Blanc, site of the Romantic sublime, now "looked to him what it was—a chaos of anarchic and purposeless forces." History follows shortly, for it is 1870, and in a few weeks most of Europe will be "in full chaos of war."[19]

The condensation of history and nature in the metaphor of woman expresses the disturbance of Eliot's post-Romantic subjectivity. The identification of woman with a saving knowledge of the truth is an old *topos*, one Eliot will later endorse in his discussion of Dante's "sublimation" of Beatrice in the *Vita Nuova* (SE, 235). In Eliot's modern revision the lover falls far short of any ecstatic communion and turns much of the blame rhetorically on the anomalous "she," who gives "too late" or "too soon" her epistemological favors. In a manner that reflects well on Eliot's study of Elizabethan drama, Gerontion's speech employs a language that reveals its duplicitous motivation. An emotional tumult has been stirred within him by Lady History, expressed in a diction that also owes much to the philosophical psychology of F. H. Bradley. At the heart of Gerontion's spiritless autobiography is a nature full of deceptions, ambitions, vanities, distractions, confusions, appetites,

18 Eliot Poetry Notebook, Henry W. and Albert A. Berg Collection, New York Public Library. On Adams, "Gerontion," and history see Harvey Gross, *The Contrived Corridor: History and Fatality in Modern Literature* (Ann Arbor, 1971).

19 Ernest Samuels (ed.), *The Education of Henry Adams* (Boston, 1973), 268, 288–89.

beliefs, memories, passions, refusals, and fears. History and nature form a compound Muse who inspires only an elliptical and defensive confession of inadequacies.

This figural merging of historical and carnal knowledge allows for no "forgiveness," as if Oedipus' fate could extend its structure metaphorically to any relation between past and present. (Allusions to Sophocles' trilogy run from "Sweeney Among the Nightingales" to *The Elder Statesman*.) At the start Gerontion pictures his belatedness in references whose images also combine the realms of history, sexuality, and literature.

> Here I am, an old man in a dry month,
> Being read to by a boy, waiting for rain.
> I was neither at the hot gates
> Nor fought in the warm rain
> Nor knee deep in the salt marsh, heaving a cutlass,
> Bitten by flies, fought.

I shall have more to say about the poem's relation to its Victorian predecessors in a later chapter. Here we can note the overdetermination of Eliot's language. As a poet (the elderly Edward FitzGerald of A. C. Benson's biography), Gerontion listens to the words of the fathers, his own springs of originality dried up.[20] This sterility is equated with his distance from historically meaningful action, specifically the heroism in defeat of the Greeks at Thermopylae. His resignation to diminishment is further extended by the eroticism of the scene, in which a phantasmal potency, despite certain death, engages in natural actions. The poem goes on to sketch the declension of potent knowledge in Gerontion's day. "Vacant shuttles / Weave the wind" of poetic breath as the stanzas elaborate on this initial, triple decentering. "Think / Neither fear nor courage saves us." Neither a fear of past powers nor the courage to oppose them seems viable for Gerontion, since both merely repeat the fatalities of an Oedipal economy of thought. "Unnatural vices / Are fathered by our heroism." The decentering of history, literature, and sexuality ("The word within a word, unable to speak a word, / Swaddled in darkness") produces a criminal genealogy: "Virtues / Are forced upon us by our impudent crimes." To act within Gerontion's nostalgia to be the father who knows the mother of truth would be "unnatural," as would be the acts of vice resorted to by the heroism of fearful repression. "Virtues" are an imposition after the fact of unlawful desires. Gerontion's tragedy moves inexorably (or so he would hope) toward the sacred grove at Colonus, where Oedipus finds his mysterious redemption.

---

20 The indispensable guide to Eliot's echoes and allusions is Grover Smith, *T. S. Eliot's Poetry and Plays: A Study in Sources and Meaning* (2nd ed., Chicago, 1974)

"I have lost my passion: why should I need to keep it / Since what is kept must be adulterated?" Whether or not these lines, and similar ones elsewhere, refer to a possible biographical event in the relations of Eliot, Vivienne, and Bertrand Russell, they convey a deep sense of guilt as well as accusation. Why "must" something "kept" be "adulterated," unless it has already been possessed by another? Or unless the preservation of ecstasy in a world of time always means its adulteration, its involvement in nature and its imperfections? "I have lost my sight, smell, hearing, taste and touch; / How should I use them for your closer contact?" The experience of adultery, now designating the decentering of any logos (history, literature, sexuality) into a genealogy of disseminations, emasculates hyperbolically Gerontion's entire sensual being. This symbolic castration of his nature confirms the Oedipal economy of his lament, since it preserves, in its negation, the logos he has lost, the missing piece of a not always metaphysical puzzle.

Throughout his career, Eliot uses genealogical metaphors to describe poetic genesis, literary history, and the workings of influence. I shall introduce here an idea to be proved in the following chapters: that Eliot's thinking through such figures tends to support a restricted or logocentric view of poetic meaning and authority, but finds itself undone from within by the drift of tropes like castration, sterility, impotence, or adultery, which name crises of significance that exceed the system's hermeneutic control. The creations of language in time form a history of transfigured repetitions that will not obey the logocentric imperative of sameness and difference, sons and bastards, or any other dualism based on the principle of noncontradiction.[21] Hence, I will be led to assert that poems like "Gerontion" and *The Waste Land* that so lament the loss of the Center are more metaphysically idealistic than the Heraclitian meditations of *Four Quartets*.

"Gerontion" tells us that the apprehensions in the American sense of nature are linked to those of the American sense of the past. The representation of sensual life in Eliot's work, from sexuality to landscape, generally recalls the memories, desires, prohibitions, and guilts that come to him from the American scene. For Emerson, "the NOT ME, that is, both nature and art, all other men and my own body, must be ranked under this name, NATURE."[22] Consciousness as present to itself is opposed to all created, time-bound things. Nature in the colloquial sense is no different from culture, and both must be made subservient vehicles for the realization of eternal Spirit. In Thoreau's genetic oxymoron, "Chastity is the flowering of man." Though raised in Saint Louis, Eliot's upbringing continued the family's New England

21 See Friedrich Nietzsche, *The Will to Power*, trans. Walter Kaufmann and R. J. Hollingdale (New York, 1968), 278–83.
22 Whicher (ed.), *Selections from Emerson*, 22.

ways. "The standard of conduct was that which my grandfather had set; our moral judgments, our decisions between duty and self-indulgence, were taken as if, like Moses, he had brought down the tables of the Law, any deviation from which would be sinful" (CC, 44). It would be many years before Eliot could indulge the feelings he experienced in nature.

> My family did not move so often . . . because we tended to cling to places and associations as long as possible. . . . My family were New Englanders, who had been settled—my branch of it—for two generations in the South West—which was, in my own time, rapidly becoming merely the Middle West. The family guarded jealously its connexions with New England; but it was not until years of maturity that I perceived that I myself had always been a New Englander in the South West, and a South Westerner in New England. . . . In New England I missed the long dark river, the ailanthus trees, the flaming cardinal birds, the high limestone bluffs where we searched for fossil shell-fish; in Missouri I missed the fir trees, the bay and goldenrod, the song-sparrows, the red granite and the blue-sea of Massachusetts.[23]

These fond memories contrast sharply with the images in Eliot's poetry through *The Waste Land*; fragments of these visions are glimpsed only briefly amidst the "thousand sordid images" gathered in poems like the "Preludes." The disgust and fear evident in the work from 1909 through 1922 have a sexual dimension that is unmistakable, as in "Rhapsody on a Windy Night."

> The reminiscence comes
> Of sunless dry geraniums
> And dust in crevices,
> Smells of chestnuts in the streets,
> And female smells in shuttered rooms,
> And cigarettes in corridors
> And cocktail smells in bars.

Yet, even in the poems of this period, beloved natural figures from Eliot's American memory reappear fitfully, if only as reminders of what lilac and hyacinth, sea smell and wave, once promised. It is difficult to explain the repression and reemergence of these memories in Eliot's poetry unless we see that their fate is determined by Eliot's response to sensuality in general and, by a logic of autobiographical metonymy, to America itself. At about the time that Eliot enters his twenties, reads Laforgue, turns from Romantic lyricism, and writes "The Love Song of J. Alfred Prufrock," a reaction against

23 Preface to Edgar Ansel Mowrer, *This American World* (London, 1928), xiii–xiv.

nature sets in that holds, with significant scattered exceptions, until *Four Quartets*. A boy's joy in his senses gives way to an almost morbid recoiling from sight, smell, hearing, taste, and touch. The things of this earth, including women, appear largely in their negation, while poetic and critical energy is invested in the countering orders of Eliot's cultural acquisitions. The suppression of the "personal" in his poetics is an integral part of this development.[24] What has long been considered, after Pound's famous comment, the spontaneous "modernization" of Eliot's verse went by way of a revisionary repression directed at his own nature, as well as at the nature of the Romantics.

The New England version of "phallogocentrism" passed to many in each generation a deep-seated anxiety that sex was the agency of the Other—of devils, women, darkness, mortality, disorder, and those other inhabitants of Satan's, Dante's, or Freud's underworld. In an enlightening discussion of these matters, Gordon reports that Eliot's father considered sex as "nastiness": "Syphilis was God's punishment and he hoped a cure would never be found. Otherwise, he said, it might be necessary to 'emasculate our children to keep them clean.'"[25] Though such views harmonize well with passages from "The Death of Saint Narcissus," the Sweeney poems, *The Waste Land*, and the essay on Baudelaire, they do not seem to fit the late Victorian eroticism in the juvenilia. Whatever precipitated the crisis, Eliot simultaneously set out to exorcise nature, America, and Romanticism, retrospectively giving to them negative interpretations that were evidently not his first ones. His effort to control his own nature and create his own poetic style merged imperceptibly into his discourse on America, so that his eventual exile from the native landscape paralleled the asceticism of his morality and the impersonality of his poetics. The return of American images in his later poetry will likewise indicate a change in his thinking about nature, tradition, and poetic identity.

The American background to Eliot's responses may be found in the passages of Adams' *Education* echoed by "Gerontion." Gerontion cannot forgive nature and history for failing to deliver unity and identity. What he experiences instead is a chaos of emotions, most prominently of guilt and recrimination. He is yet another in the New England genealogy caught between desire and the law, where desire may also be metaphysical and the law the goddess Ananke. Like Cousin Nancy, who is a child of the "barren New

24 See John N. Serio, "Landscape and Voice in T. S. Eliot's Poetry," *Centennial Review*, XXVI (Winter, 1982), 33–50.
25 Gordon, *Eliot's Early Years*, 27.

England hills," Gerontion inherits a Manichaean tradition in which opposing forces struggle for ascendancy. Adams portrays this potentially paralyzing ambivalence (what Eliot would later call his own "aboulie") as an antagonism between New England and southern landscapes, a conflict quite evident in Eliot's sensibilities. The "passionate depravity" of the "Maryland May" educates and delights the son of Massachusetts Bay, and Adams falls "into the Southern ways of the summer village about La Fayette Square, as one whose rights of inheritance could not be questioned." The following page continues his "savage" attack against Boston's two evils, its weather and its morality: "The climate made eternal war on society, and sex was a species of crime." Adams' remark about his "rights of inheritance" is significant in a book whose chief subjects are the pressures of genealogy, history, and nature. The entire passage points back to an earlier chapter ("Washington") that recollects his first boyhood trip into the "May sunshine" of the South. Adams creates an allegory of natural determinism, with the "freedom, openness, swagger, of nature and man" in the South "almost obscuring" the cold, patriarchal atmosphere of Quincy and Boston. His "feeling caught on to an inheritance," for his maternal blood flowed partly from this warmer climate. With some relief Adams notes, "He did not wholly come from Boston himself." Within his nature course two conflicting inheritances, producing an emotional preference for maternal chaos over paternal law, as the former (in the guise of the Virgin Mary) absolves those who rebel against the latter.[26]

For Eliot, the story is repeated in a way by the distinction between the poetic and spiritual influence of his doting mother on the one hand and the forbidding, mercantile pragmatism of his civic-minded father on the other. It was not a choice between New England and "the South West," for memory cherished both. Rather, his was a choice between two inherited responses to nature, two histories that inscribed it alternately as timeless beauty or fallen spirit. Eliot usually chose to represent the sordid side of nature in his early work precisely because he held so hard to a theological concept of the beautiful and a phallogocentric concept of the sexual. The sensuous martyrdom depicted in poems like "The Death of Saint Narcissus" testifies to this tendency. The desired sublimation of the physical into the metaphysical is never achieved, despite the hyacinth girl and the Lady of *Ash Wednesday*, as long as the imagination defends itself against its own desires by portraying women with a violent physical disgust bordering on misogyny, such as in the manuscript drafts for the "Fresca" version of "The Fire Sermon" and the purged "The Death of the Duchess." Behind these poems, and *The Waste Land* as a

26 Duminaln (ed.) *The Education of Henry Adams*, 268–69, 44–45.

whole, is a terror of the differences that nature and sex make, what Sandra Gilbert in her analysis calls a "nightmare of gender disorder."[27] Woman literally becomes the place where man sees what he has "lost," the lack of center that threatens his own being. The breakdown of orderly distinctions between the sexes forms part of a larger pattern in which systems of identity and meaning come apart. As will become apparent in the course of the argument, sexuality functions as a discourse or kind of writing in Eliot and cannot be disentangled from matters that seem to belong to other realms. Sexuality entails genealogy and so provides metaphors of disorders in the structures of nature and history.

Eliot's castigations of the body were, of course, a way of retaining contact with its powers. The "impersonal" device of allusion leads us to myriad references to adultery, lust, and every form of family tragedy in the cultural artifacts of the West. His primary thesis for the construction of a literary history is the "dissociation of sensibility," that estrangement of mental and physical faculties that Eliot projects onto various authors and periods. He makes the charge in 1919 against Adams himself, indicating the extent to which it may be a congenital American disease: "It is probable that men ripen best through experiences which are at once sensuous and intellectual; certainly many men will admit that their keenest ideas have come to them with the quality of sense-perception; and that their keenest sensuous experience has been 'as if the body thought.' There is nothing to indicate that Adams's sense either flowered or fruited: he remains little Paul Dombey asking questions." This, written in the same year that Eliot lifts a passage from the *Education* for "Gerontion," should help us see how much of Eliot's condescending review of Adams' book grows out of an uneasiness with their kinship. As will so often be the case, Eliot uses the figure of a past writer to fashion a standard for himself and to ward off what threatens him. The review closes with a comparison of passages by Adams and Henry James as each arrives in Liverpool, the point being to demonstrate James's superior rendering of physical detail. Granted James's obvious superiority as a stylist, the contrast is nonetheless a massive misreading of the *Education*, which is at times a densely sensuous memoir, Jacobean in its language, of nature's chaotic thwarting of our cultural and historical senses. When one does compare passages like those on the death of Adams' sister to the writings of James, a greater level of abstraction obtrudes, to be sure, but it is with a philosophical emotion that Adams writes, and it is the content as well as the style of such

27 Sandra Gilbert, "Costumes of the Mind: Transvestism as Metaphor in Modern Literature," *Critical Inquiry*, VII (1980), 403.

paragraphs that influences Eliot. The exemplary figure of James offers the model for a more ascetic, refined sensuality of intellect, disciplined by European tradition and strengthened by its strange economy of chastity and revelation. James's bachelor visionaries trade their natures for knowledge, and despite the author's irony, Eliot finds this a more heartening tale than Adams' bitter confession of ignorance. "Wherever this man stepped," Eliot said of Adams, "the ground did not simply give way, it flew into particles," like the characters in "Gerontion" who are "whirled . . . in fractured atoms."[28] Though Eliot had to suppress the emasculated part of his legacy from James, he and Pound quickly saw that the fabulation of a European tradition could also give them a different ground to stand on. It is this adoption of Europe and its strange gods that becomes Eliot's first move in fathering a counter-genealogy.

28 "A Sceptical Patrician," *Athenaeum*, No. 4647 (23 May 1919), 362–63.

CHAPTER 2

THE IDENTITIES OF A POET

Yet if the only form of tradition, of handing down, consisted in following the ways of the immediate generation before us in a blind or timid adherence to its successes, "tradition" should positively be discouraged. We have seen many such simple currents soon lost in the sand; and novelty is better than repetition. Tradition is a matter of much wider significance. It cannot be inherited, and if you want it you must obtain it by great labour.

"Tradition and the Individual Talent"

From the start, T. S. Eliot aspired to a place in literary history. We have satisfied him, sometimes with a vengeance. Each generation since "Prufrock" and "Tradition and the Individual Talent" finds its inheritance haunted by the figures of Eliot. His words and example license us to obtain him according to our own lights, to acquire or reject him as we practice the "great labour" of interpreting the past. Like Matthew Arnold before him, Eliot pursued the writing of literary history with uncommon fervor. His criticism and poetry meant to change the canon of English literature, and he succeeded for a time quite beyond anyone's expectation. This disturbance in the shape and use of literary history is Eliot's chief critical legacy to us, and it complements a poetic practice that itself both arranges and disrupts the texts of the past. Eliot's version of the poetic canon emerged, as he often reminded us, from his own needs as a poet and more obscurely from his personal and cultural situation. To place Eliot now in literary history demands an acute self-consciousness about the entire process of canon formation, for his career reveals the intervention of self-interest in every critical decision, though I do not mean this observation as a pejorative judgment. The very possibility of writing a "literary history" or of even defining the term is vigorously debated by critical theorists in the postmodern era, and I think it no accident that the dilemma is one of Eliot's bequests to us. To understand, if not resolve, the problems posed to literary history by Eliot's modernism, we need first to reconsider the relation between tradition and inheritance.

The "wider significance" that distinguishes tradition from inheritance involves the freedom of the poet, and his guilt. In the passage preceding the one I have given as epigraph, Eliot asserts that poetic originality is not inconsistent with echoing ancestral voices. He qualifies this thesis with a distinction between passively received legacies and the values consciously appropriated by "great labour." What remains unclear, and vitally important, in Eliot's poetics is the motives and methods of this differentiation. To what extent does the present moment alter what it chooses to call its authorizing past, and with what authority? What kind of a tradition is it that can be acquired by judgment and selection? What rules, conscious or unconscious, guide the choice of a canonical genealogy?

Tradition, from its use and etymology, has usually meant a handing over, a passing on by the past of its effects. Shaped by his studies in poetry, psychology, and philosophy, Eliot knows that reception or impression is not mechanical but mediated. Our minds perceive selectively and in response to the histories that have composed them. Such an active role undermines the stability of a tradition. Is it something handed down to us or something that we clutch? Something found or something made? In fact, Eliot's idea of tradition already, in this ambivalence, exhibits the operations he will come to know later as "transfiguration."

Inheritance, in contrast, is a passively suffered bequest, a burdensome or worthless perpetuation of worn-out coinages. And yet, however debilitated, inheritance threatens to produce repetitions. Here and elsewhere, Eliot opposes tradition to inheritance in a way that suggests that the former is a response to the latter; it is a defense, evasion, erasure, or revision of what time hands down. Tradition transfigures inheritance. The repetition enacted by a "blind or timid adherence" (Oedipus' unwitting fulfillment of the oracle?) creates no new identity, is lost finally in the sands of time and death ("I will show you fear in a handful of dust"). Life inheres in novelty, in difference (as Heidegger and Derrida have argued), in the space between signifiers where structural linguistics finds the occasion of meaning in language. But a difference that cut itself off entirely from the past—if such a thing were possible—would lose identity as well and would find itself bereft of meaning. Relinquishing an inheritance, therefore, opens up an abyss, one that a newly gathered tradition must fill (or supplement). In his temerity the traditionalist denies the authority of the inheritance in order to author his own canon— a rebellion that in the poetics of modernism often wears the mask of self-sacrifice. The poet's remembrance of the past recovers the material for constructing the identity of the present; he may do so in the name of the fathers, but he will scatter their bones in gathering what he needs. As Eliot wrote in the crucial section on memory in his dissertation on F. H. Bradley, "Ideas of the past are true, not by correspondence with a real past, but by their coherence with each other and ultimately with the present moment; an idea of the past is true, we have found, by virtue of relations among ideas" (KE, 54). Eliot's poems and critical essays follow this noncorrespondence theory of truth. The "relations among ideas" form a genealogy or writing that interprets past and present in acts of figuration. Eliot's adopted traditions differ in determined ways from his inheritances, so that it is in these relations of divergence, as well as in the effects of coherence, that new meanings occur.

The espousal of "tradition," then, should not be read literally, but in the context of those things from which it is designed to differ. Dogmatic as Eliot often intends to sound, his statements operate in rhetorical and theoretical fields that, when taken into the interpretative account, alter our sense of his significance. Even an essay as conservative as "The Frontiers of Criticism" (1956), which seems so defensive in promulgating restrictions on the scope of criticism, equivocates on the critic's task. Is he to deliver the truth or point the way on a journey?

> What matters most, let us say, in reading an ode of Sappho, is not that I should imagine myself to be an island Greek of twenty-five hundred years ago; what matters is the experience which is the same for all human beings of different centuries and languages capable of enjoying poetry, the spark which can leap across those 2,500 years. So the critic to whom I am most grateful is the one who can make me look at some thing I have never looked at before, or looked at only with eyes clouded by prejudice, set me face to face with it and then leave me alone with it. From that point, I must rely upon my sensibility, intelligence, and capacity for wisdom. (OPP, 131)

The first half of the passage seems to present the familiar thesis of a timeless, "same" truth that unites Western culture in a single "spark" of poetic breath. Tradition recaptures the past logos. Yet, Eliot begins with an injunction against identification and repetition and makes the "same" an "experience," an emotional rather than epistemological event. Contradicting the Emerson of *Nature*, he employs criticism and tradition as the agents that clear up our vision for a face-to-face encounter. Again, we end with self-reliance; only here the mediation of criticism has been internalized, not repressed. Eliot leaves the figure of the reader in a kind of crisis. Reading does not bring back Sappho or the "same" identity of people, ideas, or things. Instead, it sets them in motion toward ends quite unlike their beginnings. Literary experience occasions the "same" *difference*, the experience of difference as a "spark" that begins another kind of knowing. Writing, criticism, and reading take place in the hopes that afterward things will never be quite the same.

Eliot's characterization of tradition (and of orthodoxy, monarchy, and classicism) often employed the rhetoric of loss and recovery, utilizing the conventional appeal of a return to an absolute logos, the Word as correspondent repetition rather than differing emergence. Indeed, the work up to the period from 1927 to 1933 (the six years of Eliot's second great crisis) does primarily communicate the desire for organizing fragments into a saving unity of the Same. In the later 1930s and in much of *Four Quartets*, Eliot achieves in his strongest moments a break from the earlier poetics of loss and impotence, which covertly restored what it lamented. The logos of the later poems works through a transfiguring textuality that strives to relinquish the desire for the recovery of the Same; the logos of *Four Quartets* is closer to that of Heraclitus than to that of Christ, whose death-for-resurrection's-sake dominated the economy of *The Waste Land*.

Identity—a metaphysic of the Same, known and recovered in a defeat of time—haunted Eliot's imagination and lured him with its promise, dividing his poetry and poetics deeply. Laboring under the imperatives of Identity, the imagination wanders unhappily between fugitive illuminations of presence and the devastations of irrevocable losses. The anxieties of inheritance, influence, genealogy, recollection, revision, and repetition all come into play under the auspices of such a metaphysic, and they are the major terms for the ways in which Eliot thinks of both literary and psychological experience. His writings proceed as variations on the theme of intertextuality and its metapsychology, drawing repeatedly on the realms of the above terms for their metaphors of writing. From its opening choices of inheritance to its late orchestration of ecstatic repetitions, Eliot's career took shape in an effort to comprehend the paradox of Identity—to comprehend or to cure it. But the thought of a cure is one of the lures Identity holds out, and it powerfully attracted the dismembered poet of *The Waste Land* and *Ash Wednesday*. The transfiguration he achieved became possible only when he relinquished this metaphysic; only when, after years of shifting, transgressing, and retreating, he finally made his uncertain way to an accommodation with its ghostly promises.

Near the beginning of his career, Eliot sought to resolve the problem of his poetic identity with "Prufrock." The decidedly mixed result, with its condensation of literary and sexual crises, led him to the more conventional and less emotional philosophical inquiry of his Bradley dissertation. This sequence is important to note if we are to appreciate the intertextuality of identity, whether in literature, psychology, or philosophy. The metaphors of inheritance, tradition, and genealogy point to the kinship between the processes that produce the person and those that produce the text. Eliot's work on Bradley allowed him to translate his personal, national, and literary dilemmas into the abstract formulas of philosophy. Though Eliot emerged as decentered as when he started, philosophy enabled him to go on analyzing his concerns through a language that was eminently impersonal. It is the first of his many covert autobiographies, one that spells out the noncorrespondence between Identity and representations.

No more than in "Prufrock" do the mermaids sing to the protagonist of the Bradley thesis.[1] The dualisms of real and ideal, knower and known, past and present collapse under the skeptical young philosopher's withering, albeit confused, critique of the circular discourse that makes up Western metaphysics and epistemology. By the end one can see why Eliot renounced this particular pulpit. The Absolute remains unknowable, and Eliot argues that knowledge appears only through an objectification and abstraction from particulars that he explicitly associates with the origin of language (KE, 132). Hence the mediate nature of human being: "Immediate experience . . . is a timeless unity which is not as such present either any*where* or to any*one*. It is only in the world of objects that we have time and space and selves. By the failure of any experience to be merely immediate, by its lack of harmony and cohesion, we find ourselves as conscious souls in a world of objects" (KE, 31). Eliot's narrative here seems that of a paradise lost and recalls Emerson's observation, in "Experience," that "it is very unhappy, but too late to be helped, the discovery we have made, that we exist. That discovery is called the Fall of Man." (The line of descent here runs through William James and American pragmatism.[2]) The self, too, is a figure mediated by the figures that precede it and vice versa. "The self, we find, seems to depend upon a world which in turn depends upon it; and nowhere, I repeat, can we find anything original or ultimate" (KE, 146).

For the Eliot of the Bradley thesis, the dissociated sensibility is articulated as a multiplicity of "points of view," the self occupying different "finite centres," often heterogeneous, sometimes simultaneous. Identity may at best be inferred from memory and language: "A reference to an identity . . . *is* the identity, in the sense in which a word *is* that which it denotes" (KE, 143). Eliot strains here, and in his argument for the continuity of symbol and thing symbolized, to retain a notion of identity despite the implications of his analysis. His opening strategy is to posit the experience of "feelings," the associated sensibility of thought and sensation, as the a priori of knowledge

1 See J. Hillis Miller, *Poets of Reality* (New York, 1969), 136–41; and Richard Wollheim, "Eliot and F. H. Bradley: An Account," in Graham Martin (ed.), *Eliot in Perspective* (New York, 1970), 169–93.

2 See Walter Benn Michaels, "Philosophy in Kinkanja: Eliot's Pragmatism," *Glyph*, VIII (1981), 170–202.

that no knowing can know, for all knowing names and so falls. (As the paradox indicates, the role of thought in such feelings is here minimal and awaits the definition it will receive when Eliot applies the theory to poetry). Self-knowledge likewise disseminates its object yet remains committed to the job of pulling itself together. "The point of view (or finite centre) has for its object one consistent world, and accordingly no finite centre can be self-sufficient, for the life of a soul does not consist in the contemplation of one consistent world but in the painful task of unifying (to a greater or less extent) jarring and incompatible ones, and passing, when possible, from two or more discordant viewpoints to a higher which somehow shall include and transmute them" (KE, 147–48).

The use of "transmute" in this hesitant formula of dialectical overcoming indicates the Hegelian inheritance with which Eliot is struggling. The key to Hegel's idealism and to his narrative of Spirit's inevitable Unity in History is the sublation, or *Aufhebung*, the critical motion that somehow both negates and preserves the past, controlling the lineage of generation in a restricted economy of ever more proper identities. This conceptual structure yields the Word that recovers the dead and saves the wasted, leaving no remainder; it is, Derrida has argued, the ideology common to Platonism, Christianity, and most Western thought. The program of the *Aufhebung* defines logocentrism and constantly tempts Eliot's divided soul with a promise of redemptive synthesis. "There are two (or more) worlds," he writes, "each continuous with a self, and yet running in the other direction—*somehow*—into an identity" (KE, 143; italics Eliot's). This reiterated "somehow" becomes the subject of Eliot's poetry. Such passages reveal a pathos in his otherwise cool rejection of idealism and epistemology. The labor of inheritance, as a structure of diverse negations and acquisitions, applies to the text of the soul as well as to those of the tradition and the poem.

The identity of a new text is composed by appropriation and violation of its sources, and that of the mind is composed by a like rewriting of influences. One need only recall that knowledge, even self-knowledge, comes to composition through the arrangement of representations. To the interpreting mind, experiences are texts. The quality, character, and identity of a mind are just such an interpretative arrangement, as a poem or fiction is an interpretative organization of acquired or fashioned signs. Personal identity and textual identity both undergo a problematic bout with originality and a troublesome quest for authority. I want to suggest, without simplifying, that the patterns of Eliot's poetics and those of his life often coincide, or determine each other. It is not at all a matter of reducing the poetry to biography or vice versa. Rather, it is a question of seeing how poetry and biography are after all two constructed, self-regulated, and artificial discourses dividing seamless experience between them. Neither discourse has a transcendent privilege of domain. If a system or systems of representation, or of feelings about representations, inhabit and structure the events in both domains, then they must be read together. Taking the opposite track from reduction, the reader can expand the conception of literature and of the self until their joint participation in a common effort of "writing" can be read. In this way psychological patterns, such as the Oedipus complex, become constituents in the interpretation of texts and histories.

The Oedipus complex, in fact, ought to be thought of first as an interpreter's hypothesis, a theory of the relationship between two (or more) "textual" identities in human time. The myth of Oedipus and Freud's myths about it are central in the canon of works on tradition and the individual talent. Raised to a theoretical level, psychological terms become literary tropes, as Harold Bloom has somewhat overzealously demonstrated. Neurosis, too, loses its reductive stigma when understood as a description of the anxiety built into the transmission of representations and identities through time. Jacques Lacan, for instance, in one of his relatively lucid moments, speculates that "neurosis is a question that being poses for the subject 'from where it was before the subject came into the world' (Freud's phrase, which he used in explaining the Oedipal complex to little Hans)."[3] As I read it for my purposes here, Lacanian neurosis can be historically conceived by reference to the subject's beginning insertion into the signifying structures of family, language, and culture that precede his origin. In his essay on the "mirror stage," Lacan narrates the development of the "I" as a proceeding from a self-conception of uncoordinated parts ("the fragmented body") to a vision of wholeness ironically predicated on a specular image or representative, an "other" who is, but who also recognizes, the self. "It is this moment that decisively tips the whole of human knowledge into mediatization through the desire of the other," as the "I" will go on seeking its identity through recognitions, desiring the desire of the other and confusing itself by identifying with the objects of the other's desire (the origin, thereby, of "phallogocentrism").[4] In these identifications, the "I" becomes inserted into a complex "symbolic order" wherein identities, like words, receive their meanings from

3 Jacques Lacan, *Ecrits: A Selection*, trans. Alan Sheridan (New York, 1977), 168. For an excellent elucidation of Lacan, see Fredric Jameson, "Imaginary and Symbolic in Lacan: Marxism, Psychoanalysis, and the Problem of the Subject," *Yale French Studies*, Nos. 55/56 (1977), 338–96. For clarification of many psychoanalytic terms and concepts, see J. Laplanche and J.-B. Pontalis, *The Language of Psycho-Analysis*, trans. Donald Nicholson-Smith (New York, 1973).

4 Lacan, *Ecrits*, 5, 198.

structures and relations. Like Freud, Lacan sees neurosis as an exaggerated version of everyone's inevitably subverted subjectivity. He sets out a theory of the primally decentered subject, of identity as imitative from the start, influenced in its very formation by the mediation of precursors that are signifiers, or texts, though they come in the shape of people.

Identity, in Lacan's argument, arises out of recognitions and so entangles the "I" in its desire for the desire of the other. This initiates the complex economy of "the family romance," in which desires and objects suffer elaborate transferences and transpositions that make up the rhetoric of personal life, for "the moment in which desire becomes human is also that in which the child is born into language." Governing this signifying economy, prescribing the rules of desire, is the logos of the symbolic order, called by Lacan the *non du père*—the Law of the Name and the No of the Father. His regulating and introjected interdiction establishes the restraint whose metaphor is castration.[5] This theory of identity considerably extends that of Freud's Oedipus complex, by way of Hegel, Saussure, and Heidegger, transforming it into a general philosophical psychology of language, cognition, and temporality. For poetics, as the work of Bloom shows, these hypotheses invite adaptation by the theorist of literary history and poetic genesis, who must account for the effects of the writer's insertion into the symbolic order of tradition and the subsequent procedures of imitation, repression, and transferred desire that follow. Tradition poses a problem for the poet, poses the poet himself as the question of poetry's new identity. Answering this imposition, the poet repositions himself, yet always in a relation, however negatively conceived, to the inherited law of the other. The poet's subjectivity has a place in response to what it shall be or mean to enact poetry now, again, here, when so much has already been said, including one's own name. "Modernism" as the desire for the new start, the new subject, replays the Oedipal theme and is thus usually, in whatever time or place, a neurosis. To make the equation more bluntly, the identities of the "I," the poet, and the poetic text may all be read as the results of intertextuality.

Psychoanalysis, however, offers more than a method for interpreting the advent of twentieth-century modernism. Freud's theoretical elaborations on generational conflict, the distortion of memory and representation, and the psychological economy of cultural history were themselves products of modernism's self-conscious parturition. Freud's texts at once participate in this insurrection and propose a reading of it. Carl E. Schorske has argued that the origin of psychoanalysis is inseparable from its particular setting in

5 Ibid., 69, 281–91.

Austro-European history. Like many of his counterparts in England and America, Freud confronted the inadequacies of rationalist humanist idealism and romantic selfhood. The "collective oedipal revolt" of the *fin de siècle* generation "against the authority of the paternal culture that was their inheritance" involved the nascent modernists in a paradoxical "search for new self-definitions. . . . Here historical change not only forces upon the individual a search for a new identity but also imposes upon whole social groups the task of revising or replacing defunct belief systems. The attempt to shake off the shackles of history has paradoxically speeded up the processes of history, for indifference to any relationship with the past liberates the imagination to proliferate new forms and new constructs."[6] *History* also denotes the specific temporal lineage of any human enterprise, and Schorske ties Freud's psychoanalytic modernism to the literature, architecture, painting, and music of the time. He subordinates all these modernisms a little too neatly to the crises of Austrian "liberalism," but the intersection charted between the diachronic analysis of a particular art form's changes and the synchronic analysis of contemporary developments in various fields remains pertinent. A knot quite difficult to interpret ties together a poet's response to past poets with his response to society, politics, and his own personal "case history." This overdetermination of the living subject or artistic text makes the temptation of "indifference" all the more intense, since a pure identity would free one from the network of differential struggle.

After psychoanalysis, or after our recognition of the traces that cannot be obliterated from (inter)textuality, no such liberating "indifference to any relationship with the past" can rest easy. Paul de Man explores this dilemma in his essay "Literary History and Literary Modernity," in which Nietzsche's call to forget or annihilate "anteriority" is shown to have the opposite result. Nietzsche's "parricidal" account of modernity perpetuates time and genealogy in the very refusal of them. This "temporal chain" constitutes a "literary history" as manifest discontinuities and latent continuities. Like Bloom, de Man adopts Freud's antithetical reading of denial: "The more radical the rejection of anything that came before, the greater the dependence on the past."[7] Yet, unlike Bloom (and here the difference is also Bloom's from Derrida, or in a way yet to be articulated, the difference of the early Eliot from the late), de Man holds out no promise that active forgetfulness, or repression, will bring a new sublimity. On the contrary, for Lacan's inserted sub-

6 Carl E. Schorske, *Fin-De-Siècle Vienna: Politics and Culture* (New York, 1980), xxvi, xviii.
7 Paul de Man, "Literary History and Literary Modernity," in *Blindness and Insight: Essays in the Rhetoric of Contemporary Criticism* (New York, 1971), 161.

ject, for de Man's literary artist, and even for Eliot's "traditional" poet, there is no subject, no text, except in distorted and displaced response to the discourse of the other. This structural involvement with anteriority, with the texts of the pasts in their various historical and formal divisions, is further reinforced as modernism turns to the cultural storehouse for the authorizing figures it requires to empower its own project. The neurotic entanglement in the demands of past voices results in another hearing, a troubled transfiguring of what is necessarily recalled and redeployed in the hope of making it, the text, and the poet "new."

CHAPTER 3

MODERNISM AND ARCHAEOLOGY

If modern civilization at the beginning of this century was, as many thought, thoroughly neurotic, it was a neurosis stemming from a radical ambivalence toward the role played by the past in the identity of the present. The saving uses of the past were products of interested interpretations. The political concerns of the modernists were thus linked to their poetic worries. The work of Eliot, Pound, Joyce, and others became explicitly, often pedantically, didactic and revisionary. Whether in poems and novels of densely packed allusions or in essays defining the "classics" and "kulchur," they purposively lifted elements from the cultural archive. These recoveries were not random: they made up a program, often inchoate or naïve, for poetics and society. As we shall see, for every recovery of a lost authority there was a corresponding expulsion from the canon, so that the new tradition was designed to cure the ills of modern life and poetry. Though it can be agreed that modernism has neither an absolute meaning nor a single historical incarnation, the question of specific modernisms, their geneses and fates, still pervades our contemporary quest in criticism and literature to "make it new." However insecure temporal categorizations of literary history may be, the need of each generation to name and substantiate itself by producing an interpretation of cultural antecedents persists. Eliot's critique of the objectivity of personal memory is equally relevant to literary history: "In short, it appears that the past in the sense in which it is supposed to be recalled, in popular psychology, simply never existed; the past lived over is not memory, and the past remembered was never lived" (KE, 51).

This thinking of the past as history, as an otherness to be approached, excavated, restored, and interpreted, accelerated greatly in the West in the time following the eighteenth century. Previously sanctioned systems of cognition, historiography, metaphysics, science, and poetics were rapidly transformed, and in each the perceived discontinuity of times, the distance and difference of history, was a crucial factor. Many accounts have been offered of the great break that seems to occur in Western thought during the nineteenth century. For my purposes I wish to accentuate the problematization of history that took place and its effects on the forms of literature. Michel

Foucault argues that the discourse of history replaced the "Classical meta-physic" by articulating temporal narratives of "that gap between order and Order, between classifications and Identity, between natural beings and Nature." History "will be Metaphysics, therefore, only in so far as it is Memory, and it will necessarily lead thought back to the question of knowing what it means for thought to have a history." Historical self-consciousness "from Hegel to Nietzsche and beyond" darkens present knowledge with the shadows cast by the figures of time.[1]

What occurred, and what problematized history, was a proliferation of discourses shattering the taxonomical table of Classical Order, upon which all discourses had founded a single History. The variety of independent histories—in economics, politics, literature, biology, philology, and philosophy—left man without a single History, adrift in the uncoordinated interplay of all his histories. The writing of history now becomes a yoking of disparities in the waste land of the present. All philosophies become philosophies of history, and all disciplines constitute themselves through strategies of representation that attempt to narrate the effects of time. The rise of archaeology and classical philology, for example, in late-eighteenth-century Germany has an immediate impact on the development of Romanticism, and its repercussions are still being felt in the works of Pound, Joyce, and Eliot. Museums and libraries in the modern sense, with their systematic representations of the past, replace the old "cabinets of curiosities" with interpretative structures.[2] A catastrophe in the Western discourse on time, order, and knowledge results in the dissemination of historical inquiries and the historicization of science, education, aesthetics, and literature.

> So that man found himself dispossessed of what constituted the most manifest contents of his history: nature no longer speaks to him of the creation or the end of the world, of his dependency or his approaching judgement; it no longer speaks of anything but a natural time; its wealth no longer indicates to him the antiquity or the imminent return of a Golden Age; it speaks only of conditions of production being modified in the course of history; language no longer bears the marks of a time before Babel or of the first cries that rang through the jungle; it carries the weapons of its own affiliation. The human being no longer has any history: or rather, since he

1 Michel Foucault, *The Order of Things: An Archaeology of the Human Sciences* (New York, 1973), 219–20.
2 On the representational theories informing the encyclopedia, the library, and the museum see Eugenio Donato, "The Museum's Furnace: Notes Toward a Contextual Reading of *Bouvard and Pécuchet*," in Josué V. Harari (ed.), *Textual Strategies: Perspectives in Post-Structuralist Criticism* (Ithaca, 1979), 213–38. Donato persuasively challenges aspects of Foucault's archaeological method

speaks, works, and lives, he finds himself interwoven in his own being with histories that are neither subordinate to him nor homogeneous with him. By the fragmentation of the space over which Classical knowledge extended in its continuity, by the folding over of each separated domain upon its own development, the man who appears at the beginning of the nineteenth century is "dehistoricized."

And the imaginative values then assumed by the past, the whole lyrical halo that surrounded the consciousness of history at that period, the lively curiosity shown for documents or for traces left behind by time—all this is a surface expression of the simple fact that man found himself emptied of history, but that he was already beginning to recover in the depths of his own being, and among all the things that were still capable of reflecting his image (the others have fallen silent and folded back upon themselves), a historicity linked essentially to man himself. But this historicity is immediately ambiguous. Since man posits himself in the field of positive knowledge only in so far as he speaks, works, and lives, can his history ever be anything but the inextricable nexus of different times, which are foreign to him and heterogeneous in respect of one another?[3]

The Waste Land, the Cantos, Ulysses—the texts of modernism—would try their hand at weaving "the inextricable nexus of different times."

Foucault's account has been challenged, and it seems itself to posit a Golden Age before the nineteenth century. Yet, he remains substantially correct. The surge of historical thought in that century marks a change in Western life. The past now appears in desperate need of being accounted for, while the present seems unable to know itself except through a story of origins, evolutions, teleologies, and ends. Previous discourses in theology, cosmology, and natural philosophy had placed the temporally precedent in a spatial location that was, like the metaphysical system, always present in an eternal explanation. The difference between past and present was a difference of place in a structure that transcended time. During the nineteenth century, in a variety of disciplines and institutions, the past ceases to be present in this way and thus becomes highlighted as a locus of inquiry. Gothic romance and the tales of Poe disclose the past as a nightmare, a series of figures that haunts the consciousness of the present. The past looms as a distant, discrete, discontinuous, and dispersed question that history must shape into meaning. Doubtless this is true, in some degree, for all ages, but the self-consciousness and explicit thematization of the historical in the nineteenth century indicates the scope of its anxious privilege over other modes of knowing. Coupled with the simultaneous rise of the subjective mind in epistemology and

3 Foucault, The Order of Things, 368–69.

literature, the work of historical knowing becomes the art of memory, and memory a form of history. History and memory lend new directions and problems to each other, creating a rebus whose interpretation inspires the texts of Freud and so many other modernist writers.

What one reads, in this light, in Proust, Pound, Eliot, Joyce, and Mann is the various effects of having metaphysics replaced by memory and of memory's discovering that it cannot master the history that inhabits it. But this kind of remembrance, like archaeology, seeks to balance restoration in and of the present with a concern for exhibiting the artifacts in the integrity of their "original" state. Modern archaeology makes artifacts into texts as, following in the tradition of German scholarship, the past becomes fossil poetry. No longer are missing arms to be restored to torsos, as if past and present were one. Cabinets of curiosities give way to epistemological displays, and the museum houses history's encyclopedia for all to read. The archaeological representation retains, however, the strangeness of the artifact, the ruin of its "presence" in the present. It is as much a didactic reminder of what has been lost, of times irrecuperable, as it is a living part of a continuing culture. The attempt at constructing a modernity with history's leftovers checked its own presumption by guarding a degree of the artifact's integrity, as a scholar checks exactness of dates and quotes before presenting the argument. The modernism of Eliot and Pound was "archaeological," prompted by the breakdown of History into histories and borrowing from the new disciplines their methods and concerns. What is *The Waste Land* if not a library of past voices? What are the *Cantos* but a wild flight on the wings of comparative literature, philology, and history? Pound, with a bit of gleeful pride, admitted that "Yeats used to say I was trying to provide a portable substitute for the British Museum." Eliot was elected to the presidency of the London Library, on which occasion he declared that "the disappearance of the London Library would be a disaster to civilization."[4] In poetry, allusions and quotations can be treated as artifacts, and intertextuality can be a form of remembrance with affinities to scholarship and criticism. The inheritance lies in ruins; the writer digs up the fragments to compose his own contributions from the shares of others. Posing as archaeologist, the poet arrives late among the rubble, as if he had no role in tearing down the temples. Modernism has long been perceived as a reaction to a felt death of the gods, but the overshadowing power of the past may have its ironic testimonial in so many

4 D. D. Paige (ed.), *Selected Letters of Ezra Pound* (New York, 1950), 257; *An Address to the Members of the London Library* (London, 1952), 5. Eliot goes on to explain, "I have an accumulation of books so various, so recalcitrant of order, that when I want to consult some book I know I possess, I cannot find it, and have to borrow it from the London Library."

funerals for the deities. Lacan observed that the myth of God's death is perhaps "simply a shelter against the threat of castration."[5] The guise of homage to the restored pantheon obscures the transgression of the newcomer.

Intertextuality is the mode of poetic archaeology. It is that sometimes wonderful, sometimes deadly game of reference and usurpation played by books, discourses, events, or any system that constructs worlds of meaning from representations. The comparison with archaeology notes an actual lineage of influence that ran from the German scholars, art historians, classicists, and philologists through the English Romantics and the Harvard faculty under C. W. Eliot to T. S. Eliot and his contemporaries. The two great scholar-modernists of the archaeological tradition were Erich Auerbach and Ernst Robert Curtius.[6] Like Pound and Eliot, both made Dante the central figure in their very different efforts to construct a historical continuity and unity for Western literature. Auerbach's *Mimesis* and Curtius' *European Literature and the Latin Middle Ages* bear a striking formal and strategic similarity to the *Cantos* and *The Waste Land*. Auerbach fashions the plenitude of each chapter in his literary history by an inspired reading of a single passage, a luminous detail found at hand in his exile's library at Istanbul. His theory of *figura*, first worked out in his early book on Dante, is a historicist's and realist's attempt to revise the Christian and Hegelian philosophies of temporality and representation, though finally, as we shall see, the most erudite philological effort cannot prevent the dissemination of the *figura*. Curtius' artifacts (his forefathers were pioneers in German archaeology and comparative philology) are his *topoi*, radiant gists of textuality that are gathered to compose a unifying rhetoric for the West. His "Romania" is fabulated as a prescription for the disease of modern European disharmony, but his compendium of conventions only subverts mystified notions of creation, originality, authority, and unity. The chapters on the "Ancients" and the "Moderns" and on canon formation definitively expose the historicity and relativity of such concepts, thereby contributing to the modernist's malaise.

The purposes informing the narratives and methods of Auerbach and Curtius are akin to the desires of other modernists, "critical" or "creative." And they share with them a common fate. An intertextuality is set to work whose

---

5 Jacques Lacan, *The Four Fundamental Concepts of Psycho-Analysis*, trans. Alan Sheridan (New York, 1981), 27.

6 Eliot greatly admired Curtius' work, which he published in the *Criterion*, and Curtius reciprocated with praise of Eliot's criticism and poetry, translating *The Waste Land* into German. The two had a falling out in later years over Goethe. See "A Commentary," *Criterion*, XII (October, 1932), 73–79; "Brief über Ernst Robert Curtius," in *Freundsgabe für Ernst Robert Curtius* (Bern, 1956); and Ernst Robert Curtius, *European Literature and the Latin Middle Ages*, trans. Willard Trask (Princeton, 1953), 597–98.

results no center will hold, not even one transfigured from those so passionately found in the past. *Tradition* was Eliot's word for the intertextual debates of the past, present, and future voices. The term was a holdover from English criticism; with characteristic subtlety he refashioned it, together with the legacy it nominated. In *The Sacred Wood* Eliot tried to convince himself and his readers that he was advocating a tradition chosen only for artistic and technical reasons. He charged Arnold, his major precursor in English criticism, with hunting "game outside of the literary preserve altogether" (SW, xiii). The book, though, makes its choices for reasons personal, political, and philosophical. The last essay, his first on Dante, expressly if awkwardly defends both philosophical poetry and philosophical criticism. The 1928 preface acknowledges Eliot's change in attitude, though it persists, as Eliot will, in believing that there can be a purely technical literary criticism: "When we are considering poetry we must consider it primarily as poetry and not another thing" (SW, viii). This dogmatic command lacks convincing argument, and the position is ultimately untenable. Eliot hopes to retain this thesis while hunting other game, but the contradiction remains unresolved, and the force of the movement away from technical criticism dominates. "I by no means disown it by having passed on to another problem not touched upon in this book: that of the relation of poetry to the spiritual and social life of its time and of other times" (SW, viii).

In a search that culminated in "The Social Function of Poetry" (1945), Eliot tried other terms, such as *culture* and the *classic*, to expand the province of inheritance and intertextuality to all human affairs. His promotion of a classical curriculum in "Modern Education and the Classics" responded to the liberalization of Harvard's curriculum under his distant cousin C. W. Eliot and to the general secularization of education that refused to select according to a strong "philosophy of life" (SE, 452). Curricular reform was another version of canon formation, and in both discourses Eliot vainly sought a single, stable, ideal order. *The Idea of a Christian Society* and *Notes Towards the Definition of Culture* simply put Christian "culture" in the place of literary tradition and educational classics with about the same degree of success. One can trace this pattern through the more voluminous and strident tracts of Pound, who actually wrote "textbooks" like *ABC of Reading* and *Guide to Kulchur*.

Eliot's conservatism became a kind of antithetical conservationism that displaced while it preserved. Remembrance, however, carries with it the knowledge of loss, and loss the implication of the inadequacy or inevitable doom of the forgotten. If this were a study chiefly of Eliot's social theories, I would take some time to argue that the positions he adopts, his notorious

Anglican royalist classicism, are constructed in the way his literary canons are propounded, as corrective fictions for a diseased time. There is no more or less reality to Eliot's ideal of a Christian society than there is to his portraits of Dante, Shakespeare, or Virgil. The power of the criticism generated by these constructs is, nonetheless, genuine and acute. Admirable in places, the social essays are embarrassing when Eliot forgets the fabulous nature of his orders and seems to call for their enactment rather than for a study of their "idea" (see ICS, 6). So we may blush when we are told that "the first educational task of the communities should be the *preservation* of education within the cloister" (SE, 460) or that "if you will not have God (and He is a jealous God) you should pay your respects to Hitler and Stalin" (ICS, 50).

Without necessarily impugning the sincerity of Eliot's social essays, we may observe that this work amounts to a massive investment in what Freud called the *Über-Ich* (or superego), the internal and external discourses of restraint, repression, and sublimation. The almost obsessive articulation of impersonal orders to which we might sacrifice ourselves indicates, by that logic of denial and negation so characteristic of the unconscious, the power within of other desires. The transferences and identifications Eliot made between his ideas of literary order and those of religion, politics, economics, and education resulted in blunders as aptly titled as *After Strange Gods*. The structure or economy of thought he developed psychologically and poetically was uncritically applied to targets outside the literary arena; so although a homology exists between his theories in those disparate fields, he rarely developed a theory (except in poetry) out of material experience. His social criticism is a poem, oddly coherent in itself but hopelessly out of touch with the tangible experiences of those human masses he hopes to save.[7] Eliot borrows from the orders of civilization the authority he requires to deal with his own discontents. In this way he circuitously regains the stature and identity that would perhaps have been his familial, native one had his American inheritance not come to him so divided.

Inheritances are often entailed, binding the legatee to circumstances beyond his control. Of this Eliot was personally and painfully aware, for his father had met the son's expatriate estrangement from familial, national legacies with a matching proscription, aimed straight at the disobedient marriage that had sealed Eliot's exile. Henry Ware Eliot, Sr., so disapproved of his son's decision to stay in England that he rewrote his will. T. S. Eliot's share, unlike those of his sisters and brothers, was not left outright, but entailed in a trust. In the event of the young poet's death, the bequest would

---

7 Stephen Spender concludes differently in his fine *T. S. Eliot* (New York, 1976), 11.

revert back to the family, with not a penny for Vivienne. She herself had few prospects for inheritance, and Eliot felt obliged for her sake not to undertake "adventures," since his job at the bank provided security for both of them (see WLFS, xxvii–xxviii). Ancestors may deprive their children even in death, forcing them into strategies of appropriation. It may not be insignificant that January of 1919 marks both the death of the father and the start of that difficult period in which his son was gestating *The Waste Land*, a poem devoted to assembling its cultural inheritance as it elegizes a lost figure of kingly power. By leaving America and immersing himself in a foreign tradition, Eliot had in a sense renounced his patrimony, and he was in turn renounced by it. The loss of this past was both an enrichment and an affliction, something Eliot feared as well as desired. Death and discontinuity were the opening conditions for an authorial career of reinscriptions and resurrections.

Inheritance, then, is not natural or spontaneous or free. It requires a mechanism or medium of transference, a system of exchange whose characteristics intervene to transform what is passed on. The structures of language, metaphor, and memory have their kinship with the organization of inheritance. The inheritance, like the metaphor or the memory, is somehow other than the postulated but never present original. Transmitted, it is something other than the wealth once held by previous hands in distant places at different times. Inheritance raises the question of property and of all the textual and critical puns deriving from it (propriety, the proper noun, the proper self, the properties of things, etc.). Once inheritance enters a metaphorical reading, passive reception gives way to the spectacle of an arduous recollection, self-conscious about the adequacy of its procedures and the nature of its gains. Writing as inheritance begins in disinheritance, which it has either willed or embraced as a *felix culpa* into difference and modernity. To return to an earlier metaphor, it is not a matter of receiving archaeological objects, but of treating the world in such a way as to archaeologize it, rendering its elements "dead" so as to require the services of an archaeologist.

Inheritance forms a network for signification Eliot never tires of exploring. Though it provides a tentative way of joining Eliot's texts, this network is also a confusing obstacle: it becomes quite impossible to entirely distinguish the analysis of any given term, since *history, time, self, representation, death,* and other such words mirror and interpret one another. Any change in one changes the others. The movement, for example, in Eliot's career from an emphasis on tradition ("a simultaneous order") to an espoused faith in the Incarnation ("The point of intersection of the timeless / With time") is at once the substitution of one metaphor of temporal readjustment for another and a wholesale shift in the range of references such intersections connote. "Incarnation" appropriates the discourses of religion and metaphysics in a thesis of salvation, surpassing the cure offered by a literary conception of "tradition." The idea of resurrection rests latently in the notion of tradition, but its extrapolation leads to "Little Gidding" and the glimpsed fusion of poetic, religious, and world-historical inheritances in an inconceivable time. Other recurrent Eliotic themes, such as impotence, askesis, misogyny, love, and childhood, play roles in the drama of recollection's quest for value. And when Eliot leads a march through the streets of London, heartily singing "Onward, Christian Soldiers" to protest the planned demolition of old London churches, the motivation resembles that behind the archaeological style of *The Waste Land*. Likewise, the impulse of "Tradition and the Individual Talent" in 1919 was still at work when Eliot served on the Commission for the Revised Psalter of the Book of Common Prayer (1958–1963) and "seldom spoke except to plead for the retention of an old phrase."[8]

To Eliot the Anglican church stood for a retained system of signs, an old text to be freshly read, a group of artifacts whose perpetuation into modernity would jar memories. The church offered a continuous narrative about man, fulfilling the requirements of inheritance, but also allowing into its edifice new prayers and sermons as the times demanded. The physical church was to be preserved as a monument and as a home for the practice of spiritual rebirths. As a memorial object it recalls to the people a specific history, and potential future, of thought and feeling. These churches, like the ruins of Rome, were at once reminders of how the world had formerly been apprehended and promises of a future Empire. But the church, in the same sense as a tradition, had to be an adjustable and nourishing order. In *The Value and Use of Cathedrals in England Today*, Eliot argues that they must not be "preserved simply as ancient monuments of historical and artistic interest with turnstiles and admissions charges." The churches and the literary tradition are to be rebuilt by modernists strong enough to inherit by choice and to revise by necessity. Inheritance involves conservation, but active conservation is not to be mistaken for hollow conservatism: "While I am conservative in the matter of doing away with what is old, I deplore excessive conservatism where there is a new work to be done; and I had rather take the risk of a great modern artist, when we have one, than employ a man who can be depended on to produce a close imitation of the devotional art of an earlier age." The modern artist restoring the churches and the modern writer restoring the tradition are one. Rather than reproduce a Gothic or baroque inte-

8 Robert Sencourt, *T. S. Eliot: A Memoir* (New York, 1971), 223.

rior, a Homeric simile or Jacobean conceit, the artist makes it new. "Surely it is the great task of the religious artist, musician, and even the creative writer, to realize religious feeling in the terms of his own time."[9]

So Eliot would revere Joyce, imitate *Ulysses*, praise how the Catholic tradition saturates his pages; he would canonize Joyce beside Virgil and Dante as one who shores up the inheritance, while identifying D. H. Lawrence with that other, iconoclastic strain of his own divided soul. Whereas Lawrence painfully disturbs Eliot's control of his passions and individual talents, Joyce rights the balance: "We are not concerned with the authors' *beliefs*, but with orthodoxy of sensibility and with the sense of tradition, our degree of approaching 'that region where dwell the vast hosts of the dead.' And Lawrence is for my purposes, an almost perfect example of the heretic. And the most ethically orthodox of the more eminent writers of my time is Mr. Joyce" (ASG, 38). When faithful or dogmatic, Eliot relies on a fiction of the solidity of the church's or literature's authority. This fiction licenses the modern artist to revise within the boundaries of an already sanctified structure. Here Eliot does not admit that the church and the house of writing may already be the constructions of modern artists or that the existence of primordial structures of original authority may be one of the modern artist's most beguiling additions. In "*Ulysses*, Order, and Myth," he projects his ideal onto Joyce. "By manipulating a continuous parallel between contemporaneity and antiquity," Eliot's Joyce (and the poet of *The Waste Land*, published the year before) found "a way of controlling, of ordering, of giving a shape and a significance to the immense panorama of futility and anarchy which is contemporary history" (SP, 177). Yet, Eliot stubbornly blinds himself to the message of the scene that probably affected him the most, Stephen's talk in the library on *Hamlet*. Whereas Eliot's 1919 essay on *Hamlet* makes no mention of the paternal specter, Stephen sees the genealogical perplexities Shakespeare builds into the play and knows, as Joyce, Hamlet, and Shakespeare knew, the weighty ambiguity of the past's command. In the library, "paternity may be a legal fiction." Myth and tradition are other legalized fictions invoked by Eliot against life's turmoil and that of Joyce's book.

Modernist uses of myth and tradition induce disorder within the settled consciousness of the reader, disorienting conventions and supplementing memory. According to Lillian Feder, "Eliot considered myth a means of reaching beneath the level of present and conscious experience" to recall the ancient, timeless patterns of violence and desire that persist in the archives of our personal and cultural unconscious. Feder rightly cites Eliot's later theory

9 *The Value and Use of Cathedrals in England Today* (Chichester, 1952), 3, 9.

that the "auditory imagination" penetrates "far below the conscious level of thought and feeling, invigorating every word; sinking to the most primitive and forgotten, returning to the origin and bringing something back, seeking the beginning and the end" (UPUC, 118–19). But the mythical method fails to resolve the anarchy of contemporary life precisely because what it recalls from the past is memories or texts dramatizing the same dissensions: Osiris, Tiresias, Oedipus, Philomela, Mr. Apollinax, Sweeney, the hyacinth girl, Phlebas, and so on. The correspondence between past and present undoes beginnings and ends because it brings back a prophecy of repeated transgressions. Violence and desire rend the origin; they both initiate and exceed the economies of identity and order. Neither *Ulysses* nor *The Waste Land* gave "shape and significance" to modern history without further disrupting it: "There can be no reconciliation, Stephen said, if there has not been a sundering."[10] Odysseus and the Fisher King were authorized ghosts, compounded to reign over the salutary dismemberment of conventional laws.

The modern artist's proclaimed departure from the past constitutes the moment of greatest danger, for in that reactionary moment the influential power of the past bears down hardest, and denial evidences the present's continuing involvement with the past. The announcement of a modernity depends upon an interpretation of the past, upon a way of remembering that dissimulates itself as forgetfulness or rebellion. As de Man observes: "As soon as modernism becomes conscious of its own strategies . . . it discovers itself to be a generative power that not only engenders history, but is part of a generative scheme that extends far back into the past. . . . When they assert their own modernity, they are bound to discover their dependence on similar assertions made by their literary predecessors; their claim to being a new beginning turns out to be the repetition of a claim that has always already been made."[11] The modernism of the twentieth century starts with this predicament, made more acute by the literature inherited from Romanticism and its Victorian heirs, which thematized the dilemma. The cultivation of historical and literary erudition by Eliot and others was, I hope to show, a tactic designed to circumvent two possible fates: a modernism doomed to belatedness by its naïveté, and a traditionalism doomed to banal imitation by its complacency.

The modernist rejection of Romanticism was conditioned by the prospects of these twin fates. The Romantic perception of precursors as overwhelming

---

10 Lillian Feder, *Ancient Myth in Modern Poetry* (Princeton, 1971), 122; James Joyce, *Ulysses* (New York, 1934), 192.

11 Paul de Man, "Literary History and Literary Modernity," in *Blindness and Insight: Essays in the Rhetoric of Contemporary Criticism* (New York, 1971), 150, 161.

deities could be reversed with the axiom that the true gods, the true tradition, the true Paideuma had vanished. This stance had the advantage of miti-
gating the modernist's debt to the Romantics, providing a model that questioned the stature of past figures. Modernism could take its cue from the
archaeological element in Romanticism itself, which had its own deep concerns about ruins and faded myths. The anti-Romantic modernists dug up
the neoclassicism of Romanticism for their own purposes, leaping past the
degenerate Romanticism of more immediate precursors. In this way the poet
gained a new view of his vocation, envisioning himself in Eliot's or Pound's
case as a heroic "bricoleur" of fallen worlds. Thus, the resurrection of tradition is a kind of massive troping of the titanic fathers into dead prophets, like
Tiresias in Hades, who can only be heard when exiled, wandering poets descend into time and bid them speak.

For this trope the modernists turned to the passages in Frazer's *Golden
Bough* on Attis, Adonis, and Osiris that Eliot cites in his notes to *The Waste
Land*. Pound writes a series of articles called "I Gather the Limbs of Osiris," a
disquisition on the "new method of scholarship" that is one with the new
method of poetry. The limbs of Osiris represent the archaeologically recovered fragments gathered by the poet in allusive combinations. He calls it
"the method of Luminous Detail, a method most vigorously hostile to the
prevailing mode of today—that is, the method of multitudinous detail, and
to the method of yesterday, the method of sentiment and generalisation."
Luminous Detail opposes the chaos of multitudinous detail and produces a
kind of revelation by synecdoche.

> In the history of the development of civilisation or of literature, we come
> upon such interpreting detail. A few dozen facts of this nature give us intel-
> ligence of period—a kind of intelligence not to be gathered from a great
> array of facts of the other sort. . . . The artist seeks out the luminous de-
> tail and presents it. He does not comment. . . . The luminous details re-
> main unaltered. As scholarship has erred in presenting all detail as if of
> equal import, so also in literature, in a present school of writing we see a
> similar tendency. . . . We advance by discriminations, by discerning that
> things hitherto deemed identical or similar are dissimilar; that things hith-
> erto deemed dissimilar, mutually foreign, antagonistic, are similar and
> harmonic.[12]

It is the method of the *Cantos*, and it parallels the theory behind *The Waste
Land*, spelled out by Eliot in analyzing the Metaphysical poets, whose "effects are secured by brief words and sudden contrasts," a "telescoping of im-

12 Ezra Pound, *Selected Prose, 1909–1965* (New York, 1973), 21, 22–23, 25.

ages and multiplied associations" creating "a degree of heterogeneity of material compelled into unity by the operation of the poet's mind" (SE, 242–43).

Quoting the *Oxford Companion to Classical Literature*, Hugh Kenner reminds us that "it was Osiris, 'the male principal in nature,' who became when
his scattered limbs had been regenerated the god of the dead (of Homer, of
the Seafarer poet, of Arnaut Daniel), but also the source of renewed life."[13]
Jessie L. Weston's *From Ritual to Romance* extended Frazer's conception of
the vegetation god to the Arthurian cycle and the Grail quest, trying unsuccessfully to erase the theme of guilt built into the accounts of Freud and
Frazer. In the legends, the parts of the god have been disseminated about the
land or thrown into the waters. The corpse/corpus has been mutilated in the
cause of fresh fertility: its return from the dead promises a transumption for
all of nature and culture. The phallus of Osiris, however, in many of the versions Frazer surveys, is never found. If this vital, procreative member is missing, at least two contradictory interpretations arise. On the one hand, the
past's preeminence is restored: it had what today is lost. On the other hand,
the relation of the present to the past may be seen to follow the path of the
Derridean "supplement," a replacing that wavers between restoration and
usurpation.[14] The castrated god of time past figures both a potency the new
generation lacks and an impotence in need of the modernist's vitality. In this
play of supplementation the modernist poet's pen assumes the place of the
lost organ of the gods—a fitting irony, for that pen was also the sword of the
sacrificial wounding. The order created in this new writing is, then, not the
past's at all; nor is it perhaps totally the present poet's.

> And what the dead had no speech for, when living,
> They can tell you, being dead: the communication
> Of the dead is tongued with fire beyond the language of the living.
>
> (LG, I)

The authority for ordered meaning, so strenuously sought after in the wake
of divinity's death, ends by putting into even greater prominence the insecu-
rity of order and authority in the genealogy of human temporality. Denied
the assurances of an external support in the guise of an eternal Father, the
poet is again thrown back onto the problem of his own, and his writing's,
capacity to arrange the dislocated signifiers into a readable script.

The modern emphasis on criticism and scholastic method, and thus of past
texts as pretexts, highlights an old truth about representation, though one

13 Hugh Kenner, *The Pound Era* (Berkeley, 1971), 150.
14 See Jacques Derrida, *Of Grammatology*, trans. Gayatri Spivak (Baltimore, 1976),
141–64.

never perhaps so consciously articulated as in the period following the eighteenth century. Writing and consciousness both compose themselves through rearrangements of what "East Coker" calls "old stones that cannot be deciphered." Archaeological intertextuality assumes an indelible spot of the undecipherable in every inscription, no matter how familiar, and interprets that strangeness by redeploying it. Eliot's iterative weaving of Ariel's song from Shakespeare's *The Tempest*, "Full fathom five thy father lies," in *The Waste Land* is a case in point.[15] The quotation is dismembered, like the body of Osiris spread about the land, a disseminated luminous detail. Re-collected and re-membered by the poem in numerous contexts, it fertilizes the waste land. The father who has suffered this decomposing sea change is Shakespeare, and also his song, father of Eliot's music by other waters. Eliot's use of them has made both more mysterious, "rich and strange," and yet set them in a system of affinities where they are reborn from the waters of cultural convention. They arrive home for the reader, but estranged and far from their origin. In the literary museum of *The Waste Land* there is no single room dedicated to Shakespeare, no one pedestal for Ariel's song. Bits of the song appear in a number of the poem's exhibits, creating a series of dense interpretive palimpsests. The drowned king, the Quester, the land, the precursor, the present poem, a friend or lover—all are figures that supplement Ariel's fanciful elegy. We should not forget that the death of Ferdinand's father is a fiction. The song as pretext is refigured, taken apart and put together until it means so much that we cannot be sure what it meant at all, originally. And Ariel's song resists reading because it is itself a metaphor of reading, an image of the transformations that writing and interpretation perform on received materials. Ariel's song and Eliot's use of it provide an allegory of the new method in scholarship and poetry: the drowned and revived fathers emerge rich *and* strange, like the texts of their literary sons.

15 The drafts for *The Waste Land* also include two dirges and an untitled fragment that rewrite Ariel's song. See WLFS, 119–23.

CHAPTER 4

THE GRAIL OF AUTHORITY

Romanticism and its popularizers emphasized novelty, change, revolution, modernity, individuality, spontaneity, and originality as part of the nineteenth-century approach to history and to what it saw as the stifling neoclassicism of its immediate forebears. Like every modernism, however, Romanticism fell victim to its own contradictions. This was not a phenomenon that escaped thinkers of the time, even those who were, or were seen to be, promulgators of the progressive, the new, the liberated present. But politics, literature, and philosophy were all embarrassed by the recurrent power of the old, by the shackles every revision seemed held by. The fate of the French Revolution, the return of the antique forms of tyranny, monarchy, and empire, was exemplary of a common failing. Karl Marx spoke for many when he wrote: "The tradition of all the dead generations weighs like a nightmare on the brain of the living. And just when they seem engaged in revolutionizing themselves and things, in creating something that has never yet existed, precisely in such periods of revolutionary crisis they anxiously conjure up the spirits of the past to their service and borrow from them names, battle cries, and costumes in order to present the new scene of world history in this time-honored disguise and this borrowed language."[1] What we can sense from this passage is the predicament of generations, including Eliot's, that inherit such pronouncements, which remind them, before they start, of the repetitiveness of their modernity. The experience of their immediate ancestors seems to have taught Eliot and company what Paul de Man has figured by theory and Marx by historical observation: the establishment of a new order had best try to wrest a degree of active control over the inevitable return of the dead. The sometimes parodic, sometimes prophetic neoclassicism of twentieth-century modernism willingly conjured the gods and spirits of the dead, putting them into service, borrowing their names and costumes for modernism's own dramas.

De Man would appreciate the irony of his nonoriginality, and Marx is cer-

---

1 Karl Marx, "The Eighteenth Brumaire of Louis Bonaparte," in Karl Marx and Friedrich Engels, *Basic Writings on Politics and Philosophy*, ed. Lewis Feuer (Garden City, N.Y., 1959), 320.

tainly not the only precursor one could cite on the subject. Most pertinently, Eliot delivered in 1953 this assessment of the century's effort at freshness:

> From time to time there occurs some revolution, or sudden mutation of form and content in literature. Then, some way of writing which has been practiced for a few generations or more, is found by a few people to be out of date, and no longer to respond to contemporary modes of thought, feeling and speech. A new kind of writing appears, to be greeted at first with disdain and derision; we hear that the tradition has been flouted, and that chaos has come. After a time it appears that the new way of writing is not destructive but re-creative. It is not that we have repudiated the past, as the obstinate enemies—and also the stupidest supporters—of any new movement like to believe; but that we have enlarged our conception of the past; and that in the light of what is new we see the past in a new pattern. We might now consider such a revolution as that which has taken place in poetry, both in England and America, during the last forty years. (CC, 57)

This retrospective rationale by one of modernism's principal instigators tries, like many of Eliot's later essays, to contain in calm formulas the stormy controversies of the years 1914 through 1928. (Specifically, this version waters down the more heterodox account Eliot gave in the third paragraph of his 1917 "Reflections on Vers Libre," reprinted in *To Criticize the Critic*.) Some of Eliot's listeners must have been surprised at this claim "that we have enlarged our conception of the past." His criticism shifted the emphasis given certain authors in literary history, but he made few if any discoveries. More pointedly, this enlargement came at the cost of some sizable exclusions, for Eliot was a man whose taste in literature, despite his apparent catholicity, was very limited. The "new pattern" that his modernism had imposed on the past did aim to repudiate some parts of it. However, the insistent return of those rejected voices in Eliot's own verse gave back enlarged conceptions and new patterns sometimes quite different from those put forward in his essays.

Eliot's explanation of twentieth-century modernism also obscures its relation to the wider context of those cultural conditions to which it was a response. Why do "a few people" find "some way of writing which has been practiced for a generation or more" suddenly "out of date"? Eliot cites a disjuncture between the inherited style and "contemporary modes of thought, feeling and speech." Is modernism, then, simply a mimesis of social change, a record of developments outside of literature? Or are "contemporary modes of thought, feeling and speech" themselves what Foucault would call a "discursive practice" and thus within a history of writing in the extended senses of *écriture* and textuality? Does not the emergence of this modernist disruption outside of literature in fact follow the same lines of development concerning the paradoxes of identity and temporality that literature displays? These "modes" are brought into being by revisionary interpretations and contradictions in the general systems by which values are produced, institutionalized, distributed, and enforced. The political, economic, and moral dimensions of the modernist movement were far more important than Eliot's retrospect implies, as the direction of his own career demonstrates. Poetic change follows from comprehending and formalizing the transience and strangeness of anarchic lives. It may also occur out of a desire to differ from prior poets, but this process cannot be divorced, in theory or practice, from the "nonpoetic." The poet inherits not only the library of literature and the museum of culture, but also the received disposition of power, wealth, and opportunity. Poetic revolutions do not proceed effectively for very long without taking cognizance of the worldly, material domains in which they struggle. Given these platitudes, it remains for every generation to estimate the value of its specific conditions and to map its plans for succeeding in the face of them. It will be seen that Eliot's approach to this question took a variety of turns before coming to rest in the proposition that linguistic renovation is an oblique but promising act of social and human reformation (see OPP, 12).

In Eliot's career, at least two sociopoetical legacies come together. One is Victorian and Arnoldian, conceiving the poet in terms of duty to society, culture, and human improvement. The other, also a force in the nineteenth century and even then not unrelated to the former, takes a more dismal view of the would-be revolutionary's situation. The "decadent" or purely "aesthetic" artistic type, often associated with Baudelaire, Mallarmé, Wilde, or Pater, mocks "art for civilization's sake" during the *fin de siècle*. For such artists Arnoldian responsibility for "culture" was a relic from a history that had ended and from which they had emerged into a monstrous and dazzling world without bottom or limit. Morally or socially redemptive poetics were seen as bankrupt and stuffy delusions, harnessing the intrinsic independence of art to an alien machinery. Of course, a literature at this extreme of estrangement may have been more directly respondent to the sociopolitical climate than that of culture's defenders. The tradition of irreverence, craftsmanship, and disgust had, as is known, a tremendous influence on Eliot's generation. This awkward division is only provisionally useful, in history or theory, obscuring as it does the character of each antithesis as a dialectical mask. Nevertheless, and in part because of its usefulness to poetic change, such a division and such a reading of the nineteenth century was a constituent of Eliot's inheritance.

This acrimonious divergence of opinions on art's role in the life of civilization seemed to some to portend, by the triumphant division of art from history, the obsolescence of the historical itself. Historiography and literature both provided spokesmen to announce the end of history.[2] In "The Eighteenth Brumaire of Louis Bonaparte," Marx had opened with a little fable of historical change as an ironic eternal recurrence. While they mark the end of history at the end of capitalism, his options are either a series of repetitions each more farcical and degrading than its predecessor or a break with the past so convulsive that two histories would have to be spoken of thereafter. The revolution of the proletariat and the establishment of its unchanging utopia was in the early Marx precisely a vision after the end of history: of history, that is, conceived as a succession of brand new events or as the operation of metaphysical Ideas in the drama of their telos. The debacle of belatedness Marx portrays inaugurates a different history altogether. In the history of philosophy it is the time after Hegel, after the self-conscious exhaustion of Spirit realizing itself, only to find that absolute knowledge ends history, too, leaving the prospect of a bleak future of nonchange and repetition. But the end of history that Marx describes leads to irony also, to a literature of incessant reversal and subversion.

The figure of the end of history converges with the myth of the death of the gods, for both Historical Truth and God belong to the mainstream of metaphysical thought from Plato to Hegel.[3] The crumbling of that philosophical edifice and of the secure values that went with it preoccupied many during the nineteenth century. Speculations about the death of the gods and the end of philosophy can be found throughout history, and one suspects they will preoccupy authors in the future. Regardless, the twilight of the idols was a formative experience for this century's modernists, who spent much of their time poetically resuscitating Osiris, Adonis, Attis, Apollo, Artemis, Aphrodite, the Virgin Mary, Christ, Buddha, and Krishna, not to mention, from a different sphere but in the same movement, Homer, Confucius, Propertius, Ovid, Virgil, Li Po (Rihaku), Arnaut Daniel, Dante, Shakespeare, Baudelaire, Laforgue, and Browning; nor should we omit Sigismundo Malatesta, Lancelot Andrewes, or any other of the authorizing personnel brought back from Hades to populate in unforeseen textual cohabitations the landscape modernism had wasted. Suddenly the pantheons were overflowing, much to the dismay of the average reader, who was just getting used to an absence of deities. This superfluity of transcendental per-

2 See Alexander Kojève, *Introduction to the Reading of Hegel* (New York, 1969), 158n–162n.
3 On the *topos* of the death of the gods, see Eugenio Donato, "Divine Agonies: Of Representation and Narrative in Romantic Poetics," *Glyph*, VI (1979), 90–122.

sonages descended like a homemade deus ex machina on modern poetry and its readers, who had been accustomed to a less heterogeneous, more systematic and inspirational presentation of mythology in Romantic verse. Eliot's conversion to the Anglican church could itself be read as the staging by a tragic poet of a god the audience had presumed dead. The superhuman powers abundant in modernist writing are not the outgrowth of a firm sense of belief, nor is the spectacle they present one of a codified and harmonious universal order. It is rather, in Claude Lévi-Strauss' term, a *bricolage* of the gods.[4] With an irreducibly Puritan temperament and a Christian philosophy of man's fallen state, Eliot could never affirm the knowledge of God's presence without committing heresy. For Pound, always the pagan, his own poetry allowed space for the imagining of an annunciation more beautiful than the flittings of one in Eliot's. At the end, Pound would write:

> The hells move in cycles,
>   No man can see his own end.
> The Gods have not returned. "They have never
>   left us."
>   They have not returned.
> Cloud's processional and the air moves with
>   their living.[5]

The gods began in ancestor worship. Ritual and reverence were the machinery of a remembrance that instilled in each generation the obligation to repeat the progenitors, thereby guarding the continuity of the sociocultural inheritance; its persistence through time depended upon a continuous, educational retelling that claimed its authority from the dead themselves. The stability of a system of transcendence or kinship works to guarantee the smooth transmission of properties, identities, names, truths, and meanings from one generation to the next, creating the illusion of a coherent culture unified in history. The *Götterdämmerung* coincides with the dissemination of the paternal fortunes or even with the revelation that the ancestral mansion had been acquired long ago in some obscure act of foul play and usurpation, the guilt for which would eventually fall upon the cursed children.

The mystery surrounding the death of the gods, and the culpability of the modernist in that passing, can be approached by reassessing the thesis of Jessie L. Weston's *From Ritual to Romance*. Her argument offers a parable of

4 Claude Lévi-Strauss, *The Savage Mind* (Chicago, 1966), 16–33. See the pertinent deconstruction of the *bricolage*/engineering distinction in Jacques Derrida, *Of Grammatology*, trans. Gayatri Spivak (Baltimore, 1976), 138–40.
5 Canto 113, *The Cantos of Ezra Pound* (New York, 1972), 787.

the poet's career useful for the explication of modernism. Weston's reading of the death of the Fisher King and the role of the Quester in the myth tries to restore a vision of creative, redemptive genesis unclouded by belatedness or guilt. The relation between the Fisher King and the Quester mythologizes that of past to present, ancient to modern, tradition to individual talent.

Analyzing the differences between the various Grail legends that have come down to us, Weston notes that there are really two major explanations for the desolation of the land. One attributes it directly to the sickness, impotence, castration, or death of the Fisher King, whose fallen state the Quester must somehow restore. The second sees the responsibility for the land's deprivation as "directly attributable to the Quester himself." The association of the Quester with the poet is suggested in two of the passages Weston cites in documenting this latter tradition. In one the hero's "word," his question concerning the nature of the Grail, frees the waters that restore the land.

> All this was done by what he said,
> This land whose streams no waters fed,
> Its fountains dry, its fields unplowed,
> His word once more with health endowed.

In the second, "the misfortunes of the land are not antecedent to, but dependent upon, the hero's abortive visit to the Grail castle," where he asks not about the nature of the Grail but whom it serves. This was the wrong thing to say.

> If you had found the word to say,
> The rich king who in distress does lay
> Would of his wound be fully healed,
> But now his fate is truly sealed,
> Never to rule his land in peace.[6]

Certain words, certain overwhelming questions, must be posed and spoken by the Quester-poet to rejuvenate the king and land. The attribution of guilt to the Quester-poet implies his part in the wounding of the king, as one might suspect in light of this myth's similarity to that of Oedipus. The Quester-poet imitates Christ, searches for the Word unheard. The assimilation of the legend to a Christian model deflects the question of the Son's guilt, of the authority by which he puts his own testament in place of the Old

6 Jessie L. Weston, *From Ritual to Romance* (Garden City, N.Y., 1957), 14–16. Standard accounts of Eliot's use of Weston's book include Cleanth Brooks, "*The Waste Land*: Critique of the Myth," in *Modern Poetry and the Tradition* (Chapel Hill, 1939), and Grover Smith, *T. S. Eliot's Poetry and Plays: A Study in Sources and Meanings* (2nd ed., Chicago, 1974).

Testament. Ideally, the Incarnation of Christ balances tradition and the individual talent perfectly, recovering the newcomer from Oedipus' tragedy. But the Quester-poet has himself overthrown authority, richness, plenitude, fecundity, and life. He acts in a doubled space of impotence, the king's and his own, as he seeks the revivifying word of a modern resurrection. The Fisher King diminishes in importance in this heretical tradition in proportion to the increased concern with the Quester's task. The king's demise is prerequisite to the quest: "There is here no cure of the King or restoration of the land, [and] the specific task of the Grail hero is never accomplished."[7]

The alteration of the myths disturbs Weston, for it throws into doubt the entire scheme of naturally divine resurrection, founded in the vegetation god stories. The shift toward an emphasis on the Quester, his guilts and inadequacies, displaces the king from the centering role he had played in a legend of wondrous recuperation. To Weston, then, "the dependence of the Curse upon the Quester reduces the story to incoherence." Her book subordinates this latter unorthodox narrative to the primacy of the "original" myth: "Does it not inevitably follow, as a logical sequence, that such versions as fail to connect the misfortunes of the land directly with the disability of the king, but make them dependent upon the failure of the Quester, are, by that very fact, stamped as secondary versions?" Weston construes her evidence according to a conventional logic that privileges the "coherence" of displaced orthodoxy and then simply assumes its chronological priority. The guilty Quester does not appear as such until apparently recent versions. Yet, could this have not been in part a suppression or displacement, and does not the thesis of the Quester's culpability only make manifest what was latent all along, what Freud and other students of the anthropology of sacrifice have shown—that the creation of the father-king-god begins in murder and castration? What the "secondary" texts imply is this procedure. Its exposure undermines the system of the myth as a foundation for a theological recuperation of lost plenitudes and fecundities. Weston promotes "the conclusion that the woes of the land are directly dependent upon the sickness, or maiming, of the King, and in no wise caused by the failure of the Quester."[8] A happy solution for scholars and textual positivists, but not one accepted by *The Waste Land*.

The Quester had to be Eliot's chief interest, for it was he, and not the Fisher King, who provided an allegory of the poetic condition. Had not the avowed modernist participated in the ritual death of the previous authorities? Was it not the poet who was caught between his guilt in wasting the fathers and his impotence to make their fragments cohere against ruin?

7 Weston, *From Ritual to Romance*, 17.
8 *Ibid.*, 17, 62, 63.

The line between the king and the Quester begins to dissolve as they are seen to share the fate of castration and infertility. The poet cannot speak the words to inseminate the waste land again. Or if he does, his utterance comes out as the ventriloquial dissemination of voices borrowed from the dead. In *The Waste Land* and the *Cantos*, the questing protagonist-poet castrates himself, too, suppressing himself through "impersonality" and stylistic dismemberment. In so doing, these poems reverse Weston's hierarchical ranking of the versions of the Grail, putting forth instead an interpretation of belatedness that clearly places the guilt for the death of the gods and the Fisher King on the Quester-poet's shoulders, though such knowledge came more easily to the Hawthornian soul of Eliot than to Pound's arrogant spirit.

The king's fall grants the new poet his saving vocation, a quest that fosters an identity in the search for one. It restores to poetry a sacred, world-historical mission. The lament for the king does not testify to the loss of a real, past fullness, though it may reflect the universal longing for the Golden Age. The trope of Utopia uses the legend of a waste land as the vehicle for recuperation, as the king uses his wounding as the vehicle of his reestablishment. Except that there has been no Fall. Neither plentitude nor castration is original: both are readings of an experience of difference. Strategically, the mark of death that designates the king clears the way for his heirs. It frees them from repeating the past, frees them to take on other names. These guilty progeny are modernists, to be sure, but the present they construct is haunted by the means of its production. The inquiries of the Quester, in his self-conscious trial, have brought him news of his own guilt, have brought to the surface what Weston and the legends hoped to bury: that death, absence, castration, and waste exceed the recuperative economy of the quest. Cut off, by his own pen, from the line of benevolent descent, the Quester-poet breaks the circuit of property and deconstructs the elementary structures of kinship. Discontinuity threatens to leave him adrift in the waste land he has created, self-castrated by a slash indistinguishable from writing. The selective resurrection of deities is then a strategy to re-form inheritance, to supplement the freedom-in-impotence of the modernist with the helpful authorial figures produced and controlled by the restricted economy of recuperation. These new deities occupy an anomalous Olympus. From there they can be invoked to support and justify the poet, but they cannot, ideally, weigh upon him as an eternally powerful, anxiety-inducing presence.

The confusion, to the point of identification, of the king and Quester indicates that the king was himself once a Quester, that he acceded to his throne through the same process of usurpation and decipherment enacted by the Quester. The king's mysterious demise may result from his own guilt in a prior ritual of sacrificial replacement, a primal scene endlessly repeatable and variable, every beginning an end and every end a beginning. Kings and Questers, ancients and moderns, supplant each other relentlessly, making time. So are transient knowledges enthroned, Fisher King-Questers doomed to dismemberment at the hands of their own offspring. The children rise up, and the dead gods come to life in their images: "To become renewed, transfigured, in another pattern" (LG, III).

The transfiguration of the dead and the rewriting of their literature requires of the poet countless deaths, his present self always under revision in a dialogue with compounded ghosts. This self-erasure and wounding, this askesis of impersonality, is a dangerously ironic way of arriving at creative potency. It risks a great deal, for what guarantees that precursor or ephebe will emerge strengthened, significant, or useful? What can stop the influence of the dead from silencing the nascent voices of those who turn to the past in hopes of recollecting a language for the living? How is the nightmare of history to be transformed into dawn when every day begins as the knowledge of night? Poetics-as-inheritance must devise solutions, or answering questions, to these riddles. This poetics steps into the Quester's role, knowing its kingship will pass, watching that passing with the ancient, glittering eyes of Yeats's chinamen. The spectacle is often comic, as Old Possum sometimes lets on. The theater of modern poetry includes a vaudeville of motley figures, got up in purloined rags and fineries. Such texts work the stage of borrowed languages and hand-me-down costumes set up by history. But they take their irony and play seriously, perhaps too seriously at times, and with an earnestness that expresses an almost innocent desire to restore poetry to a status it once (or so it seems) enjoyed. Yeats, Pound, Eliot, and others thrust upon poetry prophetic duties it could rarely, if ever, perform without stumbling into the ridiculous on the way to the sublime. Prufrock's "overwhelming question" is laughable, yes, but somehow it manages to become our own.

Taking up Arnold's cry for salvation through culture, practicing the techniques if not accepting the premises of "art for art's sake," Eliot's modernism did for a time dream of a kingly poetry. Such a program for writing includes a reevaluation of critical and poetic inheritances that makes the two inseparable. The Quester-poet examines the particular woes of contemporary history, searches the library and the museum as well as the street for luminous details to decode or decompose. The abstract pattern of usurpations and replacements yields little, however, until filled in with the concrete occurrences of time. These accumulate as experience, before language brings them to awareness. Like all human efforts at cognition, this unknown history is an immediacy inapprehensible by any method dependent on repetition. This kind of history is the inexpressible adversary of discursive attempts at order and is the origin of belatedness. Yet, it is also the breeding of difference that energizes life and writing. Histories of writing should care scrupulously for this record of formulations transgressed by events, lest the history of poetry be reduced to merely formal reactions. The endless destruction of identities by time Eliot took as a major reason for poetic change.

> But people do not only experience the world differently in different places, they experience it differently at different times. In fact, our sensibility is constantly changing, as the world about us changes; ours is not the same as that of the Chinese or the Hindu, but also it is not the same as that of our ancestors several hundred years ago. It is not the same as that of our fathers; and finally, we ourselves are not quite the same persons that we were a year ago. This is obvious; but what is not so obvious is that this is the reason why we cannot afford to *stop* writing poetry. (OPP, 10)

Time allows for a difference from ancestors and fathers. The documentation of these differences is "history," written in prose and poetry, which interpret differences, giving them a reality and direction neither wholly the event's nor wholly disconnected from it. This faith in time appears as the obverse of belatedness, as an antithetical temporality of difference rather than sameness. Conceiving time in these terms, Eliot finds a way out from underneath his ancestors, though at the cost of securing any stable identity for the self. So we will find him saying in "Burnt Norton," "Only through time time is conquered." That will mark the beginning of the end of Eliot's quest, of his struggle with the dead, of his effort to hold to the myth of Identity unchanged in time. In "The Dry Salvages," "Time the destroyer is time the preserver," and the transfigured time of "Little Gidding" is "not in the scheme of generation." There the "broken king" finds:

> Either you had no purpose
> Or the purpose is beyond the end you figured
> And is altered in fulfillment.

(LG, I)

PART TWO

ELIOT IN BLOOM

We dwell with satisfaction upon the poet's difference from his predecessors, especially his immediate predecessors; we endeavour to find something that can be isolated in order to be enjoyed. Whereas if we approach a poet without this prejudice we shall often find that not only the best, but the most individual parts of his work may be those in which the dead poets, his ancestors, assert their immortality most vigorously. And I do not mean the impressionable period of adolescence, but the period of full maturity.

"Tradition and the Individual Talent"

CHAPTER 5

FATHER FIGURES AND LITERARY HISTORY

By traditional criticism we may mean that which follows the same methods, aims at the same ends, and expresses much the same state of mind as the criticism of the preceding generation. Or we may mean something quite different: a criticism which has a definite theory of the meaning and value of the term "tradition," and which may be experimental in reverting to masters who have been forgotten. . . . For it is obvious that every generation has a new point of view, and is self-conscious in the critic; his work is twofold, to interpret the past to the present, and to judge the present in the light of the past. We have to see literature through our own temperament in order to see it at all, though our vision is always partial and our judgement always prejudiced; no generation, and no individual, can appreciate every dead author and every past period; universal good taste is never realized.

"Experiment in Criticism"

Experimental literary criticism since the 1960s has largely chosen to forget T. S. Eliot. Swept aside in the reaction against the New Criticism, Eliot may now be reverted to by another generation. The principal attack on Eliot came from the partisans of Romantic poetry, who have since succeeded in reversing (at least in the United States) the judgments that preferred Marvell to Wordsworth or Donne to Shelley. The victory has been so extensive that many take for granted Eliot's place in a lineage he often derided. The new and sometimes experimental readings of Romanticism were often developed directly in response to Eliot's positions and thus should shed considerable retrospective light upon them. At the same time, an inquiry into Eliot's theorizing may suggest a reassessment of recent issues in American criticism.

Of course, interpreting the relation between Eliot and his critical heirs involves the whole range of problems taken up in previous chapters, including influence, literary history, originality, authority, and identity. Since the latter terms are themselves adopted from contemporary criticism, a "hermeneutical circle" shapes the argument. Nonetheless, the gains made through investigating these concepts in Eliot's poetics suggest the degree to which we have inherited our problems from him and extended our understanding of them by opposing him. I do not intend, however, to offer an exhaustive reading of Eliot's theories of Romanticism or of his reactions to nineteenth-century British poetry. George Bornstein's recent work covers those topics in detail.[1] Here I will look instead at Eliot's critical statements on the stages of influence in a poet's development and then at the evidence of the poetry from 1907 through 1919.

Discussions of poetic influence today cannot evade the speculations of Harold Bloom. The flaws in his work have been widely noticed, yet more than any other theorist of his generation, Bloom has profoundly altered the way we think about poetry.[2] No single critic has so provocatively challenged our approach to poetry since, well, T. S. Eliot. In part this is no accident, for Bloom's constant antagonist in establishing his theories of anxiety, influence, misreading, and transumption has been the author of "Tradition and the Individual Talent." Like most in his generation, Bloom (mis)read Eliot as a believer in benevolent influence and set out to revise his precursor's vision of literary history and canonical poets: "Since poets also idealize themselves, and their relations to other poets, there is already an excessive self-regard in poetic and critical tradition. Modern theories of mutually benign relations between tradition and individual talent, including those of T. S. Eliot and Northrop Frye, have added their idealizations, so that it becomes an enormous labor to clear away all of this noble obfuscation." Bloom's brief epics unfold as a revision or misprision of his critical father. By initially turning to Milton and the Romantics, beginning with the much-maligned Shelley, he represses Eliot's voice (though phrases borrowed from Eliot dot his prose) to experience the "Counter-Sublime . . . daemonization" of his love for the "Visionary Company." This sets the stage for Bloom's own critical swerve in *The Anxiety of Influence*. "Poetic history, in this book's argument, is held to be indistinguishable from poetic influence, since strong poets make that history by misreading one another, so as to clear imaginative space for themselves. My concern is only with strong poets, major figures with the persistence to wrestle with their strong precursors, even to the death. Weaker talents ideal-

---

1 George Bornstein, *Transformations of Romanticism in Yeats, Eliot, and Stevens* (Chicago, 1976). Bornstein is finally a little too hard on Eliot for refusing to be a romantic, and he too readily employs the term *imagination* as the romantic logos that Eliot lacked (112). See also C. K. Stead, *The New Poetic: Yeats to Eliot* (New York, 1966), and Frank Kermode, *Romantic Image* (London, 1957).

2 For especially valuable commentaries see Frank Lentricchia, *After the New Criticism* (Chicago, 1980); Geoffrey Hartman, *Criticism in the Wilderness: The Study of Literature Today* (New Haven, 1980); Paul Bové, *Destructive Poetics: Heidegger and Modern American Poetry* (New York, 1980); and Joseph N. Riddel, "Juda Becomes New Haven," *Diacritics*, X (June, 1980), 17–34.

ize; figures of capable imagination appropriate for themselves. But nothing is got for nothing, and self-appropriation involves the immense anxieties of indebtedness, for what strong maker desires the realization that he has failed to create himself?"[3]

The goal of Bloom's strong poets is the transumption, or victorious interpretative troping, of the precursor's figures, the images and echoes of the dead who return in the moment of *apophrades*.[4] Bloom acknowledges that in *The Waste Land*, "Eliot too became a master at reversing *apophrades*," but he excludes Eliot from the canon of strong poets. "Eliot is a poet whose poems, with some exceptions, tend to become weaker rather than stronger, the more provocatively they trope, defensively, against the burden of anteriority."[5] What brings Bloom to a boil, then, is Eliot's movement away from a "Romantic" belief in the poetic subject's achievement of sublime immortality. Eliot gradually relinquishes the quest romance for Identity and submits both himself and writing to time and history. Bloom's transcendentalism, as his "religious" turn in *Agon* shows, surpasses in metaphysical faith Eliot's Pascalian wager with Anglo-Catholicism.[6]

Eliot repeatedly characterizes his poetic childhood as a time without models or influences: "The conventional literature of America is either wretchedly imitative of European culture, or ignorant of it, or both" (1921; compare Emerson's "The American Scholar"); "What the help and encouragement of men of an older generation may be like, what it feels like, what useful stimulus or perhaps misdirection it may give, I do not know. At a time which may be symbolized by the figures 1910, there was literally no-one to whom one would have dreamt of applying" (1935). And in 1946, a comprehensive narrative.

> Whatever may have been the literary scene in America between the beginning of the century and the year 1914, it remains in my mind a complete

3 Harold Bloom, *Poetry and Repression: Revisionism from Blake to Stevens* (New Haven, 1976), 95; Bloom, *The Anxiety of Influence: A Theory of Poetry* (New York, 1973), 5.

4 Transumption, or metalepsis, is actually a revisionary defense that turns *apophrades*, or the return of the repressed, into an act of the poetic will to power. For a splendid definition, history, and critical application of transumption, see John Hollander, *The Figure of Echo: A Mode of Allusion in Milton and After* (Berkeley, 1981). Hollander explicitly associates transumption with Hegel's *Aufhebung*.

5 Bloom, *The Anxiety of Influence*, 142; Bloom, *Poetry and Repression*, 80. He can be even harsher, as in these remarks, quoted by Hilton Kramer: "Most overrated: T. S. Eliot, *all* of him, verse and prose; the academy, or clerisy, needed him as their defense against their own anxieties of uselessness. His neo-Christianity became their mast, hiding their sense of being forlorn and misplaced. His verse is (mostly) weak; his prose is wholly tendentious." Hilton Kramer, "The Triumph of Misreading," *New York Times Book Review*, August 21, 1977.

6 Harold Bloom, *Agon: Towards a Theory of Revisionism* (New York, 1982).

blank. I cannot remember the name of a single poet of that period whose work I read; it was only in 1915, after I came to England, that I heard the name of Robert Frost. Undergraduates at Harvard in my time read the English poets of the '90s, who were dead: that was as near as we could get to any living tradition. . . . But I do not think it is too sweeping to say that there was no poet, in either country, who could have been of use to a beginner in 1908. The only recourse was to poetry of another age and to poetry of another language.[7]

This description of the weak state of English poetry from 1880 to 1915 is not without justice and has been taken up by eminent scholars of the subject. But influence is not bound by mere chronology. Eliot admitted in 1959 that the void was not a hindrance: "I think it was rather an advantage not having any living poets in England or America in whom one took any particular interest. I don't know what it would be like but I think it would be a rather troublesome distraction to have such a lot of dominating presences. . . . There was really nothing except the people of the 90s who had all died of drink or suicide or one thing or another."[8] Here Eliot represents the troublesome distraction of "dominating presences" as limited to the poet's contemporaries. Bloom, on the other hand, rightly thinks of influence over longer time spans—Milton to Wordsworth, Emerson to Stevens. Eliot sees this when recalling his own maturation as a poet; he had early on recognized the inter- or intratextual ontology of literary history and the inevitable agon it seemed to prescribe. "No poet, no artist of any art, has his complete meaning alone. His significance, his appreciation is the appreciation of his relation to the dead poets and artists. You cannot value him alone; you must set him, for contrast and comparison, among the dead" (SE, 5). Certainly through *The Waste Land*, Eliot continues a romantic quest for a victory over belatedness. This rivalry presupposes a logocentric poetic history wherein poets struggle for the single position of self-fathering Divinity. Bloom's criticism presents the Father Text as Wordsworth or Milton or Emerson or the Hebrew Bible, each a figure of a Center that governs and transcends poetic history. Bloom affirms the existence of "a central text that perpetually possesses authority, priority, and strength, or that indeed can be regarded as *text itself*."[9] This onto-theological textuality guarantees a literary history, for it creates a narrative of

---

7 "London Letter," *Dial*, LXX (1921), 450; "Views and Reviews," *New English Weekly*, September 12, 1935, p. 351; "Ezra Pound," *Poetry*, LXVIII (1946), 326–27. See also Introduction to *The Literary Essays of Ezra Pound* (New York, 1935), xiii; CC, 58–59; and OPP, 306.
8 Interview by Donald Hall (1959), reprinted in *Writers at Work: The "Paris Review" Interviews, Second Series* (New York, 1965), 94.
9 Harold Bloom, *A Map of Misreading* (New York, 1975), 4.

the Fall from sublimity and the ephebe's struggle to regain Paradise. To question this metaphysical and ahistorical model for the recollection of Identity through writing, as the later Eliot did, produces a different poetics and an acceptance of the differences time makes.

> And what there is to conquer
> By strength and submission, has already been discovered
> Once or twice, or several times, by men whom one cannot hope
> To emulate—but there is no competition—
> There is only the fight to recover what has been lost
> And found and lost again and again: and now, under conditions
> That seem unpropitious. But perhaps neither gain nor loss.
> For us, there is only the trying. The rest is not our business.
>
> (EC, V)

"To live," Bloom counsels, "the poet must *misinterpret* the father, by the crucial act of misprision, which is the rewriting of the father." If Bloom's reading of Eliot as a weak poet unable to face the anxiety of influence is necessarily a misinterpretation, this does not keep the misprision from telling us essential things about Eliot's poetics. Bloom's rejoinders change the way we hear well-known Eliotic pronouncements, such as the following from his essay on Massinger: "Immature poets imitate; mature poets steal; bad poets deface what they take, and good poets make it into something better, or at least something different. The good poet welds his theft into a whole of feeling which is unique, utterly different from that from which it was torn; the bad poet throws it into something which has no cohesion. A good poet will usually borrow from authors remote in time, or alien in language, or diverse in interest" (SE, 182). Roger Sharrock cites this passage as embodying "almost all of what Harold Bloom had to say over fifty years later." On the contrary, Bloom forces us to question Eliot's epigrammatic confidence and the conscious, controlling choice it emphasizes. An interest in metaphorical language will prompt us to speculate on the distinction between "immature" and "mature." The poststructuralist critic may ask how this "whole of feeling" can govern, from the inside, an intertextual economy that itself produces this "unique, utterly different" poetic identity from stolen parts. We may also wonder why good poets "borrow from authors remote in time, or alien in language," rather than from close relatives. Bornstein makes fine use of Bloom's perspectives, arguing that "in attacking Romanticism Eliot combated not a historical force but a projection of his own problems."[10] If

10 *Ibid.*, 16; Roger Sharrock, "Eliot's 'Tone,'" in David Newton-De Molina (ed.), *The Literary Criticism of T. S. Eliot* (London, 1977), 171; Bornstein, *Transformations of Romanti-*

Bloom's theories merely repeated his precursor's or were a weak misprision of them, the comparison would teach us little about either critic. But Bloom's agon with Eliot produces at least two key insights, revisionary corrections of Eliot's poetics that uncover a far more complex attitude toward the past than had been supposed.

First, Bloom develops a rhetoric or tropology for the analysis of poetic history. This "diachronic rhetoric" calls attention to the figural language of poetic theories and influence relationships. More important, he argues that poetic careers are a series of figurations, the poet dynamically altering or troping the powerful images of the dead. For Bloom, "Poems . . . are not tropes of being or of knowledge, but rather are tropes of action or of desire." He insists upon this distinction to defend himself against deconstruction, which he construes as a critique of epistemology and rational subjectivity. Although this seems to deflect logocentrism and embrace a Nietzschean will to trope as the play of poetics, Bloom's ultimate goal is a closed tropological economy that will recenter man and poetry in a "Gnostic" American religion he finds prophesied in Emerson. The transumptive troping of inherited figures aims to defeat time, Bloom's greatest enemy, thus allowing the pneuma, or "inmost self," to breathe more easily. This troping of time's threats seeks to counter the deconstructor's undoing of Hegelian sublation, or *Aufhebung*, proposing a recuperative Gnosticism that travels backward in time to seize the purity of Absolute Spirit. The American call for originality, according to Bloom, announces "American poetry as the new possibility of a Negative that perpetually might restore a Transcendental Self."[11] Like Eliot's, Bloom's anxiety in the face of history and nature leads him to espouse a "religious" poetics as a defense against the deconstructive undoing of transcendental signifieds by the temporality of language.

Second, Bloom's poetics reconceives the relations of literary history through genealogical metaphors. His "family romance" of poets owes much to recent French readings of Freud that emphasize linguistic theory and the textual ontology of subjectivity.[12] Bloom's use of Freudian terms turns them into names for intertextual relationships. At the same time, the metaphors of father and son for precursor and ephebe suggest the possible overdetermination of an individual poet's attitude toward authority and identity, for the structure of a family history may determine a poet's concept of literary his-

---

cism, 116. Leonard Unger also notes the Eliot-Bloom connection, and some good reasons for Bloom's avoidance of his precursor, in *Eliot's Compound Ghost: Influence and Confluence* (University Park, Pa., 1981), 95.

11 Harold Bloom, *The Breaking of the Vessels* (Chicago, 1982), 103; Bloom, *Agon*, 335.

12 See Freud, "Family Romances," *Works*, IX, 235–44.

tory, or vice versa.[13] Yet, like Bloom's transcendental tropology, this kind of genealogical poetics orders time and identities in timeless schemes. The family metaphor, Joseph Riddel observes, "guarantees an orderly displacement of the father or the precursor, and, therefore, a 'literary history.'" Genealogy appears to be another restricted economy, though Bloom moves increasingly away from the dangers of the kinship trope toward his Gnostic repudiation of any temporality of mutabilities. "The primary teaching of any Gnosis," he declares, "is to deny that human existence is a historical existence."[14] Such a denial would not only be the abolition of time; it would be Oedipus' final revenge, "historical existence" being a grand trope for the Father.

The application of genealogical metaphors to the construction of historical or literary orders is an ancient tradition, as kinship systems are a kind of narrative and a spatial ordering of time. Indeed, the use and theory of spatial form in modern literature responds to the same need to stop or control time that genealogical anxiety expresses. The Romantic and Victorian thematics of mutability, history, and decadence bequeath a crisis of temporality to modernism. Eliot's frequent use of family metaphors for literary history reflects, then, his American sense of the past, his English quest for order, his Romantic war with time, and his modernist's rage for individual identity. All converge in an extraordinary passage from his "Reflections on Contemporary Poetry," written in 1919.

> There is a kind of stimulus for a writer which is more important than the stimulus of admiring another writer. Admiration leads most often to imitation, we can seldom remain long unconscious of our imitating another, and the awareness of our debt naturally leads us to hatred of the object imitated. If we stand toward a writer in this other relation of which I speak we do not imitate him, and though we are quite as likely to be accused of it, we are quite unperturbed by the charge. This relation is a feeling of profound kinship, or rather of a peculiar personal intimacy, with another, probably a dead author. It may overcome us suddenly, on first or after long acquaintance; it is certainly a crisis; and when a young writer is seized with his first passion of this sort he may be changed, metamorphosed almost, within a few weeks even, from a bundle of second-hand sentiments into a person. The imperative intimacy arouses for the first time a real, an un-

13 Of course, Bloom and Eliot's masculine kinship systems need feminist deconstruction. For progress on this front see Sandra M. Gilbert and Susan Gubar, *The Madwoman in the Attic: The Woman Writer and the Nineteenth-Century Literary Imagination* (New Haven, 1979); Margaret Homans, *Women Writers and Poetic Identity: Dorothy Wordsworth, Emily Bronte, and Emily Dickinson* (Princeton: Princeton Univ., 1980); and Elaine Marks and Isabelle de Courtivron (eds.), *New French Feminisms* (Amherst, 1980).

14 Riddel, "Juda Becomes New Haven," 23; Bloom, *Agon*, 177.

shakeable confidence. That you possess this secret knowledge, this intimacy, with the dead man, that after a few or many years or centuries you
should have appeared, with this indubitable claim to distinction; who can
penetrate at once the thick and dusty circumlocutions about his reputation,
can call yourself alone his friend; it is something more than *encouragement*
to you. It is a cause of development, like personal relations in life. Like
personal intimacies in life, it may and probably will pass, but it will be
ineffaceable.

The usefulness of such a passion is various. For one thing it secures us
against forced admiration, from attending to writers simply because they are
great. We are never at ease with people who, to us, are merely great. We are
not ourselves great enough for that: probably not one man in each generation is great enough to be intimate with Shakespeare. Admiration for the
great is only a sort of discipline to keep us in order, a necessary snobbism to
make us mind our places. We may not be great lovers; but if we had a genuine affair with a real poet of any degree we have acquired a monitor to avert
us when we are not in love. Indirectly, there are other acquisitions: our
friendship gives us an introduction to the society in which our friend
moved; we learn its origins and its endings; we are broadened. We do not
imitate, we are changed; and our work is the work of the changed man; we
have not borrowed, we have been quickened, and we become bearers of a
tradition.[15]

Eliot never republished this disturbing account, which appeared some six
months after the death of his father and in the same year as "Gerontion,"
"Hamlet and His Problems," and "Tradition and the Individual Talent." The
condensation of familial, erotic, and literary figures in Eliot's rhetoric illustrates the overdetermination of the poet's textual subjectivity. Especially baf-
fling at first is the metaphorical identification of fathers, lovers, and past authors. The equation supports a structural and psychoanalytic analysis that
would subsume familial, erotic, and literary metaphors in a common economy of the desire for identity. In the implicitly homoerotic relation to the
father-lover-author, poetic narcissism fulfills itself by transference onto the
father figure. The love affair with the prior poet is an act of self-figuration,
troping or metamorphosing the newcomer "from a bundle of second-hand
sentiments into a person." In the mirror that is the beloved precursor, the
speculative new poet imagines himself.

We notice, however, that this passionate affair is not the first one, but is
entered into to resolve a prior confusion of identity. This temporal sequenc-
ing may be, in fact, a mythology for representing simultaneous ambivalences

15 "Reflections on Contemporary Poetry," *Egoist*, VI (July, 1919), 39.

toward the same dead father. The adopted parent of the second stage is also a reading of the parent in the first, as Eliot's readings of Dante and the Metaphysicals were defensive responses to Shakespeare and the Romantics. The favored precursor is "probably a dead author," preferably distant in time and language, because his function is to mediate the influence of the first and closer relative. In the first, immature stage, imitation blocks originality and instills a belated consciousness, resulting in a "hatred" of the precursor.

The latent rivalry here is for the recognition of one's different poetic identity, a recognition whose genealogical metaphor is the Mother's Love and whose sexual metaphor is genital narcissism. For Freud, the passing of the Oedipus complex hinges on the successful completion of the castration complex, which diverts desire from prohibited objects, introjects the Father's No as the beginning of socialization, and replaces libidinal satisfactions with the culture of sublimation. Neurosis signals the failure of this castration economy to regulate and restrict identities and desires in time. The "hatred," or death wish, directed at the Father turns castration back upon its author. Yet, this wounds the son as well, for it subverts the phallogocentric and genealogical economies that valorize the authority and identity he desires. Woman disappears from the scene because the sight of her only confirms the "reality" of the castration threat. Misogyny dramatizes the breakdown of repression, for woman continues to be the signifier of a difference that has never been resolved, of desires blocked but not sublimated. When the truth of identity becomes confounded with the presence or absence of the Phallus, the Father, the Logos, and the Law, the restoration of one's self-image becomes a process of identifying with a series of substitute figures for the Father, each a supplement to an "original" identity that was itself an imitation. The erotic language of the attachment to this Father may indicate a consequent regression to, and fixation on, the stage of primary phallic narcissism. The prohibited love of the self for itself achieves its goal by way of the substitute father, who displaces the original Father of the Law, thus freeing desire. Yet, as a father figure he reinstitutes the fiction of genealogy and the identities it makes possible.[16]

Castration, then, is a metaphor of logocentric economies of meaning in

16 See Freud, "The Dissolution of the Oedipus Complex," *Works*, XXV, 173–79, and "Some Psychical Consequences of the Anatomical Distinction Between the Sexes," *Works*, XXV, 243–58; and Jacques Lacan, "The Signification of the Phallus," *Ecrits: A Selection*, trans. Alan Sheridan (New York, 1977). Of course, the Phallus is not a penis, says Lacan, but part of a discourse: "The phallus is the privileged signifier of that mark in which the role of the logos is joined with the advent of desire" (287). Thus, the excess that is desire succumbs to sublation: "The phallus is the signifier of this *Aufhebung* itself, which it inaugurates (initiates) by its disappearance" (288).

general. It highlights the way that a beginning difference, in sexuality the difference between little boys and little girls, is interpreted hierarchically as a difference between identities, between presence and absence, truth and non-truth, vision and ignorance. The incomplete installation of the castration complex derails the organization of the logos. Difference, nonidentity, and gender remain in their beginning mobility, in what Derrida calls a disseminated economy, or the undecidability of *differánce*. The strategy of castration anxiety, like the lamentation for the death of the gods, enforces a restricted economy upon the body of nature and of history. A castration thematics in literature represents not the trauma of literal emasculation but, on the contrary, the desire to be "castrated," the desire for Truth.[17] An understanding of castration *topoi* as indicators of a certain crisis in textual or psychological economy will, I believe, explain much about Eliot's choice of precursors in his criticism and redirect our readings of the sexual signifiers in his poetry.

For the poet, the Phallus of the precursor is his poetic Truth and his priority in the canon of authors. The genealogical metaphor intervenes with a psychoanalytic resonance to establish the order of literary history and to make it a metaphysics. Using "personal relations" for his figures, the poet-critic organizes textuality into a regulated temporality wherein freedom from imitation and achievement of a new identity can be had without guilt and without a radical break from the continuity with past authorities. The "family romance" defends against time, against textuality, and against desire. The imposition of father figures on literary history, however, like the castration complex, will inevitably betray the fantasy at its origin.

In other accounts Eliot modifies the chronology of influence given in his "Reflections." Before examining these changes, we should note that the passage from "Reflections," though bolder in its imagery, does not tell us much more than the comparatively restrained rhetoric of "Tradition and the Individual Talent." Wherever the genealogical metaphor is at work, the story it presents of literary history will exhibit the same limitations and contradictions. (Obviously this holds for the present study as well, which hopes to inhabit the genealogical structure of literary history while simultaneously inquiring into its foundations.) I make the point because Bloom himself cites the passage defensively, to show that he does not "underestimate Eliot here, or elsewhere." He finds it "totally at variance with Eliot's 'official' view,"

17 On woman, truth, and castration, see Jacques Derrida, *Spurs: Nietzsche's Styles*, trans. Barbara Harlow (Chicago, 1979), and "The Purveyor of Truth," *Yale French Studies*, No. 52 (1975), 31–114; and Samuel Weber, "The Sideshow, or: Remarks on a Canny Moment," *Modern Language Notes*, LXXXVIII, (1973), 1102–33. My thanks to Andrew Parker for his help on this topic.

which he locates in the "deceiving" rhetoric of the paragraphs in "Tradition and the Individual Talent" on the "great labour" of acquiring the "simultaneous order" of tradition: "Eliot's idealized fiction here is that vision of a 'simultaneous order' that releases literary time from the burden of anxiety that is always a constituent of every other version of temporality."[18] Of course, Bloom is right to see that this simultaneity is a modernist spatial metaphor troping time into order, but as I have tried to show in the last chapter, this simultaneity is also a trope for textuality in general. The "simultaneous order" is the strange presence of history's archive as it weighs upon us at any moment, and the work of "great labour" implies the selection and exclusion that go into constructing this "whole of literature." Eliot's logocentrism chooses his spatial metaphor, but the essay's genealogical rhetoric and its expression of the new poet's own labor of acquisition belie the metaphysical figuration of tradition. There appears to be an aporia—an impasse or undecidable contradiction—between the genealogical rhetoric and the statement of tradition's wholeness, an aporia also cutting through the presentation of burdensome and benevolent fathers in the "Reflections."

Bloom has written elsewhere that Eliot's "fiction is a noble idealization and as a lie against time will go the way of every noble idealization." He has since turned the lie against time into his religion, evading the fatal lesson his own analyses point toward. To see that the same aporia runs through both of Eliot's versions of literary history is to see a major problem in the writing of any poetics, including Bloom's. To use Paul de Man's terms loosely, a poetics, as a literary history, is subject to that aporia between rhetorical figures and meaningful statements that critics can always take as the occasion of deconstruction. De Man finds the genetic and organic metaphors illusory. "Within an organically determined view of literary history, Romanticism can appear as a high point, a period of splendor, and the subsequent century as a slow receding of the tide, a decay that can take on apocalyptic proportions. A reversed image of the same model sees Romanticism as a moment of extreme delusion from which the nineteenth century slowly recovers until it can free itself in the assertion of a new modernity. . . . No father, no son can be God, but the history of the struggle between fathers and sons remains in essence divine."[19] De Man's critique is a powerful blow in an increasingly sharp debate between him and Bloom. Though I sympathize with many of Bloom's rejoinders to de Man's privileging of the "language machine" over either his-

18 Bloom, *The Breaking of the Vessels*, 17–18.
19 Bloom, *A Map of Misreading*, 30; Paul de Man, *Allegories of Reading: Figural Language in Rousseau, Nietzsche, Rilke, and Proust* (New Haven, 1979), 80–81.

torical materialism or the writer's subjectivity, Bloom remains unable to erase the epistemological moment from his own discourse, though his Gnosis attempts it.

In *Allegories of Reading*, on the other hand, de Man tries to write a nongenetic, deconstructive literary history. Careful misreaders, however, will find an aporia even here. De Man's subtitle is *Figural Language in Rousseau, Nietzsche, Rilke, and Proust*, seeming to promise another conventional and progressive genealogy. But the table of contents shows that the chapters analyze these figures in a reversal of chronological order, beginning with Proust's preference of metaphor over metonymy and ending with Rousseau's multiplicative textual ironies. The effect should be the undoing of our genetic notion of literary history. Yet, at another level we do have a teleology, for the narrative is shaped quite demonstrably to exhibit an ever-increasing complexity of dizzying aporias and to bring about the complete displacement of all textual determinants (history, psychology, reference, etc.) by "linguistic" problematics. In the scheme of de Man's canon of strong deconstructors, Rousseau indeed comes first. De Man's statements against genetic and teleological literary history are themselves unsettled by the aporia between them and his rhetorical staging of progressively more intricate representational ironies culminating in Rousseau. Between genetic and disseminated versions of literary history there is no choice, but an undecidable relation, for the two depend upon each other. Thus, although a critique of genealogical metaphors in literary history is salutary, we cannot help inhabiting them, ironically or otherwise.

In analyzing the metaphors of Eliot's "Reflections" passage, Bloom himself attempts a de Manian reading by underscoring his precursor's genealogical terms: "This language of metamorphosis and awakening is the language of the family romance, and not of a simultaneous order defying temporality." Yet, how can Bloom criticize Eliot's "simultaneous order" when his own agon is for a "mastery over time"? What Bloom has actually taught us to see is that Eliot's "simultaneous order," his "whole of literature," documents an anxious poet's "family romance." What Eliot teaches us to see is that Bloom's "family romance" is a "simultaneous order defying temporality." After all, does not *any* literary history lie against temporality? Eliot's canon of Virgil, Dante, the Metaphysical poets, the Jacobean dramatists, Dryden, Johnson, Tennyson, Arnold, Laforgue, and Baudelaire is no more or less metaphysical, defensive, and revisionary than Bloom's pantheon of the Hebrew Bible, Milton, Wordsworth, Shelley, Wilde, Pater, Emerson, Whitman, Stevens, and Ashbery. Bloom further tries to argue for the heretical status of the "Reflections" passage by stating that "the language of kinship and crisis was discarded by Eliot because it placed the principal emphasis upon personality, and upon the fantasies and defenses of a poet's personality."[20] Here misreading lapses into mere inaccuracy, for Eliot's use of family metaphors, as we are about to see, *increases* in later years, and finds its fullest flowering in "East Coker." As late as 1961, Eliot was still saying that his critical generalizations arose from a "feeling of kinship with one poet or with one kind of poetry rather than another" (CC, 20).

20 Bloom, *The Breaking of the Vessels*, 20, 52, 21.

CHAPTER 6

POETIC ORIGINS AND DAEMONIC POSSESSION

🌹 During the crucial year of 1919, Eliot published a piece entitled "The Education of Taste," the first of many similar versions he would give of his own poetic genesis under the influence of nineteenth-century British poetry.

> The first step in education is not a love of literature, but a passionate admiration for some one writer; and probably most of us, recalling our intellectual pubescence, can confess that it was an unexpected contact with some one book or poem which first, by apparent accident, revealed to us our capacities for enjoyment of literature. The mind of a boy of fourteen may be deadened by Shakespeare, and may burst into life on collision with Omar or the Blessed Damozel. And none of our tutors could have guessed what piece of printed book would precipitate this crisis.[1]

It is not clear at first what relation this account bears to the one (analyzed in the previous chapter) in his "Reflections on Contemporary Poetry," published a month later. Here "passionate admiration" characterizes young Eliot's pubescent love for FitzGerald's *Rubáiyát of Omar Khayyám*, whose echoes continue into *Four Quartets*, and Rossetti's melancholy Pre-Raphaelite eroticism, redone in "La Figlia che Piange" and *The Waste Land*'s hyacinth girl. What it means to be "deadened" by Shakespeare goes unexplained, but the "crisis" of reading these new precursors brings the boy to life. The "Reflections," on the other hand, relegated this "admiration" to the period of immature imitation, while "crisis" and "passion" were reserved for subsequently discovered authors. Shakespeare there is again among the "merely great," admired but not loved. Though never named, the object of Eliot's "feeling of profound kinship" in the "Reflections" may still be his Romantic, Victorian, or Pre-

---

1 "The Education of Taste," *Athenaeum*, No. 4652 (27 June 1919), 521. In his 1929 essay on Dante, Eliot confesses that "Rossetti's *Blessed Damozel*, first by my rapture and next by my revolt, held up my appreciation of Beatrice by many years" (SE, 223). See Ron D. K. Banerjee, "Dante Through the Looking Glass: Rossetti, Pound, and Eliot," *Comparative Literature*, XXIV (Spring, 1972), 136–49: "'La Figlia che Piange,' surely, is not Eliot's 'Blessed Damozel' . . . but an exorcism of Rossetti by way of Laforgue" (148)

Raphaelite precursors. But this is 1919, and Eliot has already graduated from his tutorial under Laforgue to an intense study of Elizabethan and Jacobean literature. The "Reflections" marks a critical transition in Eliot's recollections of his poetic development, for in it he begins to repress the "intimacy" he felt for nineteenth-century British poets, who are later replaced by the supplement of long dead or foreign fathers.

Eliot's revision of his own literary history appears clearly in his "On the Development of Taste in Poetry," an extensive autobiographical note appended to the first chapter of *The Use of Poetry and the Use of Criticism* (1932–1933). Eliot now divides the poet's genesis into three stages. The prepubescent enjoyment of verse is shared by all children. This is also the time of a forced admiration for Shakespeare. The second stage coincides with the awakening of sexuality: "I can recall clearly enough the moment when, at the age of fourteen or so, I happened to pick up a copy of Fitzgerald's *Omar* which was lying about, and the almost overwhelming introduction to a new world of feeling which this poem was the occasion of giving me. It was like a sudden conversion; the world appeared anew, painted with bright, delicious and painful colours. Thereupon I took the usual adolescent course with Byron, Shelley, Keats, Rossetti, Swinburne" (UPUC, 33). The significant metaphor of conversion would not have been lightly used by Eliot, who had joined the Anglican church in 1927. In his youth, Eliot took Romanticism as his religion, a heresy he often denounced later in others. A new self and new world bloom in this ecstatic encounter, erotically "painted with bright, delicious and painful colours." As Eliot goes on to describe this second stage, the language parallels that of the "Reflections," although now he rejects the poetic identity formed in this love affair.

> At this period, the poem, or the poetry of a single poet, invades the youthful consciousness and assumes complete possession for a time. We do not really see it as something with an existence outside ourselves; much as in our youthful experiences of love, we do not so much see the person as infer the existence of some outside object which sets in motion these new and delightful feelings in which we are absorbed. The frequent result is an outburst of scribbling which we may call imitation, so long as we are aware of the meaning of the word "imitation" which we employ. It is not deliberate choice of a poet to mimic, but writing under a kind of daemonic possession by one poet. (UPUC, 34)

Once more we encounter a figurative condensation of poetic and erotic object choices. This stage, seemingly celebrated by the account in "Reflections" of the poetic love that metamorphoses the young writer "from a bundle of second-hand sentiments into a person," now becomes decidedly the time of baleful "imitation." A third stage will be added by Eliot—"when we cease to identify ourselves with the poet we happen to be reading" (UPUC, 34). The description of "immature" and "mature" stages uses the organic diction of biology and genealogy. The critic may ignore the rhetoric as merely instrumental or ornamental, taking the passage as an unproblematic statement of event and its theory. Or criticism may read such texts with the same care it shows for other uses of figurative language and may consider these accounts as themselves "poems" not unrelated to "Prufrock," *The Waste Land*, and *Ash Wednesday* in their movement toward an ascetic withdrawal from passionate desire.

Harold Bloom's poetics provides a ratio of askesis, which follows the phase he names "Daemonization or The Counter-Sublime": "But truly, the strong poet is never 'possessed' by a daemon. When he grows strong, he becomes, and is, a daemon, unless and until he weakens again. . . . Turning against the precursor's Sublime, the newly strong poet undergoes *daemonization*, a Counter-Sublime whose function suggests the precursor's *relative weakness*." Eliot's countersublime, however, does not come through daemonic identification with a force including and transcending the precursor, as does Bloom's. Instead, he opens himself to a counterdaemonization by the poets and dramatists of his revisionary "tradition," which constantly accuses Romanticism of a "relative weakness." First, however, an askesis is required, a turning against the internalized Romantic self. Askesis is an art or trope of "self-purgation" (Arnaut Daniel's "Poi s'ascose nel foco che gli affina") aiming at "a state of solitude." The poet "yields up part of his own human and imaginative endowment, so as to separate himself from others, including the precursor," and in the process "the precursor's endowment is also truncated." But Bloom doubts that "sexual distaste or anxiety was at the root of Eliot's aversion to his own experience of poetic origins."[2] While avoiding a sexual myth of origins for Eliot's poetics, Bloom substitutes a poetic myth of origins that characteristically divides the "poet as poet" from other modes of human being. But the repeated entanglement of sexual with literary discourses in Eliot's texts cannot be so summarily evaded.

Before proceeding, however, into another "psychoanalytic" speculation that may test the patience of already skeptical readers, I should offer some thoughts—provisional and heuristic—on the relation between literature and psychoanalysis. The major objection to "Freudian" criticism has rightly been directed at its genital reductionism and its allegorical sexual semiology. Ev-

2 Harold Bloom, *The Anxiety of Influence: A Theory of Poetry* (New York, 1973), 100, 15; Bloom, *The Breaking of the Vessels* (Chicago, 1982), 21. See also Thomas Weiskel, *The Romantic Sublime: Studies in the Structure and Psychology of Transcendence* (Baltimore, 1976).

erything had its origin in an empirical sexual fact, and all representations could be decoded to reveal their "true" sexual content. The great advantage of poststructuralist psychoanalysis comes in its theoretical repudiation of this empiricism and literalism, as instanced in the analytic replacement of the penis by the Phallus-as-signifier. French-inspired rereadings of Freud, including Bloom's, approach subjectivity as langauge and writing and thus situate the self in a "symbolic" register whose relation to empirical events always involves the paradoxes and limitations inherent in representation. Freud himself, developing his "metapsychology," moved increasingly toward describing the phantasmal status of childhood traumas, understanding the girl's "seduction" and the boy's "castration" as deferred interpretations (*Nachträglichkeit*). The subject invests past events with meanings derived from a response to present disturbances in psychical economy: "The first thing the introduction of the notion does is to rule out the summary interpretation which reduces the psycho-analytic view of the subject's history to a linear determinism envisaging nothing but the action of the past upon the present. . . . In actuality Freud had pointed out from the beginning that the subject revises past events at a later date. . . . On this view interpretation is a way for the subject to escape from the present 'demands of reality' into an imaginary past. . . . Consciousness constitutes its own past, constantly subjecting its meaning to conformity with its 'project.'"[3] Sex, then, in the literal sense is not the referent of psychoanalytic criticism. In fact, it is the "absence" of the referent, or more exactly, the representational status of all referents and object choices in economies of desire, that psychoanalysis traces. The connection to literary studies emerges in this shared concern with the workings of representation.

Freud's tropological view of the mind's operations broke with any simple or restricted economy of representation. Dreams, symptoms, slips of the tongue, religious rites, civilized norms come under the heading of readings whose self-proclaimed statements of meaning differ from the significance legible in the processes of their symbolic construction. Here one should recall that the interpretation of dreams focuses on the *dreamwork* itself, and not on the "latent content," as the simple referent of dream symbolism. Freud's practice of interpretation struggled precisely there at what de Man has named the aporia between grammar and rhetoric. For Lacan, the place of subjectivity *is* the aporia, for the subject is a linguistic one and thus both the gov-

3 J. Laplanche and J.-B. Pontalis, *The Language of Psycho-Analysis*, trans. Donald Nicholson-Smith (New York, 1973), 111–12. *Nachträglichkeit* also plays a key part in the fundamentally symbolic ontology of all sexuality. See Jean Laplanche, *Life and Death in Psychoanalysis*, trans. Jeffrey Mehlman (Baltimore, 1976).

erning identity of a grammatical expression and the construct figured by rhetorical differences. The primacy of sexual thematics in psychoanalytic criticism derives from the exemplary undecidability of the subject or the object in sexuality, and thus in turn from the dynamic or economic "writing" of identities that constitutes the tale of sexuality. It is because our sexuality is nothing more and nothing less than a discourse on who we are that psychoanalysis attends to it. The ensuing problems of essence, origin, referent, influence, history, structure, and interpretation may be subsumed under the general heading of textuality or of *écriture* in the extended sense. Here they meet up with literary textuality insofar as it is read otherwise than through the restricted or logocentric heremeneutics that also characterizes a reductive Freudianism.

Returning to Eliot's narrative of love, poetry, and daemonic possession, we find a doubly deferred interpretation, or *Nachträglichkeit*. First, the Eliot of 1932 rewrites the accounts of 1919, producing a defensive negation of passionate poetic love and systematizing the ambivalence already evident in previous versions. The inspiration that made him a "person" now appears as "daemonic possession," or a loss of self through an extreme identification with the father-precursor. The "new and delightful feelings" that produced "an outburst of scribbling" were his countersublime, doomed by its imitativeness to embrace an askesis that truncates or "castrates" poet and precursor through a counteridentification with the Father-as-Phallus. The result is a conflation of the earlier two stages of imitative admiration and passionate love, making way for the revisionary effort of Eliot's discipleship under Laforgue, Dante, and the Elizabethan and Jacobean poets. The "classic" and the "tradition" composed by these adopted figures occupy the place of the poetic Phallus, controlling the anxiety of influence in two ways: by enforcing a renunciation of the desire for the Romantic precursor's Muse-Truth and by "murdering" the precursor-father through an antithetical canon formation. If this scenario makes any sense, then it should be clear that Eliot's writings on the Romantics and his many echoes of their poetry are defensive testimonials to their continuing daemonic possession of his poetic unconscious. It also follows that Eliot's essays on classic and traditional writers obey the same logic, troping and transfiguring the identity he received in his first, most passionate love affairs.

Yet, at least a second deferred interpretation of the past complicates this rather-too-neat scheme. The scene of instruction "at the age of fourteen or so" presents a retrospective interpretation of puberty that invests Eliot's reading of nineteenth-century British poetry with all the traumas of sexual anxiety. Or to put it the other way, Eliot's *Nachträglichkeit* retrospectively invests both puberty *and* early childhood with all the anxieties of the young writer. Can we privilege either "poetry" or "sexuality" as the original referent of Eliot's metaphorically condensed account? Clearly we cannot, for they have become figurations in a larger problem of unresolved differences. In the best overview of Eliot's early rejection and later acceptance of the Victorians, A. Walton Litz finds Eliot suppressing his American memories of the natural world in order to distinguish his verse from post-Romantic nature poetry. But this neo-Bloomian explanation yields to the biographical origin: "The repression of sexual energies, a dominant theme in Eliot's early poetry, was partly responsible, one suspects, for the suppression of the 'Nature poet' within."[4] Litz's caution is exemplary, but it obscures that troubling difference within post-Romantic nature poetry that Eliot's deferred interpretation eventually converted into the difference *between* Romantic and modern.

The problem here, as with Eliot's own critical statements on the Romantics, concerns the characterization of post-Romantic "nature poetry" as a direct and personal expression of sympathetic feelings toward the external world. Scholarship now severely qualifies this interpretation, demonstrating that Romantic poetry's principle concern is with the poet's quest for an imagination powerful enough to negate the things of time. Granted that a saccharine celebration of man's unity with nature pervades minor nineteenth century verse, the fact remains that the moderns inherited from Romanticism a complex ambivalence toward the natural world. One can find it in Eliot's pre-1910 juvenilia, such as "Before Morning" and "On a Portrait," where Keats, Rossetti, and Swinburne preside over visions of "fresh flowers, withered flowers, flowers of dawn" and the apparition of "a pensive lamia in some wood-retreat, / An immaterial fancy of one's own" (PWY, 19, 21). The drive to suppress obdurate nature and the common self in a transcendent imaginative vision was common in the negative sublime from Hegel to Wordsworth, Shelley, Keats, and Tennyson. It left its ruined project to the late Victorians and their immediate heirs, creating a generation of time-weary, historically burdened, and culturally smothered "nature poets."[5]

Eliot's early reworking of his inheritance may be seen in "Song," published in 1907.

> When we came home across the hill
>   No leaves were fallen from the trees;

---

4 A. Walton Litz, "'That strange abstraction, "Nature"': T. S. Eliot's Victorian Inheritance," in U. C. Knoepflmacher and G. B. Tennyson (eds.), *Nature and the Victorian Imagination* (Berkeley, 1977), 478–79.
5 For this reading of Romanticism see the essays collected in Harold Bloom (ed.), *Romanticism and Consciousness* (New York, 1970).

The gentle fingers of the breeze
Had torn no quivering cobweb down.

The hedgerow bloomed with flowers still,
  No withered petals lay beneath;
  But the wild roses in your wreath
Were faded, and the leaves were brown.

(PWY, 18)

These lines, indebted especially to the time-blown "Rose of Yesterday" and hyacinth garden scene from the *Rubáiyát* and to Swinburne's "A Forsaken Garden," rehearse *The Waste Land's* hyacinth girl and the openings of "Burnt Norton" and "Little Gidding." Despite its rather fine and subdued execution, the poem remains within a late-nineteenth-century sensibility aptly summarized in the contrast of titles between Shelley's "The Triumph of Life" and Swinburne's Whitman-daemonized "The Triumph of Time." In 1920 Eliot would repeat the accepted view that Shelley is "the master of Swinburne" (SE, 283). (By 1936, however, this title would go to Tennyson.) In contrast to Swinburne's imitative generalities, which resembled those of his own early verse, Eliot offered the "clearly and simply expressed" beauty of this lyric from Shelley:

Music, when soft voices die,
Vibrates in the memory;
Odours, when sweet violets sicken,
Live within the sense they quicken.

Rose leaves, when the rose is dead,
Are heaped for the beloved's bed;
And so thy thoughts, when thou art gone,
Love itself shall slumber on.

"His song," writes Eliot of Shelley, "has what Swinburne has not—a beauty of music and a beauty of content" (SE, 283).

Eliot's "Song," though echoing the conventional treatments of time's victory over love (as in Swinburne's "The Garden of Proserpine"), moves technically in Shelley's direction. If there is a "nature poet within" Eliot here, he has already internalized the difference between nature and human desire. The seeming immortality of the hedgerow's flowers exists in a world other than that of human love, whose roses of perfection fade into imitations of mortality. The power of the desiring imagination to trope nature into eternity ends with these roses, which have become the signs of love and poetry. Their fading achieves a negative sublime and an erotic morbidity in the cleverly effective final two lines, where the impersonality of a speaker's quiet shock and distance seems almost to accuse the girl of complicity with those disappointing flowers. The shadow of death that falls across passion here may be linked to sexuality's place in time. For the narcissistic self, loving the truly other involves detaching love (or cathexis) from oneself and risking it on another who, unlike oneself, may not always reciprocate. Loving the other literally requires self-sacrifice, differing from oneself, and thus a submission of identity to time. As in subsequent poems, the figure of woman represents loss and thus indicates a poetics already "traditional" in its use of a belated castration logic for the making of absence into truth.

The modernist substitution of hard, precise images from urban life for the supposedly vague, sentimental naturalism of the nineteenth century was an aesthetic, not a generic, discontinuity. Poetry continued to probe the differences between poetic consciousness and the objects it set in order. Historical and social temporality replaced nature's mutability as the poet's nemesis. The Romantic poetic subject was constantly undone by the nature with which, despite heroic imaginative efforts, it was not identical. The modernist misreading attributed to Romanticism a simple-minded victory of solipsistic pantheism, despite poems such as "Tintern Abbey," "To a Sky-Lark," and Keats's odes. Following Irving Babbitt and T. E. Hulme, Eliot accused Romanticism of lacking a sense of Original Sin! As if Milton were not the arch-Romantic and his tale of the soul's fall from godhead and subsequent quest for a release from death were not *the* Romantic theme. When Eliot opened *The Sacred Wood* with an approving citation of Arnold's dictum that the Romantics "did not know enough," he unwittingly repeated Arnold's own defensive posture toward precursors whose poetic knowledge was nearly unbearable. What Eliot (like Arnold) inherits from Romanticism *is* the poetics of Original Sin, a negative theology perfectly suited to a genealogical recuperation of literary history as rebellion and restoration. Eliot's denials defend him against the negative capabilities of his ancestors and plant his own negative authority in the place of former laureates. His "classical" doctrines of restraint, discipline, and authority turn Romanticism's agon with nature into his own internalized quest romance, constructing his logos as an evasion of the deconstruction of identity inherent in the Romantic project.

The various renditions Eliot gives of his youthful development cannot be decoded allegorically to reveal their "true" poetic or sexual referent, since it is the production of the literary and erotic subject that the metaphors retrospectively figure. The tactic of self-fashioning suggested by the condensation of these two figural languages can be named, after Freud, "narcissism."[6] The

6 Freud, "On Narcissism: An Introduction," *Works*, XIV, 69–102. This volume also contains Freud's other papers on "metapsychology." See also the entry for narcissism in Laplanche and Pontalis, *The Language of Psycho-Analysis*.

apparently passive position of the young poet ravished by the predecessor who invades and possesses him turns out to be (or so it is refigured) an active projection of internal autoaffection and self-knowledge. Precursor poems or poets are not "something with an existence outside ourselves; much as in our youthful experiences of love, we do not so much see the person as infer the existence of some outside object which sets in motion" feelings that give a sense of a bodily self or poetic identity other than the self-consciousness that observes it. To take this image of the self, whether bodily or literary, as the object of one's own affections, as the figure to which cathexis is directed or energy attached, begins the constitution of narcissism. Feeling or attachment is withdrawn from objects outside the self and redirected toward an image of the self. In the ensuing "fantasy" or "poetic career," the subject may internally occupy all the various sites in the economy of desire, alternately passive and active, father and mother, parent and child, precursor and ephebe. The tropes of identification, condensation, displacement, and projection make possible this metaphorical resolution of instinctual or literary frustrations.

What is the function or value of such a narcissism? In broad terms, it enables an evasion of the mediating and symbolic discourses that inscribe subjectivity or poetic identity in the ultimately ungovernable relationship of interpersonal and intertextual life. Freud first sketched his theory of narcissism after observing that it provided a recourse and relief for persons who, for a variety of reasons, had not successfully introjected the laws of society and consequently had not accepted a structure of "proper" object choice and identity. Narcissism seemed a "regression" to a time before the crises named by the Oedipus and castration complexes, which were designed to foster the transition from the infant's "primary narcissism." In Freud's elaboration of the myth, the mother replaces the child as the provider of identity-affection, or "ego-libido." The intervention of the Father's No and its introjection as "conscience" paves the way for sanctioned object choice, while the internalization of an "ego-ideal" fashioned after the Father and the Law provides a substitute source of affection and approval. "Secondary narcissism" would occur at times of crisis, such as the ending of the latency period in puberty or at any moment when sexual identity was at stake. The recourse to narcissism indicates a decentering of the Father's No and of the castration-logocentrism it constructs. The return of repressed differences, once ruled out by the metaphysics of the Father, destabilizes identity and prompts the recourse to a restricted economy of unmediated imaginary knowledge.

Bloom understandably argues that the myth of a "primary narcissism" disguises the real referent, the writer-poet's essential desire to be the only Author of the Word. By turning against the introjection of a Father (the greatness of Milton or Emerson or any precursor), the Son wars against Time by

seeing all things as images of himself. Belatedness is reversed, tropes are
transumed, and the Son authors the Father in the ultimate dream of narcissism. To switch to another famous figure of the poet, "there never was a
world for her / Except the one she sang and, singing, made." I allude to Stevens' "The Idea of Order at Key West," in Bloom's view a canonical poem.
When Stevens' "single artificer of the world" sang, "The sea, / Whatever self
it had, became the self, / That was her song." Bloom calls this union of voice
and natural universe an "argumentative or topical failure," an insufficient solipsism because it slights the alienation between singer and world, thus un-
derestimating "the power of the mind over what Milton had called a universe
of death."[7] The drive of this reading toward a tenuous affirmation of a transcendent poetic spirit raging to order nature evades the deep pathos of Stevens' "never," his truly modern uneasiness with the Romantic solipsism and
estrangement that he inherits and that his poetry beautifully repeats. Bloom
identifies the Ramon Fernandez of the poem's close as "a Gallic equivalent of
Eliot or Tate," a "formalist" and "anti-Romantic inquisitor . . . admonished"
by Stevens' closing stanzas. But even Bloom, with a teleological eye on his
upcoming readings of "Notes Toward a Supreme Fiction" and "The Auroras
of Autumn," acknowledges that Stevens' achievement here is less than triumphant. The admonitions to "pale Ramon" are a little too eloquent, mask-
ing the identity of that "anti-Romantic inquisitor" who is primarily a part of
Stevens himself. When Eliot closes *his* inquiry into voice, nature, and self
with "Shall I at least set my lands in order?" the earliness and new beginning
have been earned by a terribly costly askesis of the Romantic poetic spirit.
Eliot's negative sublime at the end of *The Waste Land* tropes, as we shall see,
the boats and oceans that figure the poetic quest in Milton, Shelley, Whitman, and Tennyson. Sitting upon the shore with the arid plain behind him,
Eliot's voyager surfaces from disemberment with a different, if not
greater, strength than that rhetorical power conjured by Stevens' gorgeous,
puzzled vision of the already ordered harbor. When Stevens, in the closing
lines of "Key West," speaks of "The maker's rage to order words of the sea,"
he no doubt, as Bloom argues, tropes against the "Death, death, death,
death, death" that is Whitman's word from the sea in "Out of the Cradle
Endlessly Rocking." But Stevens also uncannily echoes the agon with Whitman's elegiac and erotic feeling for nature and the soul that inspires Eliot's
countersublime at the end of *The Waste Land*. Was it Eliot, too, whose
"words out of the sea" told "of ourselves and of our origins, / In ghostlier
demarcations, keener sounds"?

When Eliot internalized the poets of nineteenth-century Romanticism as

7 Harold Bloom, *Wallace Stevens: The Poems of Our Climate* (Ithaca, 1977), 102, 96.

his "ego-ideal," what he took was no identity based on a clear separation of nature and self; it was the aporia of their difference. That impasse also figures the crisis in the young poet's identity, split between an image of himself as passionate Romantic poet and the desire for a self free of nature, time, and influence. The sexual metaphors in Eliot's deferred interpretation revise his Romantic precursors into "natural" and genealogical roles. The "nature poet within" Eliot already interprets what it internalizes, makes of Romanticism something he can form an identity in opposing. But the pole of opposition is itself inherited from an inherent Romantic agon with nature. Eliot ascribes nature to Romanticism and an alien part of himself and turns to his "classical" purposes the antithetical spirit that had always been a part of Romanticism's difference with itself. The strategy allows him to narrate a recovery from the deconstruction of stable identities, poets, texts, or metaphysics that comes down from Romanticism and the nineteenth century. Once he has made this difference within into a difference between, Eliot is on his way to founding the logos of the modernist.

Eliot's reaction against "daemonic possession" underscores, however, the threat of imitation that unsettles the self-enclosure of the narcissistic identity. Lacan's theory of the "mirror stage" modifies the hypothesis of a primary narcissism, as the child's first idea of itself comes in an image, reflection, or speculation that produces identity through the mediation of another figure. "It is an experience," writes Lacan, "that leads us to oppose any philosophy directly issuing from the *Cogito*."[8] In the beginning, the subject is a question that finds its answer in an image and through the modes of sameness and resemblance. The cogito of the mirror stage is the product, not the origin, of reflection. Lacan also locates the beginning of aggressivity and rivalry here, for identification with others leads to competition for what the other desires. Lacan calls the structure of this mental stage and its operations Imaginary. The way out of this endless doubling and demand for immediate knowledge is what Lacan calls the register of the Symbolic, the subject's insertion into a reality structured like a language. Rivalry with the father, for example, ceases when the biological father is replaced by the abstraction of the Name-of-the-Father, a linguistic and social site that the child may eventually (if he obeys the No of the Father) occupy. For the young poet, "daemonic possession" results from the narcissism of a textual mirror stage. Eliot's version of the accession to the Symbolic order is his "third, or mature stage of enjoyment . . . when we cease to identify ourselves with the poet we happen to be read-

8 Jacques Lacan, *Ecrits: A Selection*, trans. Alan Sheridan (New York, 1977), 1. See also Lacan's follow-up essay, "Aggressivity in Psychoanalysis," 8–28.

ing" (UPUC, 34). This is the ratio of askesis that truncates the precursor's, and the poet's, natural endowment, compensating for these losses with the functions of power and authority. Identification is transferred to the new "ego-ideal" of "classical" restraint. The repression of the daemon inspires the new logos.

But Eliot never ceases to identify with the poets he reads and writes about. Among his most often quoted statements are these: "The best of my *literary* criticism . . . consists of essays on poets and poetic dramatists who had influenced me. It is a by-product of my private poetry-workshop" (OPP, 117); and "in writing about authors who had influenced me, I was implicitly defending the sort of poetry that I and my friends wrote" (CC, 16). These influences were mainly antithetical fathers, antagonists to the daemons within, as Helen Gardner notes: "Eliot sent himself to school, consciously and deliberately, to widen, deepen, and correct his inheritance as a late-nineteenth-century poet." Gardner adopts Eliot's perspective on values and corrections, but she is not far from seeing what a Bloomian reading would suggest. The transition to a "classical" or Symbolic poetic discourse never quite succeeds in escaping the lures of a "Romantic" or narcissistic and Imaginary poetics. What Freud calls a "compulsion to repeat" evidences itself in Eliot's verbal echoes of the Romantics and in his frequent use of mediating figures (Dante, Baudelaire, Laforgue) to reenact his agon with his precursors. "In such cases," Freud writes, "we attribute a 'daemonic' character to the compulsion to repeat."[9] In "The Three Voices of Poetry" and *Four Quartets* (as a later chapter will show), Eliot names the "exorcism of this demon" as the origin of poetry (OPP, 107) and dramatizes the results in his meeting with the "familiar compound ghost / Both intimate and unidentifiable" in "Little Gidding."

9 Helen Gardner, *T. S. Eliot and the English Poetic Tradition* (Nottingham, 1965), 7; Freud, *New Introductory Lectures on Psychoanalysis*, in *Works*, XXII, 107.

CHAPTER 7

FIGURES OF THE POET
Prufrock, Narcissus, and Gerontion

Eliot's poetry from 1907 through 1919 practices its own deferred interpretation of literary history and daemonic possession. In these poems the dispute with Romanticism and the acquisition of a counterinheritance may be read in both the protagonists who figure the poet's crisis and the techniques that treat it. Eliot's discovery of Jules Laforgue in 1908 sparked a counterdaemonization, what he described later as "a sort of possession by a stronger personality."[1] In "Nocturne," "Humoresque," "Spleen," and "Conversation Galante" Eliot skillfully imitates his adopted master's style (and that of Baudelaire), turning out thin but accomplished exercises in renovating the Georgian vagaries of diction and feeling. The distance and lateness of desire, however, continue to be his chief themes. Though Laforgue substitutes irony for sentiment, his verse still turns on the absent truth behind vain and transient appearances. Moreover (and this seems to have been most attractive to Eliot), Laforgue, under the influence of Eduard von Hartmann's theory of the unconscious, portrays sexual relations as inevitably degrading and disappointing. No reconciliation between conscious and unconscious forces seems imaginable, so that the only alternative is to renounce women, as Laforgue's references to Hamlet's "Get thee to a nunnery" show. His various "Complaintes" and the monologues of *Dernier Vers* (written while Laforgue translated Whitman) supplement Eliot's reading of Browning and Henry James by explicitly making sexuality the principal dramatic metaphor of philosophical and psychological crisis. "Any particular influence," Eliot observed in 1928, "is both of form and content."[2]

The results of Eliot's first French affair are complicated by the overt discontinuity between author and speaker in Laforgue. Eliot incorporates this irony as a poetic (and often personal) "ego-ideal," but it leads to a second irony, turned against the dandy disillusionment of Laforgue's speakers. The *fin de siècle* rejection of Romanticism turns out to be a defense against women,

1 Quoted by Ronald Schuchard, "'Our mad poetics to confute': The Personal Voice in T. S. Eliot's Early Poetry and Criticism," *Orbis Litterarum*, XXXI (1976), 214.
2 John Porter Houston, *French Symbolism and the Modernist Movement* (Baton Rouge, 1980), 67–83; Introduction to *Selected Poems of Ezra Pound* (London, 1928), xiii.

time, and nature, and so represents an ironic stage on the way to askesis. Adoption of the Laforguian pose in "Portrait of a Lady" and "The Love Song of J. Alfred Prufrock" only multiplies images of impotence and belatedness. In "Portrait," the speaker's "self-possession" depends upon a repression masked by the stance of weary sophistication.

> I remain self-possessed
> Except when a street piano, mechanical and tired
> Reiterates some worn-out common song
> With the smell of hyacinths across the garden
> Recalling things that other people have desired.

The representation of desire as a "worn-out common song" partially protects the speaker from the common desires of other voices, internal and historical. It would seem that the traditional music is "mechanical and tired," but in "Recalling things that other people have desired," it analyzes belatedness quite precisely, as it ambivalently combines inability with repudiation. Paralysis occurs in the self-consciousness of the mimesis of desire, in the unoriginality of wanting what the other wants. Sexuality is "common," as Hamlet punningly reminded his mother, and does involve the repetition of the father's (or mother's) role. For the poet of young Eliot's cast it also means repeating the "worn-out common song" of previous love poets.

Eliot will often associate sex with the dissolution of identity, with the loss of stable, understood differences. During an analysis of "self-expression" in Thomas Hardy, that "powerful personality uncurbed by any institutional attachment or by submission to any objective beliefs," Eliot judges him interested only in "emotions," not "minds": "It is only, indeed, in their emotional paroxysms that most of Hardy's characters come alive. This extreme emotionalism seems to me a symptom of decadence; it is a cardinal point of faith in a romantic age, to believe that there is something admirable in violent emotion for its own sake, whatever the emotion or whatever its object. But it is by no means self-evident that human beings are most real when most violently excited; violent physical passions do not in themselves differentiate men from each other but rather tend to reduce them to the same state" (ASG, 54–55). For the speaker of "Portrait of a Lady," self-possession similarly depends upon resistance to the seductions of emotion awakened by women and Romanticism. The negative portrait of each reduces the threat they symbolize to the speaker. At poem's end we find him "sitting pen in hand," having substituted the safety of narcissism for intercourse with the lady.

The closing maneuver reminds us that this "Portrait of a Lady" is the speaker's fiction, one that rationalizes his failure of feeling through adolescent criticisms of the woman. She is a danger, "slowly twisting the lilac stalks" of Whitman in her hand. Like any logocentric structure of exclusion, his self-possession in writing testifies to the precedent power of what he opposes. Even in death, "Would she not have the advantage, after all? / This music is successful with a 'dying fall.'" This allusion takes us to the opening of Shakespeare's *Twelfth Night*, where the music of love is "not so sweet now as it was before." Duke Orsino's "fancy" has grown "high fantastical" in the frustration of his desire for Olivia, who reserves herself for "A brother's dead love, which she would keep fresh / And lasting in her sad remembrance." The duke's problem is that of the young poet, who competes with dead rivals for the love of the Muse.

"The Love Song of J. Alfred Prufrock" treats this competition with more intensity and success. The dramatic components of the poem, the story of Prufrock and his situation, comprise an allegory of the poet's failed quest for the Romantic sublime and so continue the genre Bloom calls the "crisis ode." The achievement of the poem, however, comes in the aporia between this grammatical enunciation of belatedness and the rhetorical manipulation of borrowed voices, images, rhythms, and styles. Eliot's transfiguration of his inheritance in the verbal texture of "Prufrock" considerably qualifies the pathos of his speaker's lament.

The continuity of Prufrock's crisis with that of his Romantic precursors may be seen by comparison to an unlikely father poem, Shelley's "Mont Blanc." I do not mean, of course, to suggest this as source or influence in the literal sense. An interpretative or argumentative relation between texts does not depend upon conscious intention or even verbal resemblance, but emerges from the larger context of how writing disseminates a culture's legacies. I choose "Mont Blanc" as an extraordinary, yet still representative, Romantic exploration of the poet's unresolved dialectic with natural experience and higher powers. "The everlasting universe of things / Flows through the mind" of Shelley's speaker as he begins his antithetical encounter with the "old and solemn harmony." Gathering itself in response, his "separate fantasy" sees Mont Blanc as a figure of sublime poetic power, "Remote, serene, and inaccessible," in contrast to "*this*, the naked countenance of earth," where "So much of life and joy is lost." In the end, an audacious introjection of Mont Blanc's power silences the wind and makes "voiceless" the lightning, enabling the newcomer to speak the Bloomian question.

> And what are thou, and earth, and stars, and sea,
> If to the human mind's imaginings
> Silence and solitude were vacancy?

The imagination's lamp asserts its primary role, though Shelley's presumption to power comes in the form of a rhetorical question, still shadowed by the mountain.

Translating the Romantic agon into a modern setting, "Prufrock" opens with its own alien flow of things, ironically emptying out the landscape of the natural sublime and replacing it with the ultimately no less threatening tour of

> half-deserted streets,
> The muttering retreats
> Of restless nights in one-night cheap hotels
> And sawdust restaurants with oyster-shells.

Critics have increasingly agreed on the place of *Four Quartets* in the tradition of Romantic landscape meditations. Despite their negation of it, "Prufrock" and *The Waste Land* also spring from that tradition. The sterility of the urban scene indicates the absence of the Romantic genius loci—father archetype or natal god or spirit of place. The "sacred marriage," explains Geoffrey Hartman, "of the poet's genius with the genius loci" would unite nature, imagination, and local history in an achievement of prophetic utterance along biblical lines.[3] In the eighteenth and nineteenth centuries, the *topos* of the genius loci turns into the Bloomian Scene of Instruction. The old genius loci that would ground poetry in a national, natural, and transcendental logos turns into the hated precursor, the spirit of present cultural and poetic failures. Against the genius loci as complacent voice of traditional values, the poet seeks other daemons, specters of place who figure forth antithetical and archaic powers. Eliot stages the disappearance of the Romantic genius loci as a variation on the theme of the death of the gods. In place of Wordsworth and Shelley come the tutelary spirits of Laforgue, Baudelaire, and Henry James as geniuses of the haunted city. Prufrock's lack of spirit represents the dethroning of Romantic genius. "I am no prophet—and here's no great matter," he disingenuously declares, but the things of the city are the things of his soul and the characters of his un-Wordsworthian apocalypse. Prufrock's "overwhelming question," deprecatingly hemmed in by jingling rhymes, is still Shelley's question. Will he have the power to make himself the genius of the place, to fill the vacancy with his own imaginings? If he did, would they turn out like Orsino's, "high fantastical"?

The modernity of "Prufrock" emerged genealogically, descending from

---

3 Geoffrey Hartman, "Romantic Poetry and the Genius Loci," in Hartman, *Beyond Formalism* (New Haven, 1970), 322.

what M. H. Abrams designates the Greater Romantic Lyric (theoretical precursor to the "crisis ode" of Bloom, Abrams' ephebe). We still have an initial outdoor setting, a colloquy with a silent auditor, and a meditation on the mind's processes as it contemplates both the surrounding scene and itself. "In the course of the meditation," says Abrams, "the lyric speaker achieves an insight, faces up to a tragic loss, comes to a moral decision, or resolves an emotional problem."[4] Eliot fashions Prufrock as a figure of the poet who cannot achieve such positive ends: his is the negative version of the internalized quest romance. The effect is to turn against the lyric poets of the past by suggesting the impotence of their stance when inscribed in modern conditions. Yet, in the character of Prufrock the weakness is made his own and so implies the continuing greatness of the Romantic logos as a lost poetic paradise he would, but cannot, regain.

Eliot's distance from his Prufrockian persona, however, complicates the poem's poetics. The formal resources come, as Robert Langbaum and others have shown, from the Victorian dramatic monologue as well as from Laforgue.[5] The dramatic monologue revised the Romantic lyric, pushing into the foreground the split between author and speaker often overlooked in readings of Romanticism that underestimated its irony. The speakers who give voice to the portraits of the artist in Browning's "Fra Lippo Lippi" and "Andrea del Sarto" take up the issues of body, soul, and art handed down from Coleridge's "Dejection: An Ode," Wordsworth's "Tintern Abbey," Shelley's "Ode to the West Wind," and Keats's "Ode to a Nightingale." Browning began his career with embarrassing imitations of Shelley's lyric personality, which he exorcises in developing his dramatic technique. The post-Romantic poet had to *analyze* the speaking subject of precursor lyric poems if he was to gain a relative independence. Browning's psychologically acute monologues, in the "impersonal" distance they establish, repeat the poet's own modernized stance toward the voices of Shelley and company.

A further swerve comes in Browning's frequent use of historical scenes and characters. Culture and society replace nature as the setting for the investigation of the soul. What Browning hands on to Eliot and Pound is the use of these domains as the place to seek the lessons of the genius loci, which in Browning (as in the Jacobeans) becomes difficult to distinguish from the mental daemons who inspire murder and adultery or block the way of the artistic genius. In Eliot as well as in Browning, the use of historical allusions

4 M. H. Abrams, "Structure and Style in the Greater Romantic Lyric," in Harold Bloom (ed.), *Romanticism and Consciousness* (New York, 1970), 201.

5 Robert Langbaum, *The Poetry of Experience: The Dramatic Monologue in Modern Literary Tradition* (New York, 1963).

may denote a timeless truth behind the events of time and so serve the same logocentric function as nature once had. Or in its psychological emphasis, the allusive habit of finding resemblances between events, and between past and present, may imply that the eternal truths are metaphors of the repetition compulsion, an enslavement to a past (personal or cultural) that has come to occupy one's nature. "Prufrock" is not as concretely localized in place or time as "Mont Blanc" or Browning's "The Bishop Orders His Tomb at Saint Praxed's Church," since its landscape is even more textual, its place an intersection of poetic traditions. The character Prufrock cannot then achieve a subjective transfiguration into the genius loci, for he conceives it within the economy of repetition, as his thematics of belatedness, narcissism, and castration signify. The poetic language of "The Love Song of J. Alfred Prufrock," however, largely succeeds in becoming the genius loci of intertextuality, its voice a nonidentity of differing elements drawn from the poetic landscape. Eliot's orchestration of echoes from the Bible, Hesiod, Dante, Shakespeare, Marvell, and Donne with the sounds of his nineteenth-century French and British predecessors eschews the acquisition of a metaphysically "unique" poetic persona.

Despite this achievement, the poem does record in Prufrock himself a defeat of poetic power and so expresses the war within the poet between the desire for individuality and the need for self-surrender. The erasure of the speaker in *The Waste Land*'s even greater heterogeneity of different voices also coincides with an increase in images of emasculation, repeating the unresolved struggle at work in "Prufrock." Thus, although the ironic and critical treatment of Prufrock owes much to the mediation of Browning and Laforgue, his situation as a persona of the poet looks back to Tennyson's post-Romantic protagonists in "Ulysses" and "Tithonus." They are among the most powerful Victorian lyric evocations of the poet's attempt to begin again, to overcome time and age in an immortal embrace of original knowledge. Tithonus is granted immortality, but not eternal youth, by the beloved goddess of dawn. His erotic consummation with the deity of earliness leaves him forever estranged from the natural cycles of time. This "immortality" parallels Shelley's vision of Mont Blanc, a glimpse or promise of sublime divination while Tithonus' endless aging portrays his inability to master time with the mind's imaginings. His gift from the goddess demonstrates the double-edged experience of the Scene of Instruction, when knowledge of the precursor's union with the Muse awakens an envious desire that can never be satisfied. Tithonus longs, like the Cumaean sibyl, to die and so be free of the body's deconstruction of the soul's dreams. The embrace of dawn feels "cold," for it reminds him of the passion that taught him "immortality," yet gave not the power to attain it. The image of himself he fixed upon at that earliest moment, an image of divine poetic identity, is his only true love, a narcissistic one. Tennyson mercilessly shows that, for Tithonus, death is far preferable to the endless, melancholy mourning for that lost self-image.

Eliot's Prufrock never gets around to embracing his Aurora or asking her for the immortal youth and poetic power for which he longs. The poem sounds more radically self-conscious about its presumption to speak than most of its nineteenth-century precursors. Prufrock insists that "There will be time to murder and create," time to displace the fathers, but it is all idle talk, "a hundred visions and revisions, / Before the taking of a toast and tea." He explains his reluctance to "Disturb the universe" with his words by a litany of world-weariness. He has "known them all already, known them all." These tropes deny the power in what he has known, while simultaneously implying the sublime he fears is beyond his measure.

> I know the voices dying with a dying fall
> Beneath the music from a farther room.
>   So how should I presume?

These are not only the voices of a mundane world, but of past poets, including Shakespeare in *Twelfth Night*. The same antithetical sense is heard in the singsong of the apparently deprecatory "In the room the women come and go / Talking of Michelangelo." Most readers have joined Prufrock in over-hearing here the degeneration of the West epitomized when frivolous women use great artists as conversation pieces. This irony is rather a projection of Prufrock's own estimate of his distance from artistic mastery, perhaps suggested by Michelangelo's role in "Andrea del Sarto."

Prufrock's monologue becomes a soliloquy on procrastination, his own "To be or not to be." His sentences stutter from "and" to "and," verb tenses expertly preclude the present moment, and inaction defines itself increasingly by reference to what it comes "after." The cumulative rhetorical effect is a deferral of the Word by words. Perversely, the strategy makes an advantage of impotence, turning it into the occasion for Prufrock's own words, quite different from the Romantic logos he cannot utter. With each stanza he seems to age into a peer of Gerontion, his body's death in time figuring the spirit's defeat by the burden of the past. Yet, Prufrock is comically comfortable in the role, as if loss somehow affirmed what he truly values. "Should I, after tea and cakes and ices, / Have the strength to force the moment to its crisis?" he asks, and he follows these innuendoes with allusions to mortification and John the Baptist's decapitation. Prufrock will not disturb the castration-belatedness economy that affirms by absence and negativity the Truth of the

Fathers. Should Prufrock presume to come back from the dead, a "Lazarus" who will "tell all," it would be an act of transumption. He fears, however, that the Muse will say, "That is not it at all, / That is not what I meant, at all." His "I am not Prince Hamlet, nor was meant to be," a line Pound unsuccessfully sought to cut, obeys the logic of the Freudian denial and links Prufrock's problems to the decentering of authority, genealogy, sexuality, and poetic language in Shakespeare's play. Hamlet, too, ironically becomes a character, and himself, in deferring any certain reading of ghostly father figures. Prufrock's final renunciation of desire and consequent metamorphosis into a pathetic ancient sage yields the lyrical beauty of the final stanzas. There the music of the mostly pentameter lines recalls Shakespeare and Tennyson, drowning Prufrock exquisitely in the return of repressed voices.

The state of the poetic mind represented by Prufrock is not simply an expression or mimesis of the author's condition. From at least the time of Wordsworth, such poems on the growth (or death) of the poetic mind have formed a genre, in which Prufrock's cowardice and defeat by time appear to be conventional *topoi*. "The Long Song of J. Alfred Prufrock" is an *interpretation* of the genre. By casting Prufrock's aspirations in parody and bathos, Eliot tropes against prior accomplishments of sublime self-knowledge or negative capability and so earns for himself as poet the new beginning that eludes his protagonist. Of course, the relation between Eliot and Prufrock remains self-figurative, as his character's desires are daemons his poetry conjures. "An artist may have elements in his composition," said Eliot later, "that drive him towards excesses of one kind or another, but a failure to keep these in hand leads to a failure in his art." "Prufrock" precariously manages this balance in the tension between Prufrock's statements and Eliot's poetic language. Hugh Kenner pointedly observes that "J. Alfred Prufrock is a name plus a Voice."[6] We can take this insight a step further by saying that Prufrock's Voice is itself a textual choir of other voices from literary history. The dream of the inviolable Voice of the original poetic subject expressing his divine soul is spoken in the many borrowed figures of the dead. Two kinds of subjectivity, metaphysical and textual, engage in their own agon in the poem. Prufrock himself longs to be Bloom's immortal poet, while the poem becomes a character in an intertextual play that constantly transfigures identities. For the rest of his career, Eliot will experience his poetic identity as a struggle between the desire for an eternal logos and the equally powerful urge to "fare forward" into uncharted possibilities.

6 Quoted in John Baille and Hugh Martin (eds.), *Revelation* (London, 1937), 30; Hugh Kenner, *The Invisible Poet: T. S. Eliot* (New York, 1959), 40.

These antitheses in Eliot's work have prompted some readers to discover a submerged quest for religious conversion in the troubled years from 1908 through 1915.[7] Eliot's graduate studies in philosophy and comparative religion seem, along with the unpublished poetry of this period, to support such a view. Prufrock's withdrawal from physical life was the price he willingly paid for identity and knowledge. In subsequent poems Eliot's protagonists approach the Absolute through violent asceticism and sensual martyrdom, as in "I am the Resurrection and the Life" (WLFS, III). Christ, Heraclitus, and the Buddha fuse in this self-image or "ego-ideal" of salvation through ecstasy and masochism, and the "I" internalizes all conflict in a claustrophobic mental economy. Many of these poems, as Lyndall Gordon puts it, exhibit "an extraordinary display of willful physical self-abuse."[8] But these first poetic efforts at introjecting a religious "conscience" to order and punish the natural self repeat, with different metaphors, Eliot's earlier adoption of "anti-Romantic" literary ideals, suggesting that the rhetoric of theology proffers only another set of terms for problems that precede and go beyond it.

The most powerful counterdaemon in the development of Eliot's critical ideas from 1907 through 1911 was Irving Babbitt. His *Literature and the American College* (1908), with its essays "The Rational Study of the Classics," "Ancients and Moderns," and "On Being Original," supplies the majority of Eliot's critical principles on a number of key topics. In those pages and in Babbitt's classroom, Eliot receives the revelation that "discipline," "restraint," "selection," and "absolute values" are correctives to "Rousseauism," the "disorderly and undisciplined unfolding of the faculties of the individual" ending in "anarchical self-assertion and self-indulgence." In an insight that haunts both Eliot and Bloom, Babbitt declares that "Romanticism from the very beginning tended to become eccentric through over-anxiety to be original." True originality "nowadays" would be "to have a thorough knowledge and imaginative appreciation of what is really worth while in the literature of the past," so that the balance "between the forces of tradition and the claims of originality" would be maintained by "creative imitation" in literature and "creative assimilation" in scholarship.[9] When Eliot turns away from Babbitt's humanism in the late 1920s, calling it (as he did Romanticism) another substitute for religion, he replays the direction followed from "Prufrock" to "The Death of Saint Narcissus."

7 See, for example, Lyndall Gordon, *Eliot's Early Years* (New York, 1977), and Ronald Schuchard, "Eliot and Hulme in 1916: Toward a Revaluation of Eliot's Critical and Spiritual Development," *PMLA*, LXXXVIII (1973), 1083–94.

8 Gordon, *Eliot's Early Years*, 59. Gordon's discussion of Eliot's attitudes toward women in the early poetry is very illuminating.

9 Irving Babbitt, *Literature and the American College* (New York, 1956), 156, 74, 91.

Eliot's journey toward the Absolute, however, sticks to the *via negativa*. In 1916, when he takes up T. E. Hulme's definition of Original Sin and begins to speak in terms of the "classicist point of view . . . the necessity for austere discipline . . . *form* and *restraint* in art, *discipline* and *authority* in religion, *centralization* in government," the new logocentrism follows the old ways of negative theology.[10] "It is to the immense credit of Hulme," wrote Eliot in 1928, "that he found out for himself that there is an *absolute* to which Man can *never* attain" (SE, 437). Eliot's "religious" poetry between 1910 and 1915 continues the project of subduing the things of nature to the mind's imaginings; only now the authority for such self-transcendence is transferred to the theology of mortification. The unattainability of the Absolute is, of course, an absolute in Eliot's system, a trope of the Romantic discontinuity of subject and object and a defense against its incarnation in erotic metaphors. The doctrines of original sin and negative theology allow for a critique of the metaphysics of Western idealism, denying to man any sublime knowledge of the living presence or logos. This is their chief attraction, though it cannot finally mask the binary logic of presence and absence, fullness and emptiness, potency and castration, truth and nontruth underlying it. Eliot's critique of idealism, as his writings make abundantly clear, provides him with the position of authority, with the guardianship of truth, with a center in an eccentric world. A different critique of metaphysics and idealism has recently surfaced in the name of deconstruction, and it has been accused of being a negative theology. On the contrary, deconstruction attempts to unsettle the mirror economies of logocentrism and negative theology, both of which promise, positively or negatively, the *Aufhebung*, the Return of the Same and the recovery of Identity. The alternative (perhaps best indicated by Derrida's notion of "dissemination") is not simply "free play," but the willingness to engage in acts of creation whose results may not conform to a prior logos. This possibility appears most powerfully in *Four Quartets*, when negative theology finally relaxes its hold on the daemons who would speak.

As the early Eliot refined his strategies of the negative sublime, he supplemented Babbitt's doctrines with those he found in poring over Evelyn Underhill's *Mysticism* (1911). Her chapters on the purification and illumination of the self, voices and visions, ecstasy and rapture, the dark night of the soul, and the unitive life provided Eliot with a vocabulary he never ceased drawing upon. Here he read of the Purgative Way to the Absolute, of Dante and Saint John of the Cross and Julian of Norwich, of the mortification of the "natural" self whose senses have "usurped" Divine Reality, of "self-surrender" and

10 Quoted in Ronald Schuchard, "T. S. Eliot as an Extension Lecturer," *Review of English Studies*, XXV (May, 1974), 165.

"self-discipline": "Increasing control of the lower centres, of the surface intelligence and its scattered desires, permits the emergence of the transcendental perceptions." The mystic personality, like Poe's Roderick Usher, cultivates a sensory paranoia and morbid acuteness. "Its passionate apprehension of spiritual beauty, its intuitive perception of divine harmony, is counterbalanced by an instinctive loathing of ugliness, a shrinking from the disharmonies of squalor and disease. . . . This extreme sensitiveness, which forms part of the normal psycho-physical make-up of the mystic, as it often does of the equally high-strung artistic type, is one of the first things seized upon by the awakened self as a disciplinary instrument."[11] The sensory faculties are turned against the natural world, and exquisite pain becomes the displaced outlet for forbidden pleasures. Affection is withdrawn from external objects, the loss of pleasure compensated by the increase in pain, and the love of the other replaced by the approval of a stern deity. To switch from the mythology of the libido to the allegories of writing, the body of the signifier undergoes a restriction of its play, a prohibition of its promiscuity, and is disciplined in an authorized genealogy of proper meanings. The mortification of the signifier acts out a desire to erase the materiality and temporality of language, in order to reveal only the pure Signified, the Word in its uncorrupted transcendence.

Eliot's nomination of Narcissus to be the deluded saint of his crisis ode tells us that his reading of Underhill was as analytic as it was inspirational. The figure of Narcissus lays bare the psychology of religious martyrdom, as does Eliot's quite overt depiction of displaced sexuality in the poem.[12] The implications come surprisingly close to the propositions summarized in Freud's *Civilization and Its Discontents*, in which the authority of culture and religion is derived by a psychological genealogy from the introjection of the Father's No. The successful passage into "civilized" behavior depends upon repression and metaphor, as guilt is detached from its "original" physical desires and made an infinitely substitutable feeling available for any moral discourse. In Lacan's formula this passage is the insertion into the Symbolic register, where the elaboration of abstractions, ideas, and structure deliteralizes and desexualizes conscious mental life. Masochism resexualizes the relationship to authority, eroticizes the discourse of guilt and punishment, and so

11 Evelyn Underhill, *Mysticism: A Study in the Nature and Development of Man's Spiritual Consciousness* (New York, 1961), 226, 223.

12 For related studies see Vicki Mahaffey, "'The Death of Saint Narcissus' and 'Ode': Two Suppressed Poems by T. S. Eliot," *American Literature*, L (1979), 604–12; and Nancy R. Comley, "From Narcissus to Tiresias: T. S. Eliot's Use of Metamorphosis," *Modern Language Review*, LXXIV (1979), 281–86.

takes the sufferer back into a time before the prohibition.[13] In masculine psychology the masochist acts out the role of the father and of the sufferer. The latter occupies a "female" position, and once more the dream of narcissism, of being one's own father and possessing his Muse, is accomplished in distorted fantasy, accompanied by a guilt that pays for the transgression and thus allows it to continue. Sadism against women, visible in the more regrettable passages of Eliot's early published and unpublished poetry, redirects self-destructive violence toward she who excites the body, who awakens prohibited desire and so disrupts identity. Woman signifies the signifier, indicates a difference never wholly recuperable in a metaphysical register. She is an Other classically categorized with the daemons of evil. The sick man's violence, directed at himself or the other, is an attempt at "writing," or at translating a frightening, incomprehensible difference into the language of a phantasmal logos. This subordination of life to a compulsive prescription is directed at the difference within, at the body that is not an idea, at the word that is not the Word. In the production of a saintly self and a metaphysical truth through the denial of the flesh, mortification, too, follows the path of negative theology.

Eliot's analysis of Narcissus begins, after a portentous introduction later moved into *The Waste Land*, with the saint's discovery of his body as an object of his own desires.

> He walked once between the sea and the high cliffs
> When the wind made him aware of his limbs smoothly passing each
>   other
> And of his arms crossed over his breast.
> When he walked over the meadows
> He was stifled and soothed by his own rhythm.
> By the river
> His eyes were aware of the pointed corners of his eyes
> And his hands aware of the pointed tips of his fingers.
>
> (PWY, 28)

Echoing within these lines are the poems of America's grandest Narcissus, Walt Whitman, especially his "There Was a Child Went Forth," "As I Ebb'd with the Ocean of Life," and "Out of the Cradle Endlessly Rocking." (See also the Whitman-inspired opening of Swinburne's "A Forsaken Garden.") Narcissus experiences his incarnation, his birth as a poet of the natural self, through the inspiration ("The wind made him aware") of the genius loci. We may surmise that this genius is none other than the daemonic Walt, for

13 See Freud, "The Economic Problem in Masochism," *Works*, XIX, 157–70.

Narcissus' awareness is not of anything beyond him, but an awakening to a repressed, alternative, and attractive image of himself. This "nature" he perceives, however, remains curiously external. His body is a distant surface of sensations, one whose very intensity of feeling causes a further detachment on the part of an epistemologically oriented consciousness that would like to translate the differences of becoming into the script of a being. To borrow Heidegger's argument, we witness once more the sundering of physis from logos: their reciprocity in the emergence of being is split into an opposition between nature and logic, object and subject.[14] Narcissism's effort to restore the unity of being only exacerbates the problem, for it continues to conceive of the logos as the commandment of the One and the Same, the return to the Word, rather than the gathering of appearances. (This interjection here of a pre-Socratic perspective on Eliot's recourse to theology is supported by his graduate readings and by the strong return to Heraclitus' influence in working out the different logos of *Four Quartets*.) The repetition of "aware" characterizes Narcissus' state as somewhere between perception and knowledge, a wary confrontation with what in 1919 Eliot called "a network of tentacular roots reaching down to the deepest terrors and desires" (SE, 135). The body occupies an anomalous inside/outside region, neither consciousness nor nature. For Eliot it is the inferno of the daemonic forces, which by condensation has come to be peopled by the figures of nature, women, sex, Romanticism, and a legion of others, including Whitman.[15]

In his own version of the "mirror stage," Narcissus is undone when the cogito finds that it cannot be the same as its images or desires.

> Struck down by such knowledge
> He could not live men's ways, but became a dancer before God
> If he walked in city streets
> He seemed to tread on faces, convulsive thighs and knees.

The first draft clarifies the terror: "So because he was struck mad by the knowledge of his own beauty" (WLFS, 91), as if daemonically possessed by his own physical being, Narcissus loses himself. Unlike Ovid's Narcissus, Eliot's saint does not literally fall in love with his own image. The ecstasy he suffers in this Scene of Instruction produces his double identity. He is aware

---

14 See Martin Heidegger, *Introduction to Metaphysics*, trans. Ralph Manheim (New Haven, 1959).

15 The "homosexual" component in Eliot's poetry or in his friendship with Jean Verdenal should thus not be construed literally. Homoeroticism and its representations are integral to the economic structure of narcissism. The metapsychological analyses of these methods of self-conception, along with a Bloomian analysis of Eliot's reaction to Whitman, should prevent us from engaging in gossip disguised as a search for the "true facts."

of a part of himself created in an invasion by the other and swayed by a power so absolute in its claims that it threatens to destroy those who yield to loving it. In the draft, the streets are those of Augustine's Carthage, though they may as well be Hawthorne's New England haunts, the streets of Salem village where the daemonized figures of Young Goodman Brown and Arthur Dimmesdale walk so guiltily, projecting their own sins on everyone they meet. Becoming "a dancer before God," Narcissus displaces his feverish physical excitement into a devotional ritual. He submits to a theological Power whose edict casts down the usurping fiends. Divinity is conjured to prop up the Name and the No of the Father, countenancing the sublimation into dancing art of the "rhythm" that so disturbed Narcissus' nature walk.

The following stanzas retrace the prior stages of Narcissus' erotic/spiritual fantasies, from the primary narcissism of "First he was sure that he had been a tree, / Twisting its branches among each other," to the phase of autoerotism, "Writhing in his own clutch, his ancient beauty / Caught fast in the pink tips of his new beauty," to an oneiric playing out of all the roles in the family romance.

> Then he had been a young girl
> Caught in the woods by a drunken old man
> Knowing at the end the taste of his own whiteness
> The horror of his own smoothness,
> And he felt drunken and old.

The earlier version presents these three scenes as "wished," not "sure" or re collected. The final stanza returns to his solution, to be "a dancer to God / Because his flesh was in love with the burning arrows" (the draft reads "penetrant arrows"). The not-so-subtle imagery transforms sexual intercourse into masochistic passion, Narcissus assuming the position of reception for God's divine influx. This conversion of the pleasure principle into Thanatos, or the death instinct, would not have surprised Freud, who was driven to the outrageous trope of a death instinct primarily by his observation that the "compulsion to repeat" often involved painful experiences. The project of the death instinct is to restore an earlier state of things, a time without tension, an inorganic repose of nondifference. The rhythm of sexual crescendo and denouement borrows the drive of the death instinct for the opposing purposes of Eros.

> This tallies well with the hypothesis that the life process of the individual leads for internal reasons to an abolition of chemical tensions, that is to say, to death, whereas union with the living substance of a different individual increases those tensions, introducing what may be described as fresh "vital

differences" which must then be lived off. . . . It is clear that the function
thus described [the repetition compulsion or death instinct] would be concerned with the most universal endeavor of all living substance—namely to
return to the quiescence of the inorganic world. We have all experienced
how the greatest pleasure attainable by us, that of the sexual act, is associated with a momentary extinction of a highly intensified excitation. . . .
The pleasure principle seems actually to serve the death instincts.[16]

In poetry, we might reverse Freud's epigram and say that the death instinct or
repetition compulsion seems actually to serve the pleasure of the poetic principle. Thanatos, the anxiety of influence, and daemonic possession are various names for the dynamic economy of tradition and the individual talent.
When the poet steals from his forerunners, he returns to an earlier state of
things, not for quiescence but to introduce his own "vital differences" into
our language and our thought. A "union with the substance of a different
individual" occurs in the passionate affairs of poets. The death instinct may
be the darkest metaphor of the drive within logocentrism and lapsarian
mythologies. Against the always enticing lure of this meaningful story of
pure origins ("In the beginning was the Word, and the Word was with
God"), the poet can redirect the instinct of repetition into the Eros of writing. The poet may, as does Eliot, declare his allegiance to the Return of the
Same while that very return turns what is gathered again into an excitement
of vital tensions.

When Narcissus takes pleasure in the burning, penetrant arrows, he performs (like the hysteric in his symptoms) both the death that ends difference
and the union that creates life: "As he embraced them his white skin surrendered itself to the redness of blood, and satisfied him." As the canceled draft
goes on to say, "We each have the sort of life we want, but his life went
straight to the death he wanted" (WLFS, 93). Enraptured by negative theology and trapped in the mirror stage, Narcissus fails as a poet, since Eros is
mercilessly made to serve the death instinct. The fundamental definition of
narcissism appears here: it is the withdrawal of affection, love, or cathexis
from objects outside the self. In contrast, love is an expenditure without reserve, a self-sacrifice that does not hold out for a guaranteed return. Love and
writing risk the meaning of their identities. Fearing that risk, Narcissus con-
summates his claustrophobic romance with the Absolute.

Autoaffection and logocentric writing, argues Derrida in his reading of
Rousseau, conform to the nonlogic of the "supplement," that operation that
paradoxically both adds to a plentitude and supplants a deficient presence

16 Freud, *Beyond the Pleasure Principle*, in *Works*, XVIII, 55, 62–63.

(much in the way Eliot's "new work" of art supplements the tradition that nonetheless authorizes it [SE, 5]). Onanism, like literature and other uses of representation, works in the realm of fantasy, "permits one to be himself affected by providing himself with presences, by summoning absent beauties." In the onanistic reverie, imagination summons and masters the presence of the other. It need not risk an attachment to something external that could fail to return a like affection and so disrupt the economy of love. Autoaffection enables a "restitution at the same time symbolic and immediate," *i.e.* the immediate stimulation of the consciousness by signs. "But," and here the deconstruction intervenes, "what is no longer deferred is also absolutely deferred. The presence that is thus delivered to us in the present is a chimera. Auto-affection is a pure speculation."[17] The self and the God of Narcissus are signs and supplements. These restitutions of purified desire come only in negative tropes, in a tortuous *and* torturous writing on the body of Narcissus. The act that mortifies the flesh to represent the spirit does not *erase* the signifier's body; it *inscribes* it, requires it, and excites it. The Absolute and sexuality continue to be written, the Word unspoken: "Now he is green, dry and stained / With the shadow in his mouth."

As a crisis poem, "The Death of Saint Narcissus" falls short of "Prufrock." The elaboration of Prufrock's decaying sensuality into Narcissus' martyrdom leads quite literally to a dead end. Transumption eludes the poem itself as well. The irony of Laforgue seems utterly gone except perhaps for the choice of Narcissus as mock hero. In the verbal texture there appears little of that mediation by echo and allusion that allows Eliot elsewhere to handle the "deepest terrors and desires" emanating from his personal and literary unconscious. The poem apparently dates from the time of upheaval and transition in the months following his arrival in London in August, 1914. It is sometime after meeting Pound in September that Eliot begins again to cultivate the stylistic devices—satire, allusion, the Gautier quatrain—of "impersonality." His commitment to philosophy, already shaken by the war's abrupt termination of his studies in Germany, declines further when he meets Pound and gains his introduction to the literary life in London. He begins to write poetry again in earnest and to feel relief in his distance from Boston and Saint Louis. In April of 1916 he meets Vivienne, and two months later he marries her, sealing his exile with an act that will outrage his family and shock the saint within him. "Morning at the Window" may have been his first new effort, resembling as it does the "Preludes" and "Rhapsody on a Windy Night." "The Death of Saint Narcissus," probably antedating the 1915

17 Jacques Derrida, *Of Grammatology*, trans. Gayatri Spivak (Baltimore, 1976), 153–54.

satires, seems conceived as an obituary on the lost years and fragments of the period from 1911 through 1914, and Eliot thought well enough of it to almost publish it in *Poetry*. His killing it after preparation of the proof sheets remains unexplained.

Beyond the embarrassments of its subject matter, the poem discloses the young outsetting bard too vulnerable to unconscious voices. If we look for the precursor poem that overwhelms "The Death of Saint Narcissus" while Eliot's "classical" defenses are down, we find Whitman's "Song of Myself," especially the account of the onanistic sublime in section 28.

> Is this then a touch? quivering me to a new identity,
> Flames and ether making a rush for my veins,
> Treacherous tip of me reaching and crowding to help them,
> My flesh and blood playing out lightning to strike what is hardly
>   different from myself
> . . . .
> The sentries desert every other part of me,
> They have left me helpless to a red marauder,
> They all come to the headland to witness and assist against me.
> I am given up by traitors,
> I talk wildly, I have lost my wits, I and nobody else am the greatest
>   traitor,
> I went myself first to the headland, my own hands carried me there.
>
> You villain touch! what are you doing? my breath is tight in its throat,
> Unclench your floodgates, you are too much for me.

A later chapter will consider in more detail Eliot's ambivalence toward Whitman. Here the Bloomian critic would argue that it is Eliot's "knowledge" of Whitman's "ancient beauty" that Narcissus has made "his own," now "Caught fast" in the revisionary poet's "new beauty." That, at least, is the hope, but so daemonized is he by Whitman that askesis intervenes and he submits to another, if not stranger, god. Whitman had transformed his gigantic narcissism and correspondent homoeroticism into a sublime cosmic solipsism that includes us as Walt eludes us. His uncanny voice keeps turning up one step beyond, speaking out of the intersection of time and the timeless at the end of "Song of Myself" and most extraordinarily in his first great challenge to death, "Crossing Brooklyn Ferry." The various saints that Eliot entertains as substitute precursors form another countertradition to his American and Romantic inheritance, but they are a weak lot in comparison and of relatively little use without the supplement of Laforgue, Baudelaire, Dante, and the Jacobeans. The continuing sexual thematics in Eliot's poetry of 1914 through 1922 demonstrate an ongoing struggle to interpret and so exorcise the Whitman within him.

"Gerontion" is the only major poem of the period between "Prufrock" and *The Waste Land*. After his flirtation with martyrdom, Eliot finds sources of new strength: his exile from America, Pound's cranky erudition, French literature and criticism, the impersonality of review work, and even his tragic marriage to the Dionysian Vivienne. Eliot's first extension lectures, in 1916, are on modern French literature (these depend heavily on Babbitt's teachings) and modern English literature from Tennyson and Browning to Fitz-Gerald and Meredith. In 1917 he gives two lecture sequences on Victorian and modern English literature. (The only American writer on the list is Emerson.) After his bout with philosophy and mysticism, Eliot, admittedly for the money, returns to the nineteenth-century authors who had early formed his sensibility. Only in 1918 does the opportunity to lecture on Elizabethan literature arise, and he eagerly seizes it, already planning the essays on dramatists that begin appearing in 1919. By that year forces are pushing Eliot towards another crisis. The impact of the war coincides with the illness and death of his father, the emotional chaos and sexual frustration of his marriage, and a nagging dissatisfaction with the often minor, mannered poems of 1915 through 1917. The brilliance of "Burbank with a Baedeker: Bleistein with a Cigar," "Whispers of Immortality," and the Sweeney poems comes in their allusive inscription of Eliot's recurrent emotional themes in networks of textual and cultural echoing. Burbank, Sweeney, Origen, Oedipus, Agamemnon, and Tereus are neither many nor one, just as the verbal identity of Eliot's lines belongs to neither him nor any one of the galaxy of writers he deploys. The effect is of a severe containment and expression of disillusioned desire through satire, horror, and violent animosity.

Eliot returns in "Gerontion" to the nineteenth-century tradition of lyric meditation and dramatic monologue, now passed through the refining fire of Webster, Tourneur, Chapman, and Gautier. While Shakespeare and Henry Adams make important appearances, the key precursor (as many have begun to see) is Tennyson's "Ulysses," a poem Eliot will twice more rewrite, in the excised draft of "Death by Water" and in "The Dry Salvages." Written in the crushing wake of Hallam's death, "Ulysses" turns the loss of the beloved youth into the aged melancholy of the speaker. By identification, the mourned one is internalized as a figure of the self, of its youth and desire for immortality: "We are not now that strength which in old days / Moved earth and heaven." Bloom acutely sees that Hallam's death, in Tennyson's work, is a poetic crisis, representing the poet's late "arrival on the scene *after the event*" of Romanticism.[18] "Tennyson's Ulysses," wrote Eliot in 1929, comparing him to Dante's,

18 Harold Bloom, *Poetry and Repression: Revisionism from Blake to Stevens* (New Haven, 1976), 168. Bloom ends his remarkable chapter on Tennyson with the assertion that "time, I am persuaded, will show us how much stronger a poet Tennyson was than Eliot" (174). The

"is primarily a very self-conscious poet" (SE, 211). As others have pointed out, the apparently heroic resolve of Ulysses to begin again, "To follow knowledge like a sinking star, / Beyond the utmost bound of human thought," withers in the poem's enervated cadences and slow sounds and in such metaphorical ironies as "knowledge like a sinking star."[19] "Ulysses" portrays the revival of the Romantic subject's struggle against time, nature, and his own desires with profoundly divided results (the aporia here is between Ulysses' Shelleyan statements and his own elderly figure and again between the sentiment of energetic voyage and the dragging speech in which it is cast). The exorcism of Tennyson's "Ulysses" leads Eliot repeatedly to a comparison with Dante's more orthodox account of Ulysses' hubris in *Inferno*, canto 26.

In 1918 Eliot "did not care to pose as a champion of Tennyson," who "had a brain (a large dull brain like a farmhouse clock) which saved him from triviality."[20] Later, he called "Ulysses" "a perfect poem" though "too *poetical*" in "*forcing*" its effects in phrases like "moans round with many voices" (SE, 210). It is a line Eliot finally transfigures near the opening of "The Dry Salvages," where he asserts that "The sea has many voices, many gods and many voices."

> The sea howl
> And the sea yelp, are different voices
> Often together heard: the whine in the rigging,
> The menace and caress of wave that breaks on water,
> The distant rote in the granite teeth,
> And the wailing warning from the approaching headland
> Are all sea voices, and the heaving groaner
> Rounded homewards, and the seagull.
>
> (DS, I)

This allegory of hearing and poetic homecoming replaces the "different voices" of *The Waste Land* and before with the native sounds of Eliot's New England genius loci. He renovates the language of Tennyson and old England by becoming an American Ulysses in his youth, speaking the dialect of the Gloucester tribe. "Groaner," explains Eliot, "is the New England word

---

whole performance, of course, including Bloom's readings of "Ulysses" and "Tithonus," provides an allegory of Bloom's attempted transumption of Eliot.

19 See Robert Pattison, *Tennyson and Tradition* (Cambridge, 1979); and James Kissane, "Tennyson: The Passion of the Past and the Curse of Time," *English Literary History*, XXXII, (1965), 85–109. For relevant cultural backgrounds see Jerome H. Buckley, *The Triumph of Time: A Study of Victorian Concepts of Time, History, Progress, and Decadence* (Cambridge, 1966).

20 "Verse Pleasant and Unpleasant," *Egoist*, V (March, 1918), 43.

for a 'whistling buoy.'"[21] Throughout his criticism Eliot displaces substantive arguments with past poets onto questions of technique and so obliquely points to the tropological interplay between literary generations. "The Dry Salvages" conjures Tennyson to return, his voice easily heard in "the heaving groaner / Rounded homewards," yet made to speak in Eliot's terms. The acceptance of Tennyson, and of American beginnings, in these lines brings to the surface for a hearing the buried forces of emotional and poetic strife that so paralyze the figure of Gerontion.

The judgment of Tennyson's "too *poetical*" phrases appears in the 1929 essay on Dante in a telling place. From the *Inferno*, Eliot cites two especially memorable episodes that "first convinced" him of Dante's greatness, those of Brunetto Latini and Ulysses. "And the two may well be put together: for the first is Dante's testimony of a loved master of arts, the second his reconstruction of a legendary figure of ancient epic" (SE, 208). In his strictures on Tennyson's style, Eliot combines these two episodes, for the master Tennyson is sent to a watery critical grave, like Dante's Ulysses, for excessive interest in himself and the things of this world. In 1936 the semiautobiographical essay on "In Memoriam" continues to praise Tennyson's technique. "His variety of metrical accomplishment is astonishing," says Eliot. "He had the finest ear of any English poet since Milton" (SE, 286). (Yet, Eliot will infamously lament Milton's "bad influence" on English poetry.) But he prefers Dante's "simplification" and "clear visual images." These could restrain and focus the purported vagaries of Victorian linguistic hedonism, that indulgence in the sensual effects of sound that Eliot rejected in his essay on Swinburne's "diffuseness" and consequent lack of the sharp visual image: "The morbidity is not of human feeling but of language. Language in a healthy state presents the object, is so close to the object that the two are identified (SE, 285). This neo-Poundian doctrine of the logocentric poetic object is designed to discipline emotion and language, to fix the daemonic forces in a true vision.

The problem with Tennyson's "Ulysses," following from its verbal self-consciousness, is precisely its inability to "fare forth" from morbidity and melancholy to the askesis that promises redemption.

> Dante is telling a story. Tennyson is only stating an elegiac mood. . . . And I do not believe for a moment that Tennyson was a man of mild feelings or weak passions. There is no evidence in his poetry that he knew the experience of violent passion for a woman; but there is plenty of evidence of emotional intensity and violence—but of emotion so deeply suppressed, even from himself, as to tend rather towards the blackest melancholia than

21 Quoted in Helen Gardner, *The Composition of "Four Quartets"* (New York, 1978), 120.

towards dramatic action. And it is emotion which, so far as my reading of the poems can discover, attained no ultimate clear purgation. I should reproach Tennyson not for mildness, or tepidity, but rather for lack of serenity. (SE, 290)

The story of "Gerontion" hardly goes further than melancholia. Its suppression of emotion attains no purgation. There is an implied violent passion for a woman, however, and a kind of dramatic action in the presentation of Gerontion's blackest moods through the voices of other writers. Eliot's treatment does emphasize the ironies preventing Ulysses from leaving shore for another quest and adds to Tennyson's mythical methods and literary borrowings Eliot's own dazzling assemblage of allusions. Though the apparent heterogeneity of Eliot's yoked-together fragments outdoes his precursor's in sheer audacity, Tennyson's lifting of pieces from classical, medieval, and Romantic literature—his "passion of the past" as a device for figuring the pattern of present moments—paves Eliot's way.[22] His critique of Tennyson implicitly (mis)reads "Ulysses" as an endorsement of self-consciousness, heroic will, and secular progress; he can thus submit the figure of Ulysses to the diminution of a metamorphosis into Gerontion. The metrical and verbal ingenuities of the poem owe as much to the Victorians as to the Jacobeans, but it is the dark inflections of the latter that make possible Eliot's bitter echoing of nineteenth-century erotic melancholy in the poem's middle stanzas on failed passion. Although still sounding a bit defensive and artificial, these most memorable portions of "Gerontion" begin to utilize the tradition of the English poetic voice in a way prefiguring Eliot's style in "What the Thunder Said," parts of *Ash Wednesday*, "Marina," and *Four Quartets*.

"Old men ought to be explorers," concludes "East Coker." Gerontion's climactic speech beginning "I would meet you upon this honestly. / I that was near your heart was removed therefrom / To lose beauty in terror, terror in inquisition" ends with a litany of sensual emasculation. The poem declines into "small deliberations." De Bailhache, Fresca, and Mrs. Cammel do not follow knowledge beyond the horizon, but are

> whirled
> Beyond the circuit of the shuddering Bear
> In fractured atoms. Gull against the wind, in the windy straits
> Of Belle Isle, or running on the Horn,
> White feathers in the snow, the Gulf claims,

22 See Christopher Ricks, *Tennyson* (New York, 1972), 118–28; Arthur J. Carr, "Tennyson as a Modern Poet," in John Killham (ed.), *Critical Essays on the Poetry of Tennyson* (London, 1960), 41–66; and Langbaum, *The Poetry of Experience*, 88–94, 102–105.

And an old man driven by the Trades
To a sleepy corner.

In these lines Eliot coldly tropes the resolute pathos near the close of "Ulysses" ("It may be that the gulfs will wash us down; / It may be we shall touch the Happy Isles") to produce an ironic reading of Ulysses' striving. This "old man" in a "sleepy corner" circles us back to Tennyson's opening, its "idle king" and "still hearth," and then to Eliot's beginning: "Here I am, an old man in a dry month, / Being read to by a boy, waiting for rain." As in "Prufrock," the statement of the protagonist's defeat comes in a rhetoric that figures the poet's strength. Eliot's opener, purloined from a biography of Tennyson's friend FitzGerald, may be read as a double emblem of the poet's condition: within the obvious inscription of Eliot's belatedness we can also read his desire to reverse indebtedness, to make Tennyson, FitzGerald, Browning, and others the old men who must be read to by the new boy. This reversal points toward *The Waste Land*, in which the elegy for the vegetation god will serve to empty the past of its privilege, empower the newcomer, and seek a way beyond the economy of debilitating self-reflection epitomized in "Gerontion."

CHAPTER 8

CRITICAL FIGURAE
Shakespeare, Dante, and Virgil

In his devotion to his father [Aeneas] is not being just an admirable son. There is personal affection, without which filial piety would be imperfect; but personal affection is not piety. There is also devotion to his father as his father, as his progenitor: this is piety as the acceptance of a bond which one has not chosen. The quality of affection is altered, and its importance deepened, when it becomes love due to the object. But his filial piety is also the recognition of a further bond, that with the gods, to whom such an attitude is pleasing: to fail in it would be to be guilty of impiety towards the gods. The gods must therefore be gods worthy of this respect; and without gods, or a god, regarded in this way, filial piety must perish. For then it becomes no longer a duty: your feeling towards your father will be due merely to the fortunate accident of congeniality, or will be reduced to a sentiment of gratitude for care and consideration.

"Virgil and the Christian World"

Eliot would always be tempted to bind genealogy through devotion to a divine logos. Before undertaking a sustained reading of his mature poetic writing, it will be useful to examine this tendency at work in Eliot's critical essays on his progenitors, in which personal affections and the accidents of congeniality are made into the obligations of piety. In the case of Tennyson, I have already suggested how, following Eliot's own description of his criticism as a workshop for turning influence into poetry, a pattern of self-invention links the essays and the poems. In one way or another, all of Eliot's essays on individual writers reveal the same rhetorical staging of self-criticism. Particularly fascinating in this light are those on Ben Jonson, Blake, Pascal, Baudelaire, Lancelot Andrewes, Arnold, Samuel Johnson, and Yeats. It was Dante above all, however, who early claimed the greatest place in Eliot's esteem and represented the highest achievement by which a poet could measure himself.[1] "I steeped myself in Dante's poetry" said Eliot in

---

1 Mario Praz, "T. S. Eliot and Dante," in Leonard Unger (ed.), *T. S. Eliot: A Selected Critique* (New York, 1966), 296–318; A. C. Charity, "T. S. Eliot: The Dantean Recogni-

"What Dante Means to Me," a talk he gave in 1950. "I still, after forty years, regard his poetry as the most persistent and deepest influence upon my own verse" (CC, 125). No other writer exerted a comparable hold upon him, from the epigraph for "Prufrock" to the ghost in "Little Gidding." Yet, in reading Eliot's commentaries on Dante, we find that not even he "has his complete meaning alone," but is appreciated "in relation to the dead poets and artists," specifically Shakespeare and Virgil (SE, 4). The way that Eliot's stance toward these three is motivated and arranged often tells us more than the isolated opinions state about any one of them. Taken together, the commentaries on this trio of masters form a tale that resonates with those of his poems and indeed with that of his career in poetic self-fashioning.

His attitude toward Shakespeare hinges on and illustrates two of Eliot's theses on influence, "that every great work of poetry tends to make impossible the production of equally great works of the same kind" (OPP, 66) and that "no nation owes its great poets a debt of gratitude for their influence upon their immediate successors."[2] In another essay he elaborated, "A poet of the supreme greatness of Shakespeare can hardly influence, he can only be imitated: and the difference between influence and imitation is that influence can fecundate, whereas imitation—especially unconscious imitation—can only sterilize" (CC, 18). The passage and its procreational metaphors intend to explain Eliot's youthful preference for the Elizabethan and Jacobean dramatists over Shakespeare: "It was from these minor dramatists that I, in my own poetic formation, had learned my lessons; it was by them, and not by Shakespeare, that my imagination had been stimulated, my sense of rhythm trained, and my emotions fed" (CC, 18). He had "read them with passionate delight" rather than daemonic possession, using them to counter the style and sensibility of his Romantic inheritance and American legacy, for Shakespeare fathered Hawthorne as surely as he sired Keats and Shelley. The "minor" dramatists knew the burden of Shakespeare's accomplishment, whereas Shakespeare himself lacked any really strong precursor to intimidate him. In a belated age the modern poet looks to other anxious poets for instruction or away from poets who seem to treat belatedness (as Shakespeare did in *Hamlet*) as fatal. From this Jacobean tutorial Eliot learned "burlesque or farce. . . . an art of caricature. . . . a brutality, a lack of sentiment, a pol-

---

tions," A. D. Moody (ed.), *"The Waste Land" in Different Voices* (New York, 1974), 117–56. Alan Weinblatt, "T. S. Eliot and the Historical Sense," *South Atlantic Quarterly*, LXXVII (1978), 282–95, makes suggestive use of Walter Jackson Bate's notion of "the burden of the past" in examining Eliot's views on Shakespeare, Dante, and Virgil.

2 "A Commentary," *Criterion*, XIV (July, 1935), 612. Eliot makes the point in discussing Yeats's "disastrous" influence on Irish poetry.

ished surface, a handling of large bold designs in brilliant colors" (SE, 137–38). There is here (as in Eliot's allied affections for vaudeville, practical jokes, and Groucho Marx) a conscious drawing back from the terrifying grandeur of Shakespearean tragedy, a withdrawal from a Romanticism associated with a "raid on the Absolute," and a movement toward a style mixing the parodic and the macabre. The sexual corruption, luxurious morbidity, personal violence, social chaos, and genealogical confusion in Jacobean tragedy fed his kindred emotions and reinforced his skepticism about redeeming the vile habits of human beings.[3]

Eliot's essays on the Elizabethan and Jacobean playwrights contrast the multiplicity of Renaissance Britain to the legendary universalism of the Latin Middle Ages. Eliot characterizes the age of Elizabeth as "a period of dissolution and chaos" and "individualism" (SE, 112). The architectonic cosmos of Dante and Aquinas has, in this declension narrative, become Hamlet's vision of the earth as "a sterile promontory," the heavens "a foul and pestilent congregation of vapors." To Eliot "the philosophical basis, the general attitude toward life of the Elizabethans, is one of anarchism, of dissolution, of decay" (SE, 98). This rather unorthodox sketch of England's flowering resembles Eliot's comment of about the same time on a recent study of Romanticism: "It exhibits the Romantic Period as a period of intellectual chaos; it leads us to speculate whether the age, as an age, can ever exert much influence upon any age to come; and it provokes the suspicion that our own age may be similarly chaotic and ineffectual."[4] Eliot had once located the "dissociation of sensibility" in the eighteenth and nineteenth centuries, after the Metaphysical poets.[5] In 1927 he pushes the fall of unity back to the sundering of medieval accord. "The end of the sixteenth century is an epoch when it is particularly difficult to associate poetry with systems of thought or reasoned views of life. . . . It seemed as if, at that time, the world was filled with broken fragments of systems, and that a man like Donne merely picked up, like a magpie, various shining fragments of ideas as they struck his eye, and stuck them here or there in his verse" (SE, 118). Elizabethan England resembles *too* closely the modernity it begins. Eliot's account repudiates the poetics of *The Waste Land*, with its heap of broken images shored against ruin in a world devoid of "systems of thought or reasoned views of life."

The Metaphysical poets were supposed to have fathered a successful adhe-

---

3 R. Peacock, "Eliot's Contribution to Criticism of Drama," in David Newton-De Molina (ed.), *The Literary Criticism of T. S. Eliot* (London, 1977), 89–110.

4 "The Romantic Generation, if It Existed," *Athenaeum*, No. 4655 (18 July 1919), 616.

5 This infamous thesis has often been challenged. For a relevant discussion see Frank Kermode, *Romantic Image* (London, 1957), 138–62.

sion of "shining fragments" in *The Waste Land*. Eliot's essay on them appeared in October, 1921. He had been at work intensely on parts of *The Waste
Land* at least since the preceding spring. The nervous breakdown that sent
Eliot to Margate, Paris, and Lausanne to finish the poem began at summer's
end, when he collapsed following a visit from America by his mother. His
desk cluttered with lyrics and satires all in a jumble, his marriage in pieces,
his family relations strained, Eliot looked to his predecessors for a healing
bricolage. He hoped to revive the Metaphysicals' "telescoping of images and
multiplied associations" and their "heterogeneity of materials compelled into
unity" (SE, 243). To them Eliot attributed a "mechanism of sensibility which
could devour any kind of experience" (SE, 247). The success he grants them
is in part wish fulfillment for himself, a vote of confidence in his bricoleur's
fate. In 1921 Eliot places their accomplishment as "no less nor more than
Dante, Guido Cavalcanti, Guinizelli or Cino" (SE, 247). By 1927 Donne has
become a "magpie." This retreat from a poetics of ideas "yoked by violence
together" recalls Eliot's disingenuous assertion that his poem "was only the
relief of a personal and wholly insignificant grouse against life . . . a piece of
rhythmical grumbling" (WLFS, 1). His conversion to the Anglican church (a
compromise between the Tudor Shakespeare and the Catholic Dante) and
his abandonment of the poetics of violent yoking express a dissatisfaction
with the heterogeneous method. As his polemical disgust with the modern
world increases, so does the distance he puts between himself and the mirror-
ing age of Elizabeth. The "dissociation of sensibility" gets set back three hundred years to Dante's death as Eliot turns toward him as his major precursor.
The *Paradiso* assumes its place, in the 1929 Dante essay and *Ash Wednesday*, as
the single most important predecessor text, particularly its last canto, which
Eliot called "to my thinking the highest point that poetry has ever reached or
ever can reach" (SE, 212). It is a point he will at last confront at the close of
"Little Gidding."

Much of this Elizabethan "chaos," as well as the style of farce and caricature, appears in Shakespeare, as Eliot's many echoes of his work attest.
A discipleship under the "minor" dramatists avoided a head-on clash with
the power of Shakespeare's language, while allowing many of its lessons to
come down from Marlowe, Webster, Middleton, and Jonson. "When I was
young," said Eliot in 1950, "I felt much more at ease with the lesser Elizabethan dramatists than with Shakespeare: the former were, so to speak, play-
mates nearer my own size" (CC, 127). The predecessor who can "first introduce one to oneself" and who "gives a clue to the discovery of one's own
form. . . . is unlikely to be one of the great masters. The latter are too exalted
and too remote. They are like distant ancestors who have been almost dei-

fied; whereas the smaller poet, who has directed one's first steps, is more like an admired elder brother" (CC, 126). When Eliot discusses Shakespeare's limitations, however, he usually cites those qualities we might most readily associate with these elder brothers. Chief among them is their stylistic excess, a correlative of the themes of disorder in their plays. "In my youth, I think that Dante's astonishing economy and directness of language—his arrow that goes unerringly to the centre of the target—provided for me a wholesome corrective to the extravagances of the Elizabethan, Jacobean and Caroline authors in whom I also delighted" (CC, 23).

Eliot represents Shakespeare and Dante as an opposition of chaos and order, difference and identity, experiment and tradition, unchecked feeling and beatified Eros. The anxiety of influence becomes both a stylistic and an emotional decentering. "If you try to imitate Shakespeare, you will certainly produce a series of stilted, forced, and violent distortions of language. The language of each great English poet is his own language; the language of Dante is the perfection of a common language" (SE, 213). Dante is "the most *universal* of poets in the modern languages," while "there is greater variety and detail in Shakespeare" (SE, 200). Dante's universality goes beyond language, as it exemplifies a cultural order, literary tradition, and religious vision. Much the same contrast governs Eliot's distinction between Lawrence and Joyce or between the Blake whose mind was "unclouded by current opinions" and the Blake who "sadly lacked" a "framework of accepted and traditional ideas" (SE, 277, 279). The difference between the Blakes in the first and second half of Eliot's essay becomes the difference between Blake and Dante: "Dante is a classic, and Blake only a poet of genius" (SE, 279). Shakespeare's genius is too individual. Neither he nor his age provides figures of a new logocentrism. "If I ask myself . . . why I prefer the poetry of Dante to that of Shakespeare, I should have to say, because it seems to me to illustrate a saner attitude towards the mystery of life" (SW, x). It seems that Shakespeare's green worlds and blasted heaths contain more daemons than Dante's *Inferno*. The moderation of Eliot's attitude toward Shakespeare in his later years coincides with a gradual acceptance of returning daemons—personal and literary.[6]

The breakdown of sanity characterizes Elizabethan drama and its language to Eliot, seeming to echo Ulysses' speech on degree in *Troilus and Cressida*: "Take but degree away, untune that string, / And hark what discord follows" (I, iii, 109–10). Ulysses pronounces the deconstruction of the Great Chain of Being, vividly imagining the collapse of the Dantean world view and pre-

6 Phillip L. Marcus, "T. S. Eliot and Shakespeare," *Criticism*, IX (Winter, 1967), 63–79; James Torrens, "T. S. Eliot and Shakespeare: 'This Music Crept by,'" *Bucknell Review*, XIX (Spring, 1971), 77–96.

figuring modern prophecies of civilization's end. Dante, in contrast, stands for harmony, pan-Europeanism, and poetry's power to judge political and secular worlds. Making Latin new, Dante's Italian performs a transumption in the realm of language that likewise holds for culture and religion. Modern languages like English are plagued by "national or racial differences of thought . . . but medieval Latin tended to concentrate on what men of various races and lands could think together" (SE, 201). Eliot and Pound were schooled in the history of language as it was promulgated in the nineteenth century by German scholars of classical and Romance philology, a tradition that Auerbach and Curtius made new. English could be rejuvenated by the supplement of foreign tongues, extending the range of possible English expression and uniting it to the world history of discourse. Shakespearean English, in contrast, is the "local self-consciousness" of a "*particular* civilization" (SE, 201). To nominate Dante as one's best poetic father handily puts the English poet outside the genealogy of a native tongue and connects him to a figure representing a time before the twin falls of the Reformation and Renaissance.

Eliot's Shakespeare personifies an independent mastery of language rather than a dutiful subservience to the impersonal causes of linguistic and cultural universality. Density, detail, and recalcitrant individuality are the qualities of Shakespeare's lines. Eliot maintains "that more is lost in translating Shakespeare into Italian than in translating Dante into English" (SE, 203). Dante's "clear visual images" and similes are contrasted to Shakespeare's "complicated" metaphors. Dante's figures "make you see more clearly" and are "explanatory," whereas "the figure of Shakespeare is expansive rather than intensive; its purpose is to *add* to what you see" (SE, 205). Shakespearean language supplements and transgresses any clear vision of things. The *visual* imagination of Eliot's Dante revives the hope of a translucent knowledge of the sublime. "We have nothing but dreams, and we have forgotten that seeing visions—a practice now relegated to the aberrant and uneducated— was once a more significant, interesting, and disciplined kind of dreaming. We take it for granted that our dreams spring from below: possibly the quality of our dreams suffers in consequence" (SE, 204). Eliot's theory of the "high dream" versus the "low dream" (SE, 223) is a rejoinder to Freud, inverting the tendency toward "low dream" in Eliot's own early verse and rebuking Shakespeare for never allowing *his* high dreams to completely take flight from the lowly and mocking crowd, social and psychological.[7] Shakespeare's individual talent awakens forbidden dreams: "When I affirm that

7 For another example of this inversion see *Ash Wednesday*, the poetic contemporary of the 1929 Dante essay.

more can be learned about how to write poetry from Dante than from any English poet, I do not at all mean that Dante's way is the only right way, or that Dante is thereby *greater* than Shakespeare or, indeed, than any other English poet. I put my meaning into other words by saying that Dante can do less *harm* to any one trying to learn to write verse than can Shakespeare" (SE, 213). Shakespeare can harm the young poet by tempting him to imitation or by fostering the insanities that "spring from below."

Eliot argues that "Shakespeare understands a greater extent and variety of human life than Dante; but that Dante understands deeper degrees of degradation and higher degrees of exaltation" (SE, 214). Partisans of Shakespeare may wonder what depths of degradation or heights of exaltation are not to be found in *King Lear*. Eliot would answer that Lear's hell is an earthly one, unlike the eternal suffering of the *Inferno*, and that no exaltation in Shakespeare signifies what Dante's *Paradiso* means. The metaphors of Eliot's distinction demonstrate his keen desire to restore degree. The democratic vista of Shakespearean expansiveness lacks the vertical organization and promise of salvation in Dante's poem. Eternal damnation is a welcome relief in the form Dante presents, for it is integrated into a structure that validates the possibility of an eventual escape from all suffering emotion. Shakespeare's plays do not, in Eliot's reading, offer such a promise. "There is a relation between the various plays of Shakespeare, taken in order; and it is a work of years to venture even one individual interpretation of the pattern in Shakespeare's carpet. It is not certain the Shakespeare himself knew what it was. It is perhaps a larger pattern than Dante's, but the pattern is less distinct" (SE, 207). Shakespearean language draws one into experiences and emotions of the widest range and detail and then leaves one still in the middle of one's years in a dark wood.

The "dissolution and chaos" Eliot sees in Elizabethan life find their dramatic expression in plots of genealogical strife. Shakespeare's tragedies are, as Richard II tells us, stories of the deaths of kings. His plays highlight the breakup of kinship securities and inheritance patterns, as patrilineal descent and primogeniture are exhibited in varying states of crisis and self-destruction. Far from validating the regime of Tudor rule, Shakespeare's plays point at the fundamental disturbances that upset every effort to control time and fashion order in a generational plot. Macbeth watches in horror as the future kingly lineage of Banquo parades before him, for he is unable to extend his rule by usurpation to the tradition of rule by genealogical imperative. His nightmare vision of the dagger is a trauma dream of castration, symbolic of his sterility as his murder of the father-king Duncan severs the rule of inheritance. The comedies show new generations fleeing the strictures of the old, and sexual power overturning the controls of society, law, and language. Without a son, Lear turns two of his daughters into masculine types by impressing his words upon them; resistant to ventriloquism, Cordelia upholds her right to a husband and a new family and is banished. From early plays like *Love's Labor's Lost* through *Hamlet* and *Measure for Measure* to *The Tempest*, Shakespeare's fathers are either dead, absent, tyrannical, or derelict in their duties. These plays contrast sharply with the reconciliations between paternal figures and heirs imaged in the *Commedia*. Dante's figural theory for the continuity of poetic and cultural generations, structured in a genealogical mode, differs from the more haphazard yet incomparable incorporation of mystery plays, romances, legends, and histories in Shakespeare's plays. There is a duel between past and present texts as Shakespeare builds his plays from borrowed material, but the playwright himself does not seem to conceive of individual or textual identity as ideally the recuperation of a past significance.

Such a desire, however, does possess a number of Shakespeare's characters, notably Hamlet. His relation to his father affords little of the solace of Dante's relation to Virgil. The ghost of Hamlet's father is the voice of *Hamlet* as it has been told in story and legend before: the son-poet is commanded to obey and repeat the fathers, subsuming his identity in the ancient revenge plot that is essentially a structure of repetition that erases identity as each individual takes a place in the binary opposition of victim or avenger. Hamlet defers the revenge act, defers repetition, and in so doing opens the way to his own verbal character and initiates the tradition of the decentered hero that is characteristic of Western literature since.

Eliot's essay on *Hamlet* (1919) never mentions the ghost. A reader of that essay ignorant of the play would find no evidence that such a figure exists or is important to the drama. But when the essay criticizes the lack of an "objective correlative" for Hamlet's feelings, it is producing a blind reading of the ghost. The haunting father's questionable being suggests that "objective correlatives" are ghosts, that adequate representational figures of authoritative character are either dead or the products of diseased imaginations troubled by usurpation and female errancy. The appearance onstage of the father as a ghost throws the whole genealogical model of continuous, proper meaning into doubt. There is no objective correlative for Hamlet's emotion because the play is a dramatization of the effects of the loss or absence of such signifiers. (The same can be said for the handkerchief in *Othello*. The same drift of the signifier away from a single or logocentric signified is dramatized by Othello's response to the theft of Desdemona's handkerchief. He reads the handkerchief as a magic symbol, and is thus blind to the possibility of its theft and its consequent relativity of meaning.) The play consists of a series

of attempts by Hamlet to test the validity of that apparition's words. His so-
liloquies, jibes, inquisitions, and plays within the play attempt to decipher a
father's representations with those of the son. If Hamlet's emotion is a response to the breakdown of secure signifying systems, then the ghost *is* a
"proper" objective correlative. Rather than acknowledge this radical exposé
of genealogy and authority or its implications for language and poetics, Eliot
refuses resolutely to see the problem, or the ghost. He does so by wishing
into theory the very principle the play repudiates. The father figure and his
text in *Hamlet* are no guide to Paradise, but instead are the hell of interminable analysis resolved only by a final acceptance of a role in another play, the
duel authored by Claudius and Laertes. Hamlet's colloquies with his father
are of such a different order and significance from those encounters with the
dead in Dante that I suspect the difference goes far toward illuminating
Eliot's preference. When in later years Eliot arrives at a poetics unfettered by
this earlier adherence to Identity, he purposely combines Dante and the
ghost of Hamlet's father in the recognition scene of "Little Gidding."

Hamlet's "Get thee to a nunnery" projects onto Ophelia his own desire for
an escape from sex, genealogy, time, and death. This, along with the ghost,
drops out of Eliot's reading. Following J. M. Robertson, Eliot concludes
that Shakespeare's *Hamlet* "is a play dealing with the effect of a mother's
guilt upon her son, and that Shakespeare was unable to impose this motive
successfully upon the 'intractable' material of the old play"—the hypothetical
"Ur Hamlet" adapted from Kyd's *Spanish Tragedy* (SE, 123). Guilt goes to
the woman, and Shakespeare's play fails to overpower its precursor. The
guilty ghost (he wears the armor of the day he slew old Fortinbras, and
Shakespeare changed the date to coincide with Hamlet's birthday and the
gravedigger's first employment) and the desiring son are minimized by a
"scholarly" argument that nonetheless traces, in its displacements, projections, and repressions, the interpreter's own tale. Eliot denies this in the
Hamlet essay with a founding statement of the New Criticism: "*Qua* work of
art, the work of art cannot be interpreted; there is nothing to interpret; we
can only criticize it according to standards, in comparison to other works of
art; and for 'interpretation' the chief task is the presentation of relevant historical facts which the reader is not assumed to know" (SE, 122). The ghost is
literally "nothing to interpret" and stands for the indeterminacy of "relevant
historical facts." Eliot's strictures against interpretations are again primarily
defensive and are belied by his own reading.

Salvation from the errancies of genealogy, sexuality, and interpretation is
apparently offered by the contrasting method of Dante. Eliot turns against
the nineteenth-century Romantic appropriation of Dante and repeats his

own metaphysical *Aufhebung* of passion. "A great deal of sentiment has been spilt, especially in the eighteenth and nineteenth centuries, upon idealizing the reciprocal feelings of man and woman towards each other, which various realists have been irritated to denounce: this sentiment ignoring the fact that the love of man and woman (or for that matter of man and man) is only explained and made reasonable by the higher love, or else is simply the coupling of animals" (SE, 234–35). Beatrice and the Virgin, as Hegel argued, are the "true essence of love," the embodiments of sublation: "In her child, carried under her heart and brought to birth in pain, Mary has a perfect knowledge and feeling of herself; and while that child is indeed raised high above her, that exalted height itself belongs to her and is the object in which she at once forgets and possesses herself."[8] In Dante and Catholicism the guilt of the mother is erased, and woman is again made the vehicle of transcendence. So Eliot concludes that the *Vita Nuova* can be "described in Freudian terms" as a "very sound psychological treatise on something related to what is now called 'sublimation'" (SE, 234, 235). But for Eliot, Eros gives way to Thanatos. "There is also a practical sense of realities behind it, which is antiromantic: not to expect more from *life* than it can give or more from *human* beings than they can give; to look to *death* for what life cannot give. The *Vita Nuova* belongs to 'vision literature'; but its philosophy is the Catholic philosophy of disillusion" (SE, 235).

These concerns appear in Eliot's first essay on Dante (1920), which like most of *The Sacred Wood* revolves around the problem of "emotional significance." The contribution Eliot makes when rebuking Landor's reading of the Paolo and Francesca episode is an interpretative one, a guide to reading. Romantic misreadings of the episode stem from a "false simplification" that fails to see that "the ecstasy, with the present thrill at the remembrance of it, is a part of the torture" (SW, 165). Eliot's psychology of hell maintains that "it is a part of damnation to experience desires that we can no longer gratify," a common condition with his own enervated protagonists (SW, 166). For Eliot, Dante's authoritative originality and lasting attraction start with the dramatic imaging of emotional states in objective correlatives and progresses to their coordination in a systematic evaluation via the "scaffold" organization of Dante's allegory: "The emotional structure within the scaffold is what must be understood—the structure made possible by the scaffold. This structure is an ordered scale of human emotions" (SW, 168). Dante fathers a poetry that places for all time the traumatic feelings of passionate moments, thus re-

---

8 Henry Paolucci (ed. and trans.), *Hegel: On the Arts* (New York, 1979), 43. See pp. 47–48 for Hegel's remarks on romantic love and Dante.

cuperating emotional disturbances or "sins" in an order that restores them to a redemptive scheme. We recall Eliot's oblique words in "Tradition and the Individual Talent" about escaping emotion.

The feelings prompted by women exist *within* the scaffold now, judged properly and compassionately inside an allegory of masculine poetic generation and approach to the Heavenly Father. Though the scaffold is inspired by Beatrice, it remains a Catholic and Aquinian edifice: she is contained by it, does not exceed its law. Her intervention on the unworthy poet's behalf is typical of the Virgin, but Eliot does not choose to deconstruct the scaffold with Henry Adams' outlaw thesis that Mary absolves mankind of guilt for the disobedience of the Father's law.[9] He wants to climb up it, out of sexual and poetic hell, to an abstract, paternal, well-written paradise. In Paolo and Francesca, Eliot sees a moment his lilac-strewn and rose-filled poetry often imitates: the infinite replay of ecstasy kept and savored for its promising beauty, judged for its inadequacy, remembered repeatedly until its loss is explained or restored. Of course, it was a book that tempted them to sin, for they read of Lancelot, whose guilty love for Guinevere thwarted his quest for the Holy Grail.

The *Commedia* seems to Eliot to put the emotions eternally in their place: "Dante's is the most comprehensive, and the most *ordered* presentation of emotions that has ever been made" (SW, 168). Here, once more, Eliot immediately contrasts Dante's method with Shakespeare's. "Shakespeare takes a character apparently controlled by a simple emotion, and analyses the character and the emotion itself. The emotion is split up into constituents—and perhaps destroyed in the process. The mind of Shakespeare was one of the most critical that has ever existed. Dante, on the other hand, does not analyse the emotion so much as he exhibits its relation to other emotions" (SW, 168). "Critical" Shakespeare joins "interpretation" in Eliot's limbo, dividing and analyzing the soul while Dante constructs a universal grammar of emotions. Eliot's *Commedia* salvages emotional distress through a mastering logos. The "horrid or sordid or disgusting" becomes in a classic Christian/Hegelian justification of evil "the necessary and negative aspect of the impulse toward the pursuit of beauty" (SW, 169). Eliot ritually seals his argument with a citation from the last canto (his favorite) of the *Paradiso*: "The universal form of this knot I believe that I saw, because, in telling this, I feel my joy increases." These lines are echoed at the end of *Four Quartets*. They immediately follow the revelation of the Cosmic Text to Dante (a passage also cited at the end of Curtius' *European Literature and the Latin Middle Ages*): "In its depth I saw

9 Henry Adams, *Mont-Saint-Michel and Chartres* (Garden City, N.Y., 1959), 290.

ingathered, bound by love in one single volume, that which is dispersed in leaves throughout the universe: substances and accidents and their relations, as though fused together in such a way that what I tell is but a simple light." (*Paradiso*, canto 33).[10] Eliot's citation of this "forma universal" and divine book implies an equation with the order and scaffold he has been speaking of. Thus God, author of the cosmic volume, and Dante, master of the scaffold of orderly emotional relations, seem one, an ambiguity deeply felt throughout the *Commedia*. The resemblance of the poet's vocation to that of the divine creator attracted the poets of the Romantic age and here lures Eliot to find in Dante the figure of his own effort to unite the disseminated leaves of personal, literary, and cultural history in a salvational form. Eliot adopts from the plan of the *Commedia* the systematic humiliation of the poet, who must leave behind his earthly self and the mundane world for a terrifying voyage to the dead. Only such an askesis, followed by an emotional purgation and guided ascension, can lead to paradise or perfect poetry. Dante's double vision sees the poet as both a gatherer of dispersed leaves and as one who shatters given orders, including one's own life. Eliot, too, will submit the figure of the poet as divine creator to an askesis, but only because he so desires to author "one single volume" of divine poetry. Here again the received image of the Romantic poet as aspirant to deity undergoes a critical transfiguration, this time though Eliot's identification with Dante.

The mystery of the Trinity comes next in the canto, the "Living Light" appearing as "three circles of three colors and one magnitude." There "the third seemed fire breathed forth equally from the one and the other," the Holy Ghost's fire of love. The love breathed reciprocally between two of the circles is the love of the Father and the Son, their mutual adoration, their dialectical union.[11] It is the final consummation of the series of meetings between disciples and masters, ephebes and precursors, initiated by Virgil's meeting with Dante. Christ's New Testament is the West's grandest, most influential model for a revisionary interpretation that claims both to continue the Word of the Father and to supplement it. As Christ stands toward his Father, so Dante stands toward Virgil, and Eliot toward Dante.

The last mystery of the *Paradiso* is the Incarnation, the meeting of time and the timeless. It is the mystery of man's place in a divine order or Tradition that redeems his individual errancy. Seeing "our image within itself and in its own color" at the end of his journey, Dante "wished to see how the

---

10 Curtius' reading of Eliot shows through in his commentary on Dante, the presiding figure and culminating example of his study. See Ernst Robert Curtius, *European Literature and the Latin Middle Ages*, trans. Willard R. Trask (Princeton, 1953), 366.

11 Charles S. Singleton, *Paradiso: Commentary* (Princeton, 1977), 582.

image conformed to the circle and how it has its place therein," but for this "his wings were not sufficient. . . . Here power failed the lofty phantasy." This upper limit to human knowledge closes the interior pilgrimage of the character Dante. Descending from Heaven, he returns to earth to write his remembrance of the journey, to pen *his* "un volume." Even Dante must rest finally in representation and writing. The progression from the seeming victory of the "un volume" to the mystery of the Incarnation parallels the progression from *The Waste Land*'s striving to bind the dispersed leaves of its ruins to the *Four Quartets*' renunciation of the dream of absolute preservation and total recall. Purposes are, Eliot found, "altered in fulfillment."

Thus, the *Commedia* authorizes at the end what it practices from the start: a revision of dead voices. The *Nekuia*, or voyage to the dead, in modernist texts serves as both means and allegory of intertextuality. Dante audaciously has himself welcomed into the "bella scuola" by his precursors. The past masters (except Arnaut Daniel) must speak in Dante's language. Dante haunts the world of the dead and, unlike Hamlet, is master of his inheritance. Graham Hough has pointed out how many of Eliot's references to Dante concern disciples and masters or fathers and sons.[12] The meetings of Virgil with Statius, of Dante with Sordello, and of Guido with Daniel present clear visual images of the process of poetic genealogy. Eliot's essays on Dante, and his meeting with the "familiar compound ghost" in "Little Gidding," repeat these scenes and interpret their pattern. Eliot embraces Dante's shadow, which speaks in Eliot's English. To Dante, Eliot could repeat Statius' testimony to Virgil: "You it was who first sent me toward Parnassus to drink in its caves, and you who first did light me on to God. You were like one who goes by night and carries the light behind him and profits not himself, but makes those wise who follow him. . . . Through you I was a poet, through you a Christian." (*Purgatorio*, canto 22).

Eliot's identification with Dante yields in later years to encounters with Yeats, Johnson, and Virgil himself. The failure to actualize in his own poetry the ideals Dante stands for in the criticism prompts Eliot to seek an image for his own limits, which he found in the Virgil of "What Is a Classic?" The significance of this shift may be understood by briefly reviewing the premises behind Dante's genealogical beatitude. The relations between poets are conceived through the heritage of typological historical interpretation propounded by the church fathers. This figural reading of temporality and divinity is most richly explored by Erich Auerbach in his essay "Figura," though the theory is first worked out in his 1929 book on Dante.[13] The essay

12 Graham Hough, "Dante and Eliot," *Critical Quarterly*, XVI (Winter, 1974), 243–305. See also Bernard Bergonzi, *T. S. Eliot* (New York, 1972), 63–65.
13 Erich Auerbach, *Dante: Poet of the Secular World*, trans. Ralph Manheim (Chicago,

ends by attempting to demonstrate of the *Commedia* "that basically it is the figural forms which predominate and determine the whole structure of the poem." Auerbach finds that "figural interpretation establishes a connection between two events or persons, the first of which signifies not only itself but also the second, while the second encompasses or fulfills the first." In this plot, which means to preserve definitively the historical reality of events even as they figure a future meaning latent and in need of fulfillment, we read both the method of Dante's presentation of his personages in the *Commedia* and an allegory of Dante's relation to his forebears. Following the story of Christ's supersession of Moses, and Hegel's philosophy of the *Aufhebung*, Auerbach declares that "the risen one both fulfills and annuls the work of his precursor." In the text of the poet-interpreter the *figura* is fulfilled by its (re)placement in the scheme of a divine historical logos. A reader of *figura* assumes a significant absence of meaning in the *figura*, to be raised and revealed in interpretation. This grants a revisionary power over the old testament, creating the time for the new. The tragedy of figural interpretation, akin to the recognition of "altered fulfillment" in *Four Quartets*, is its interminable quality. Each fulfillment in turn becomes a *figura* for the next generation, and the hope of a finally mastered text is shattered.

> Thus history, with all its concrete force, remains forever a figure, cloaked and needful of interpretation. In this light the history of no epoch ever has the practical self-sufficiency which, from the standpoint both of primitive man and of modern science, resides in the accomplished fact; all history, rather, remains open and questionable, points to something still concealed, and the tentativeness of events in the figural interpretation is fundamentally different from the tentativeness of events in the modern view. . . . They point not only to the concrete future, but also to something that always has been and always will be; they point to something which is in need of interpretation, which will indeed be fulfilled in the concrete future, but which is at all times present, fulfilled in God's providence, which knows no difference of time.[14]

Auerbach's historicism is formalist and Hegelian, and thus his argument reaches at its horizon a prospect that unsettles it. Through time, time is conquered; but each new figuration, each supplementing poem, surrenders its

---

1961). Auerbach also endorses the Platonic/Hegelian reading of Beatrice: "she is transfigured and transformed while preserving her earthly form" (62). See also his discussion of the replacement of history by memory (134–46). The Dante book rehearses the argument later made in *Mimesis: The Representation of Reality in Western Literature*, trans. Willard R. Trask (Princeton, 1953).

14 Erich Auerbach, "Figura," trans. Ralph Manheim, in Auerbach, *Scenes from the Drama of European Literature* (New York, 1959), 64, 53, 51, 58–59.

claims to self-sufficiency and the presence of truth. As "Little Gidding" puts it:

> History may be servitude,
> History may be freedom. See, now they vanish,
> The faces and places, with the self which, as it could, loved them,
> To become renewed, transfigured, in another pattern.

(LG, III)

Ideally, figural interpretation founds a theory of poetics and history in which the connection between the figural occurrence and its fulfillment wipes out historical discontinuity by establishing assigned places for disparate events in an eternal taxonomy of signifying incarnations. The logos of Providence manifests itself in history's events, imprinting on them the figure of their eventual unfolding. This is time recuperated as the method of figural action, the field of Providence's self-expression. Such an interpretative system and historical theory hinges on an agreed taxonomy of figures or types— Moses-Christ, Exodus-salvation, etc. They make up the lexicon of the logos: every historical event becomes a "word" unheard to be classified. Yet, the logos both governs interpretation and is produced by it, so that the figural economy remains open after all to differences it could not foresee. Transfiguration replaces figural revelation as every new word both conceals and reveals. The teleological governance of interpretation and history weakens when each fulfilled type suffers a retrogression to the status of *figura*. The pattern is "another." To the faithful it may remain that of a mysterious Providence; to the poet of transfigurations it is a mystery, indicative of the limited recollective powers of poetry and language. In this, Eliot moves closer to a pre-Christian, pre-Socratic, or Hebraic poetics that reads logos as becoming or insists upon the noncorrespondence between vain idols and the unknowable Yaweh.[15]

As time subverts the claims to truth of each new poetic word, the sense of belatedness afflicts writer and culture alike. The historical is irremediably involved in representation and burdens consciousness with the demand to recover time in a figure whose meaning will require another break and another figure. This calamitous poetics Eliot connects with Virgil, and Auerbach extends to civilization. "Thus figural interpretation is a product of late cultures, far more indirect, complex, and charged with history than the symbol or myth. Indeed, seen from this point of view, it has something vastly old about it: a great culture had to reach its culmination and indeed to show signs of

---

15 See Herbert Schneidau, *Sacred Discontent: The Bible and Western Tradition* (Berkeley, 1976), 141.

old age, before an interpretive tradition could produce something on the or-der of figural prophecy."[16] Auerbach, Eliot, and Curtius saw the "old age" of twentieth-century Europe. The poised tension of Eliot's 1944 lecture on Vir-gil reflects this new vortex. Eliot's personal and poetic chronology crosses that of world history, as the climax of *Four Quartets* had come just two years before, ending Eliot's career in poetry, though dramas were to follow. His own poetic stance in "What Is a Classic?" is posthumous. The devastations of World War II are drawing toward a distant but foreseeable end, leaving the poet to wonder what this event figures prophetically for the future. For Eliot it is more essential than ever that a peaceful order be reestablished, that val-ues be reaffirmed. Yet, behind him lies a period of history, and a poetic life, that questions the modernist's ability to revive an idea of civilization as the ground for a new beginning.[17]

The lecture's key term, *maturity*, is again used by Eliot to transfigure the lateness of the hour. This maturity names an age of culture as well as the poet's age and rhetorically inquires whether that age is fruition or failure. Virgil's nomination as the only classic in Western literature does not demon-strate Eliot's hopeless rigidity or nostalgia. He articulates an ideal for poetry and civilization, using the hypothesis of Virgil's classicism as More had used his Utopia or Shakespeare his "green worlds": not as a portrait of actuality, but as a figure to measure the promise and performance of the contemporary. The shadow of Virgil measures the distance of the present from its fulfill-ment. Eliot shares Auerbach's faith in the historical reality of past achieve-ments, yet the self-consciousness of this figuration highlights the work of in-terpretation in the representation. Eliot devises an ironic, provisional, and admonitory tone: "We may expect the language to approach maturity at the moment when men have a critical sense of the past, a confidence in the pres-ent, and no conscious doubt of the future" (OPP, 57). Wracked by a world-wide conflagration, Eliot's audience could recognize the disparity between such a maturity and the disorder of their own time. Language and civiliza-tion can only reach maturity, preaches Eliot, when knowledge of history is critical. He lifts the audience with expectation and deflates it with a con-sciousness of its fallen state, paying his debt to the oratorical tradition of the Puritan sermon. Most of Eliot's later essays were lectures first: he enjoyed taking up the pulpit of literature and exploiting the authority granted him. The style of these late pieces mixes pomposity and insight, banality and wisdom. Eliot knows the irony of his authority and feels the temptation to

16 Auerbach, "Figura," 57.

17 For a related study see Frank Kermode, *The Classic: Literary Images of Permanence and Change* (New York, 1975).

use his bestowed and cultivated position for all it is worth. The shifts in argument and tone, not always successful, self-consciously adjust the contradictions between his priestly pose and Possum-playings.

The war itself can be read as a horrific, magnified repetition of the worst components of the human tradition. The Second World War repeats the First. Many of the younger generation who condemned the war of their fathers now find themselves carrying on the gruesome heritage. Eliot addresses contemporary history indirectly. His idea of classicism engages history as a memorial, thus poetic, problem, as he analyzes the possibilities for change and originality within a continuous culture. The reader and the poet are aware of predecessors "as we may be aware of ancestral traits in a person who is at the same time individual and unique. The predecessors should be themselves great and honored: but their accomplishment must be such as to suggest still undeveloped resources of the language, and not such as to oppress the younger writers with the fear that everything that can be done has been done, in their language" (OPP, 58). This is odd logic. Since the dead predecessors cannot be asked posthumously to refrain from oppressing the young, the determination of their relative achievements passes to the new generation. New poets are asked to (mis)read their ancestors critically, shaping transumption by a search for weaknesses, finding in past masters the figures in need of fulfillment.

Eliot proceeds from this youthful "fear" to a meditation on the poet in "a mature age" of culture. This poet "may even be in revolt against" his predecessors, "as a promising adolescent may revolt against the beliefs, the habits and the manners of his parents." This revolutionary discovers, to his chagrin, "that he is also the continuer of their traditions, that he preserves essential family characteristics, and that his difference of behavior is a difference in the circumstances of another age." In this unwilled return of the dead, language and culture use the poet, pose their questions with him, perpetuate their texts. The progression from revolution to unconscious repetition may not be as salutary as theorists of tradition might wish: "Just as we sometimes observe men whose lives are overshadowed by the fame of a father or grandfather, men of whom any achievement of which they are capable appears comparatively insignificant, so a late age of poetry may be consciously impotent to compete with its distinguished ancestry" (OPP, 58). The consciousness of impotence pervades Eliot's poetry through *The Waste Land*. Not that the poetry itself is impotent or unable to "compete with its distinguished ancestry." It lives through the awareness of its temporal predicament, recasts the shadows of its ancestors. It uses the consciousness of impotence against impotence, finding impotence in its ancestry and potency in reprojecting the ghosts of its forebears.

Eliot made much the same point twenty-seven years earlier, in the youth of his age.

> When a theory of art passes it is usually found that a groat's worth of art has been bought with a million of advertisement. . . . A mythical revolution will have taken place and produced a few works of art which perhaps would be even better if still less of the revolutionary theories clung to them. In modern society such revolutions are inevitable. An artist, happens upon a method, perhaps quite unreflectingly, which is new in the sense that it is essentially different from that of the second-rate people about him, and different in everything but essentials from that of any of his great predecessors. The novelty meets with neglect; neglect provokes attack; and attack demands a theory. In an ideal state of society one might imagine the good New growing naturally out of the good Old, without the need for polemic and theory; this would be a society with a living tradition. In a sluggish society, as actual societies are, tradition is ever lapsing into superstition, and the violent stimulus of novelty is required. (SP, 32)

This sums up the opening critical strategy of Eliot's modernism. Two traditions exist, the forgotten and the "second-rate"; theory is a necessary vehicle of poetic revolution; and the uninterrupted flow of properties from the Old to the New is only an "ideal," while actual poets require the "violent stimulus" of attacking their fathers. By 1944 Eliot is himself a tradition, and a master to be judged. In maturity the poet compares himself to his predecessors or to titanic contemporaries like Yeats with a new assumption: whereas in the past the poet, in his strategies of development, defied his fathers or chose new ones, now in late age, he contrasts his life's achievement to theirs. "Reflections on 'Vers Libre'" and "What Is a Classic?" both try to establish the theoretical grounds that can promise new poetry, despite the hegemony of the old. In the earlier tract the spectacle of unknowing repetition amuses the sardonic young Eliot, who thus separates himself from the naïve avant-garde and the second-rate. *He* will proceed to make his identity in *conscious* replays of traditions, as if this guaranteed him safety from the derivative through the critical. The elder Eliot has to judge his own poetry, looking a bit less happy at this career of making it old. A body of verse lies behind him; he is impelled to explain its lapses and pretensions and to place it for the new generation. He covertly estimates the claim of his own poetry to the status of the classic and thus the degree to which it will oppress new poets. Both estimates are made ironically through the assertion that there has never been a true classic in English.

The argument turns on the distinction between foreign and national inheritances and on a parallel division between the relative classic (Shakespeare, Milton) and the absolute classic (Virgil). Virgil's "maturity of mind" and his "awareness of history" enable him to bring his civilization and its language to a climax of maturity and exhaustion. The lesson of Virgil's use of the Greeks is meant to apply to our use of Virgil. "Consciousness of history cannot be fully awake, except where there is other history than the history of the poet's own people: we need this in order to see our own place in history" (OPP, 62). Eliot's exile from America and its literary history, and his subsequent immersion in a consciousness of English and European literature, follows this need for "other history." This cross-fertilization also saves the heirs to a language from having an absolute classic imposed upon them. Virgil's "rewriting of Latin poetry" means that "later poets lived and worked under the shadow of his greatness" until Dante escaped by creating the new Italian language (OPP, 64, 65). Thus, Eliot's judgment that all English classics are but relative ones liberates the present and future English poet. "There is no classic in English: therefore, any living poet can say, there is still hope that I—and those after me, for no one can face with equanimity, once he understands what is implied, the thought of being the *last* poet—may be able to write something which will be worth preserving" (OPP, 67). In the context of analyzing Virgil, the "*last* poet" signals the end of a civilization, the final act of its poetic mind, the utter exhaustion of a culture's resources—precisely the condition Eliot wishes to defend himself against in 1944. In fact, the concept of the last poet is a double concept. The last poet, like the *figura*, culminates the interior life of a nation in fulfillment of its prophetic promise, while simultaneously bringing the culture as a whole to a collapse that itself becomes the initial figure for future poetic readers—as Dante had read Virgil's Roman legacy. Every poet hopes to be the last poet, to have the last say. Failure to reach this height affects theory by reversing the concept so that the idea of being the last poet is strenuously opposed. Eliot's own poetry cannot be considered an absolute classic, nor can he be considered the last poet. The identification with Virgil breaks down, as Eliot falls on the wrong side of the double concept of the last poet, having failed to become a classic, while slyly suggesting by the concept's employment his own pretension to the laurel crown.

A real historical event of poetic classicism to Eliot, Virgil's *Aeneid* was also a figural prophecy of the kind of poetry a dismembered Europe should aspire toward in 1944. It represents the lost "centre of European civilization. . . . an empire and a language with a unique destiny in relation to ourselves" (OPP, 70—71). For Eliot, Virgil's assimilative universalism checks the modernist's "provincialism," an attitude "for which history is merely the chronicle of human devices which have served their turn and been scrapped, one for which the world is the property solely of the living, a property in which the dead hold no shares" (OPP, 72). This application of economic metaphors to poetic history reduces claims of poetic originality to a kind of capitalism. The present reality of ownership and control does not constitute proper authority, is not authorized by anything but usurpation. In poetry as in politics, property is theft. Returning the corporate shares of the poetic achievement to the dead reestablishes genealogical continuity as the structure determining the disbursement and significance of properties. Eliot hopes to cure the fratricidal warfare of poets and nations with a rhetoric of organic identity: "We need to remind ourselves that, as Europe is a whole (and still, in its progressive mutilation and disfigurement, the organism out of which any greater world harmony must develop), so European literature is a whole, the several members of which cannot flourish, if the same bloodstream does not circulate throughout the whole body" (OPP, 72). This ethnocentrism ignores the role played by non-European peoples in the wars as victims of colonial property struggles. The premise that "world harmony" depends on European culture repeats the very ideology that precipitated the wars in the first place.

These limits marked, Eliot's provincialism carries with it a mechanism for its own undoing in the theoretical proposition that languages and culture apprentice themselves in self-exile to foreign ways. The interior humiliation of European national provincialisms by a discipleship to Virgilian universalism halts future transformations before they cross the boundary beyond which lies the threatening external worlds of the non-Christian, the non-white, the non-European. Throughout Eliot's poetry the imagery of deserts, primitive terrors, and hearts of darkness suggests that the Third World, like woman, signified to Eliot the tempestuous other, his own version of what Edward Said calls "Orientalism."[18] Facing the self-mutilation of Europe's identity and the dislocation of Europe from its role as master of world order, Eliot prescribes the classic standard: "But the maintenance of the standard is the price of our freedom, the defence of freedom against chaos" (OPP, 73–74). These disreputable politics, a product of condensed fears and desires, should not blind us to the irony of Eliot's crafted stance. He withdraws from his absolutism (after exploiting it fully) by an invocation of Virgil's figural status in the *Commedia*, where his limits as a guide are firmly set. One could turn the implications of figural prophecy on Eliot himself and argue that Virgilian universalism figures in its limited sphere an eventual world order of all nations exceeding its Roman model. But Eliot looks askance at utopias. Such a grand impersonal order would displace forever the thought of a European identity. Even as *Four Quartets* moves away from the metaphysics

18 Edward Said, *Orientalism* (Berkeley, 1978).

of identity, Eliot continues to invest in the securities of logocentric econo-mies in culture, politics, and religion.

Guiding his listeners through the dark woods of crisis, Eliot comes to oc-cupy Virgil's position, and the audience-reader that of Dante. This allows Eliot to lead, yet it denotes figurally the limit of his comprehension. Future poets will, like Dante, carry the work of Eliot and other followers beyond what they had foreseen. This maneuver both scales down Eliot's projected stature and raises him up as the nominated father of a future potentially as bright as Dante's *Commedia*. Eliot had not found in himself the capacity to write its equivalent, and he could only approach Virgilian classicism as a the-ory of the ancient past or distant future. Eliot, too, must be left behind, his figures argue. This process of substitutions, of Eliot for Virgil, of the audi-ence and new poets for Dante, lifts the discourse into a metaphorical space that adds a poignant irony to the final injunction: "We may remind ourselves of this obligation, by our annual observance of piety towards the great ghost who guided Dante's pilgrimage: who, as it was his function to lead Dante towards a vision he could never himself enjoy, led Europe towards the Chris-tian culture which he could never know; and who, speaking his final words in the new Italian speech, said in farewell . . . 'Son, the temporal fire and the eternal, hast thou seen, and art come to a place where I, of myself, discern no further'" (OPP, 74). Christian culture and the classic poem are, to borrow the words of "Burnt Norton," "an abstraction / Remaining a perpetual pos-sibility / Only in a world of speculation." The great ghost of Eliot retires to the bounded world of his discernment. The vision to come may not be an-other *Commedia*, but a post-Christian and postmodern poetry that takes its inspiration from the more radical implications of Eliot's theorizing.

PART THREE

"TOLLING REMINISCENT BELLS"
Love and Death in *The Waste Land*

When he left for Stockholm, the Kauffers and I took him to the airport where a reporter asked, "Mr. Eliot, what book did they give you the Nobel Prize for?" "I believe it's given for the entire corpus," he replied. "When did you publish that?" the man wanted to know. When he had gone, Eliot said to us, "It really might make a good title for a mystery—The Entire Corpus."

Robert Giroux, "A Personal Memoir,"
in Allen Tate (ed.), T. S. Eliot

CHAPTER 9

DISCOVERING THE CORPUS

Then I—I shall begin again. I shall not cease until I bring the truth to light.
Apollo has shown, and you have shown, the duty which we owe the dead. You have
my gratitude. You will find me a firm ally, and together we shall exact vengeance
for our land and for the god. I shall not rest till I dispel this defilement—not just
for another man's sake, but for my own as well. For whoever the assassin—he
might turn his hand against me too. Yes, I shall be serving Laius and myself.

Oedipus Tyrannus

The detective and the literary critic are often compared. Each undertakes to solve a mystery, working from scattered clues to piece together
the meaning of disparate events. This is a hermeneutic quest, as the detective-
critic discloses at last the surprising truths behind apparently random appearances. Ideally, a "totalization" or systematic comprehension of fragments
is the result. The figure of the sleuth appeals to every reader's desire to detect
a pattern in life's haphazard flow of things; our interest is more intensely
fixed when there has been a crime, since the violation of the law stands metaphorically for the negation of meaning in general, for an outbreak of transgression that threatens to bring down the orders of significance established
by the law's logos. So it is that many critics take special interest (at least of
late) in texts that disobey laws, genres, or conventions. Theoretical critics
tend to pursue these literary felonies after the formal or aesthetic case is
closed, inquiring at the doors of philosophy, linguistics, psychoanalysis, and
history, and throughout the neighborhood of the human sciences for the
agents of disharmony.

But who has been slain in *The Waste Land*? The intrigue deepens when we
realize that the victim, the assailant, and the detective are interchangeable
metaphors. The predicament of Oedipus dramatizes this tragic condensation
of roles, the entanglements of which will preoccupy much of Eliot's poem.
We have seen in an earlier chapter the similar case of the Quester and the
Fisher King. The disturbing indistinction between, or identification of,
Oedipus and Laius or Quester and King repeats the "peculiar personal intimacy" of poetic sons and fathers. The addition of the detective (a vocation

thrust upon both Oedipus and the Quester) to this relation figures the desire to resolve its paradoxes and to reinstitute the power of the law. The poem enacts this effort to unravel the mystery and restore order. Yet simultaneously, in form and conception, it compulsively repeats the crime, transgresses the inherited rules of writing, and dismembers the unity of the fathers' words. Adding another turn of the screw, the poem presents this fragmentation of truth as the death of the speaker or author himself. We are asked to mourn his life as well, though self-murder is the planned escape from "personality" back to the soul's eternal life. The stylistic subordination of personal voice to borrowings, echoes, and allusions performs an askesis that violates the unity of self and tradition. "What happens" to the poet, wrote Eliot in 1919, "is a continual surrender of himself as he is at the moment to something which is more valuable. The progress of an artist is a continual self-sacrifice, a continual extinction of personality" (SE, 7). The body of tradition and the poet himself suffer willingly, or by the will of the poet, the ritual of the *sparagmos*. This is part of the relevance of the vegetation god ceremonies, as they too dramatize an identification of the god with the life of the people who recurrently slay him in the name of fertility. The god's resurrection and the nation's rejuvenation culminate another restricted economy of the *Aufhebung*, in which castration and death are the *via negativa* of potency and life. As I will argue later, this pattern informs *The Waste Land*'s modernist revision of the pastoral elegy, the genre whose laws the poem subjects to uncanny interpretations.

It would be nothing new simply to observe that *The Waste Land* violates literary (and other) laws or that like many such texts it places the reader quite self-consciously in the occupation of the hermeneutic detective. The criminal themes of murder and adultery serve this function and provide self-consuming models for the resolution of the poem as a whole. An avid fan of Conan Doyle and founding member of a Sherlock Holmes fan club, Eliot presents us with a puzzling array of remains that increase our suspicion that a coherent, though horror-filled, story lies behind the "heap of broken images." Dead men turn up everywhere in this unreal city, or their words float to its allusive surface. The story begins like a good melodrama at the victim's burial service and proceeds in disjointed flashbacks to piece together the tale of his loves and losses. But the victim is protean, as are his assailants, and hermaphrodite and polysemous. The corpse's casket is a library, his obituary everyman's. The poem's criminal atmosphere filches much of its scenery from Eliot's reading of Shakespearean and Jacobean tragedy, through numerous allusions to adultery and murder in Webster, Middleton, and others. Eliot's voyeuristic involvement with the sordid had also prompted his earlier verse on urban horrors, his taste for Baudelaire and for *Bubu of Montparnasse*, the story of a Parisian whore for which he wrote a preface. He was fascinated by that English tradition of popular tabloid gossip about the criminal, which seemed to be a modern Jacobeanism. With similar motives Eliot consistently ranks Poe, elegist of dead beauties and inventor of detective fictions, among the three or four American writers worthy of his attention.

The poem's origin in this tradition of low crime, sordid mystery, and dark artistry is evidenced in the manuscripts, where the original title, "He Do the Police in Different Voices," is taken from Dickens' *Our Mutual Friend*. In the passage Eliot has in mind, Sloppy performs a kind of ventriloquism as he reads the newspaper text that tells of ghastly doings, providing an obvious source for *The Waste Land*'s polyvocal method (WLFS, 125). *Our Mutual Friend* contains not only a model for Eliot's revoicings, but a protagonist come back from the dead. John Harmon rises from the waters of the Thames to inhabit London in the disguise of John Rokesmith, covertly observing the fate of his own entailed inheritance, concretely symbolized by the mounds of waste that are the novel's thematic and ironic narrative centers. In erasing his own identity, Harmon, like the Duke in Shakespeare's *Measure for Measure*, compounds and perpetuates the disharmony of his realm. Eliot may also have been thinking of Dickens' *Bleak House*, whose Detective Bucket is one of the first great English comic sleuths. That novel, as J. Hillis Miller has written, brilliantly examines the problems of wills, testaments, and legacies lost in a hopeless mire of documents and interpretations disputed interminably.[1] The novel's characters find themselves bewildered by a mountain of wastepaper. Esther Hawdon, one of the novel's two narrators, tells her tale in an effort to uncover, detective fashion, the truth of her own parentage. Her mother, Lady Dedlock, is an "exhausted deity," an artist of deceptive self-representation. Her dead father, the shadowy Captain Hawdon, was, we are not surprised to learn, a legal copyist—a textual nobody like Melville's Bartleby. His death parallels in implication the farcical court case of Jarndyce and Jarndyce: both represent the breakdown of lawful, authoritative, ordered scripts. The revelations of the novel lead in the end to Esther's marriage and the construction of another Bleak House, an edifice not unlike Dickens' book, which problematically hopes to restore what has been wasted. Eliot agreed that it was Dickens' "best novel" and "finest piece of construction" (SE, 410–11).

1 J. Hillis Miller, Introduction to Charles Dickens, *Bleak House*, ed. Norman Page (Baltimore, 1971). Eliot taught *Bleak House* in 1916, and in a 1918 letter to his mother he compared his experience with wartime bureaucracy to "a chancery suit—dragging on and on, and always apparently about to end" (WLFS, xv.).

The motifs of detection, scattered writings, adulteries, and sacred mysteries may be traced in a second deleted title. Part 2, "A Game of Chess," first bore the designation "In the Cage," the title of Henry James's tale of a young woman whose job in a telegraph-office cage makes her privy to the cryptic secrets of high-society lovers. Valerie Eliot ascribes this title instead to the passage from Petronius that provided Eliot with his epigraph of the Cumaen sibyl (WLFS, 126). Grover Smith concludes that this explanation "does not hold up," though he declares that James's story "has no particular relevance to Part II of the poem." On the contrary, it strikingly prefigures Eliot's formal and thematic concerns. James uses the figure of the sibyl ironically in his portrait of the girl whose function is "to dole out stamps and postal orders, weigh letters, answer stupid questions, give difficult change and, more than anything else, count words as numberless as the sands of time."[2] She occupies a vortex of writings, exercising her "instinct of observation and detection" in guessing "the high reality, the bristling truth" of the fragmentary messages that pass before her. Although she "was perfectly aware that her imaginative life was the life in which she spent most of her time," supplemented by "greasy" novels "all about fine folks," the girl scarcely perceives the disparity between her projections of sublime Romantic love and the seedier reality of her clients' adulterous liaisons. She finds her ladies and gentlemen "always in communication," and "she read into the immensity of their intercourse stories and meanings without end." Her folly in so mistaking her own wish fulfillment—that Romantic love might sweep her transcendentally out of the plebeian world of her intended Mr. Mudge and into the aristocratic sublime—informs Eliot's placement before his readers of the cryptic evidence of so many sordid or tragic liaisons contemporary and antique. James's tale illustrates a point Eliot would insist upon, that Romanticism looks to relations in this world for a Truth that lies beyond it. James's social point—that her sublime is a trick that cheap romantic novels play on the hearts of the lower class—becomes in Eliot the conviction that he has been seduced by his precursors' imaginative achievement of an erotic union of the mind with the world it reads.

The girl in the cage concentrates her powers upon a single case, that of the adulterous communication between Lady Bradeen and Captain Everard. (James was shameless in his names!) Like the chess game's king, Everard is the weakest player in James's complicated love game: "he only fidgeted and floundered in his want of power." In this society, like that of *The Waste Land*,

2 Grover Smith, *T. S. Eliot's Poetry and Plays: A Study in Sources and Meaning* (2nd ed.; Chicago, 1974), 303; Henry James, "In the Cage," in James, *Eight Tales from the Major Phase*, ed. Morton D. Zabel (New York, 1958), 174.

"it was much more the women, on the whole, who were after the men than the men who were after the women." Perhaps it was this underscoring of the castration thematic so recurrent in James that led Eliot to decoy his readers with a change of title. Moreover, the figure of the girl as sibyl and decoder would have been assimilated to that of Eliot himself, identifying her Romanticism as the cause of interpretative impotence, since in the end she gets it all quite muddled: "what our heroine saw and felt for in the whole business was the vivid reflexion of her own dreams and delusions and her own return to reality." This acceptance of the reality principle represents the girl's askesis. Her biological femininity does not preclude, but underlies, her participation in a castration psychology that has shaped her search for the missing truth from the start.

James's tale links Eros, truth, writing, and the phallus in the girl's pursuit of Everard's mystery. "It came to her there, with her eyes on his face, that she held the whole thing in her hand, held it as she held her pencil, which might have broken at that instant in her tightened grip. This made her feel like the fountain of fate."[3] Poor Everard! When she grasps the "truth" of his letters and affairs, she purloins the phallus and restores it to her own incomplete self. In this she, as much as any of James's bachelor epistemologists, figures the Romantic author as castrated/castrating in the quest for a condensed logos of sex, writing, and knowledge. At the end, however, she learns that her salvation of Everard through recollection of the lovers' letters only dooms him to Lady Bradeen's clutches. In the economy of phallogocentrism, the truth of the letter always requires the dispossession of its former owner: the girl has unwittingly emasculated Everard in knowing him. The truth she is left with is the "truth" of his castration, as we are left with the uncanny notion that "truth" in writing "castrates" life. Renouncing her sibyl's job and marrying Mr. Mudge, the girl gives up the Romantic and phallogocentric vocations for a less metaphysical career. Eliot's poem takes up her career once more in deciphering the logos of scattered parts. It restages the drama of James's tale, expressing once more the Romantic longing to find Truth through the incarnations of Eros, discovering once more that the truth of sexuality is loss, difference, and the adulteration of identity. In its negative theology, *The Waste Land* repeatedly returns to castration as truth, subl(im)ating the deconstruction of Romantic Eros into another quest for the divine love that can fulfill the desires human life seems to imitate with its carnal appetites. The fragmentation of truth in the poem operates, according to such logic, to spur our critical desire to locate and regenerate what has

3 James, "In the Cage," 247.

been lost, and it represses, by its very hyperbole and lamentation, the prerequisite of castration as the "original" scene of the crime. Only in aspects of its conclusion does the poem come round to a reconciliation with the desssemination of the father's word.

Correspondences with James's tale shed light on at least the first two parts of "A Game of Chess," with its evocations of insufferable women, male fear, and marital discord. At the heart of these mournful mysteries lies the retelling of paradise lost. As his footnote tells us, Eliot borrows his "sylvan scene" from Milton (and, quite tellingly behind that, from Spenser's accounts of Venus and Adonis and of the Bower of Bliss) for his own revisionary display of "The change of Philomel, by the barbarous king / So rudely forced." She becomes the genius loci of a "romantic" transmutation of loss into a redemptive, artful song. What Eliot adds to our hearing, literally so in the manuscript, is "lust," the unsublimated drive that violates the virgin garden of woman and man's identity. The element of incest in the rape of Philomel by Tereus may appear irrelevant here unless we understand desire's threat to kinship systems and thus by extension to the structuring of a stable and meaningful economy of differences. Philomel represents woman as an object of prohibited desire, and we are left wondering whether that prohibition originates in genealogy (in which case she would be a metaphor of the mother) or in a "classical" deconstruction of a "romantic" metaphysics of art and Eros.

These complex associations may be further detected, if not resolved, by reference to a clue overheard by that exceptional aural sleuth, John Hollander. He notices that the second reference to Philomel's song, in "The Fire Sermon," reads "So rudely forc'd," and he argues that "there is nothing to explain the peculiar spelling 'forc'd' at this point, except a Miltonic echo," from "Lycidas": "And with forc'd fingers rude." What correlation can there be, beyond the general "milieu of the drowned poet," between the king's rape of Philomel and Milton's untimely plucking of the berries? The answer, I think, lies in the elegiac strategy of poetic resurrection intrinsic to Milton's transumption of the genre in "Lycidas," that is, in his rebirth as a poet after this "violation" of Mother Nature and the Muse. Milton's "inviolable voice" haunts new poets with its power to create a highly individual beauty out of its "Babylonish" troping of the language and inheritance. Eliot's king is called "barbarous," meaning he literally speaks an unacceptable language, an eccentric tongue. The speaker of "Lycidas" presumes to grasp the laurel crown before his time, pressured into it, he says, by the death of Edward King. To tradition he says he must "Shatter your leaves before the mellowing year," where "Shatter" connotes not only the traditional ritual scattering of leaves but a destructive shattering as well.[4] The song of Philomel, then, once more inscribes the poet's ambivalence toward beginning again his attempt upon the sublime and condenses the problems involved with those of sexuality. Thus, the passage expresses 1) a fear of the father-precursor's prohibition, 2) a desire to scatter the words of the father by violating his Muse, 3) a dread that he may not have the power to regather the leaves in a new volume of love, and 4) a transfiguring urge to reject the whole "romantic" problematic as delusory compared to a complete askesis and retheologization of desires poetic and sexual.

The section had opened, in fact, with a revision of a precursor. Eliot twists Shakespeare's lines on Cleopatra into an elegantly suffocating portrait of the lady, thus contradicting all his warnings about Shakespeare's bad influence in the sense that his defensive parody both confirms Shakespeare's stylistic preeminence in its absence and improves upon it with additions from other dead masters. Frequently cited in Eliot's criticism, *Antony and Cleopatra* holds a high station in his canon. The play's theme of a hero led astray by his infatuation with a beautiful woman illustrates one of Eliot's key obsessions, vacillating as it does between adoration and condemnation. He had given the lines "she looks like sleep, / As she would catch another Antony / In her strong toil of grace" as an example of Shakespeare's "complicated" metaphors, remarking that the trope's additive quality was "a reminder of that fascination of Cleopatra which shaped her history and that of the world, and of that fascination being so strong that it prevails even in death" (SE, 205). The fascination of Cleopatra stands for the fascination of Shakespearean metaphor: both exceed, add, tempt one beyond confirmed identity, whereas Dante's "visual" metaphors reveal truth. Cleopatra seduces as Shakespeare's poetic style can seduce, turning her victims into predecessors of James's deluded romantic girl. Antony's fate echoes Captain Everard's, while Enobarbus is made into yet another blinded prophet. Sifting through Shakespeare's leaves, Eliot is lured but suspicious, and he mocks the folly of Enobarbus and of misreaders who have failed to hear Shakespeare's irony as he dramatically presents yet another victim of Cleopatra's self-representations. Revising Shakespeare's style, Eliot overloads the imagery of his lines to create a dissociation of sensibility. He compounds the Jacobeans, the eighteenth-century baroque, and *fin de siècle* aestheticism in a hyperbolic illustration of the snares of sensual

4 John Hollander, *The Figure of Echo: A Mode of Allusion in Milton and After* (Berkeley, 1981), 104; Ellen Z. Lambert, *Placing Sorrow: A Study of the Pastoral Elegy Convention from Theocritus to Milton* (Chapel Hill, 1976), 155.

imaginings. He brings to the surface the purport of Shakespeare's speech with the aid of its setting in his own poem, among the fearful females, deluded men, and parodied styles.

The failure of romanticism to find in human experiences the sublime it projects as lost also pervades the disharmony of the nervous couple in the subsequent lines of "A Game of Chess." As the opening section dwelled upon the femme fatale, this conversation, or lack of one, indicates the concurrent absence of the saving woman who provides access to life, creation, presence, and the Absolute. While "nothing" occurs between these two, all the action takes place offstage. The section's title and Eliot's note refer us to Middleton's *Women Beware Women* and Bianca's forced seduction, which occurs while her mother-in-law is distracted by a chess game with the procuress. "The wind under the door" sends us to Webster's *The Devil's Law Case*, in which it brings news of a man's wounding.[5] Another primal scene, then, of woman's violation and man's vital loss takes place within earshot of this couple and within an imagistic and allusive context of reiterated blindness. It was also, Grover Smith notes, "with a noise and shaking, and with a blast of wind, that the dead in Ezekiel's valley of dry bones received the breath of life and stood upon their feet."[6] In the manuscript, what the wind was doing was "Carrying / Away the little light dead people" (WLFS, 13), a theft from the Paolo and Francesca episode in *Inferno*, canto 5. Of them Eliot wrote: "To have lost all recollected delight would have been, for Francesca, either loss of humanity or relief from damnation. The ecstasy, with the present thrill at the remembrance of it, is a part of the torture. Francesca is neither stupefied nor reformed; she is merely damned; and it is part of damnation to experience desires that we can no longer gratify" (SW, 165–66). The speaker in Eliot's poem either cannot gratify his desires or gratifies them at the cost of a greater damnation. Eliot's couple, in Dantean fashion, seem eternally damned to the condition of unsatisfied longing. Intercourse of any kind appears impossible in this "rat's alley / Where the dead men lost their bones."

What obstacle prevents speech, thought, or action here? The "loss" of "bones" imaged in the man's words voices a connection between present impotence and past losses or glories. He is hardly present at all, in fact, as his mind is usurped by repetitive memories that possess him. The significance of this haunting may be seen in a look at Eliot's revisions. The printed draft reads, "I remember / Those are pearls that were his eyes." The manuscript reads: "I remember / The hyacinth garden. Those are pearls that were his

5 Eliot later denied the relevance of the phrase's context in Webster. See B. C. Southam, *A Guide to the Selected Poems of T. S. Eliot* (New York, 1968), 79.

6 Smith, *T. S. Eliot's Poetry and Plays*, 81.

eyes, yes!" (WLFS, 13). Pound left these lines unaltered, except to suggest cutting the allusion to Molly's soliloquy in *Ulysses* (a relevant tale of adulteries and wandering paternities). Vivienne Eliot inexplicably penned "Yes & wonderful wonderful" in the margin. The decision to drop this reference to the hyacinth garden was evidently Eliot's own. Perhaps he felt that having his speaker recall that former ecstasy here would be too obvious an irony. He may also have been uncomfortable with the conjunction of a lover's tryst with a father's death or of the loss of love and the loss of eyes. Some have even argued that the excision covers up a reference to Jean Verdenal and Eliot's attraction to him, a sensational and untenable speculation.[7] A more viable biographical reading would be that the passage implies that the man's memory of a former love makes his disillusionment with a present wife crippling and that Eliot would not have thrown such a message at Vivienne in public, whatever her perception of the lines' import. He was too caring and solicitous toward her feelings for that, even if the lines were simply intended to express impersonally the difference between an ideal regenerative love and a spiritless communication. The juxtaposition of hyacinth garden and Ariel's song would have been helpful, however, in pointing out the links between these two scenes of love, loss, and metamorphosis. They emerge from a "romantic" desire for translation into a beatified state, transfiguring loss into pearls as precious as Molly's final, loving affirmation of her moment as Bloom's flower of the mountain. Incoherence plagues the speaker of the scene because, by measure of past or figurally constructed images, his emotions cannot find any available or adequate object. A poetic coherence, however, holds these lines and themes and allusions in a paratactic assemblage that puts the techniques of imagism and symbolism to their best use: a vital tension stays suspended between the incoherence of the represented and the skill with which Eliot draws us on to read his articulations of its origins and ends as we play sibyl to the poem's leaves.

The foregoing investigations of a few intertextual case histories in *The Waste Land* demonstrate how quickly the poem eludes interpretative or aesthetic closure. At the risk of scattering an already shattering poem, these forays seemed strategically prerequisite to theoretical questions about how to read or name this text, since criticism and canon formation have already so tamed its uncanniness for us. It might be healthy to restore our sense of how aberrant the poem is, as any undergraduate would gladly tell us.

7 I refer to James E. Miller, Jr., *T. S. Eliot's Personal Waste Land* (University Park, Pa., 1977), which revives the thesis of John Peter's notorious "A New Interpretation of *The Waste Land*," *Essays in Criticism*, II (July, 1952), suppressed by Eliot and reprinted after his death by the same journal in April, 1969.

Reviewing Eliot's experiment after its initial publication, Louis Untermeyer wrote, "It is doubtful whether 'The Waste Land' is anything but a set of separate poems, a piece of literary carpentry, a scholarly joiner's work, the flotsam and jetsam of dessicated culture," or simply a "pompous parade of erudition."[8] These are pertinent insights, though not in the derogatory sense that Untermeyer intends. Inspection of the published manuscripts now confirms that Eliot did indeed assemble his poem from myriad jottings, some nearly ten years in the keeping. Most of the poem as we have it was set down in 1921 and 1922, undergoing a famous series of revisions at the hands of Eliot, his wife, and Ezra Pound. At the literal level this history exhibits processes ordinarily disguised in the presentation of supposedly unitary, orderly texts ascribable to a single authorial consciousness. Untermeyer's critical a priori posits the existence and privilege of a metaphysically conceived writing, set down instantaneously and forever by a voice speaking an isolable truth. This formalist object would above all things be "separate," individually differentiated, whole, and free of the past. Eliot's "poem," however, is an intertextual phenomenon, conspicuously a process of allusive appropriation. *The Waste Land* demonstrates Eliot's theory of tradition and Harold Bloom's insistence on intertextuality. There are no individual, self-contained poems. The "poem" lies in the relations between poems, in the troping of an ancestor. Has Eliot allowed us to say who "wrote" *The Waste Land*? What do we think we mean if we say that Eliot wrote:

> Frisch weht der Wind
> Der Heimat zu.
> Mein Irisch Kind,
> Wo weilest du?

These lines from Wagner were the German's property, but their properties are in Eliot's hands now.

Untermeyer's metaphors for the poem ("literary carpentry, a scholarly joiner's work") point again to Lévi-Strauss's notion of *bricolage* and to an idea of poetry as the opportune arrangement of whatever happens to be at hand rather than as the mimesis of an organic or transcendent architecture. Yet, before endorsing *bricolage* as a master metaphor of the text, we should recall Derrida's argument that "if the difference between *bricoleur* and engineer is basically theological, the very concept of *bricolage* implies a fall and an accidental finitude."[9] *Bricolage*, like belatedness and other mythologies of lost

---

8 Quoted in Jay Martin (ed.), *Twentieth Century Views of "The Waste Land"* (Englewood Cliffs, N.J., 1968), 5.

9 Jacques Derrida, *Of Grammatology*, trans. Gayatri Spivak (Baltimore, 1976), 139.

Golden Ages, retrospectively invests an absent figure with the status of an Origin. Ironically, the bricoleur's technique in *The Waste Land* rebuilds, albeit through lament and eulogy, the value of metaliterary and metaphysical constructs that writing might mirror rather than piece together: "What are the roots that clutch, what branches grow / Out of this stony rubbish?" The possibility of an organic logos springing up out of all this textual rubbish is suggested by the figural language here, but in its contextual allusion to the resurrection of the bones in Ezekiel the passage looks instead to a transcendent power for salvation. The use of *bricolage*, or the allusive method, in *The Waste Land* does transgress the conventions of poetry, but like any transgression it simultaneously re-marks the place of the law.

Bricolage and engineering, like the artificial and the organic or the chaotic and the orderly, fall into a binary opposition of the kind that Hegel puts to work in the following relevant passage.

> The encyclopaedia of philosophy must not be confounded with ordinary encyclopaedias. An ordinary encyclopaedia does not pretend to be more than an aggregation of sciences, regulated by no principle, and merely as experience offers them. Sometimes it even includes what merely bear the name of sciences, while they are nothing more than a collection of bits of information. In an aggregate like this, the several branches of knowledge owe their place in the encyclopaedia to extrinsic reasons, and their unity is therefore artificial: they are *arranged*, but we cannot say that they form a *system*. For the same reason, especially as the materials to be combined also depend upon no one rule or principle, the arrangment is at best an experiment, and will always exhibit inequalities.[10]

The distinction between the "ordinary encyclopaedia" and the "encyclopaedia of philosophy" seems to parallel the one between the nineteenth-century poem of organic unity and the twentieth-century poem of fragments. "On Margate Sands / I can connect / Nothing with nothing." How many readers of *The Waste Land* or Pound's *Cantos* have come away thinking that "they are *arranged*, but we cannot say that they form a *system*"? This is not quite the case, however, as with Eliot we have any number of systems alluded to as possible keys—myth, anthropology, mysticism, religion, the tarot, and even literary criticism. The poem experiments with these systems of interpretation by inviting the detective-critic to try them out on the aggregation of entries stolen from other encyclopedias. Eliot's famous dictum bears repeating: "The good poet welds his theft into a whole of feeling which is unique, utterly different from that from which it was torn; the bad throws it into some-

10   William Wallace (trans.), *Hegel's Logic* (Oxford, 1975), 21.

thing which has no cohesion" (SE, 182). "Torn" implicitly plays upon the metaphor of the dismembered body, utilizing the traditional aesthetic description of a work as "shapely" or "monstrous," as in the opening of Horace's *Ars Poetica*. Only if the purloined goods are re-membered in a coherent new body, "whole" and "unique," is theft pardonable.

What is this "cohesion"? In contrast to Hegel's "system," Eliot gives us an emotion rather than an epistemology. "I cannot make it cohere," wrote Pound in Canto 116, after a lifetime's work at a poem that, one could argue, never strayed from the method Eliot advanced and then abandoned in *The Waste Land*. Cohesion stems from the Latin *haerere*, to stick together. Its cognates include adherence, adhesion, and hesitation. The principle of connection in each is paratactic: discontinuous elements are held together but not integrally so, their relations being not so much of interiors coordinated as of exteriors juxtaposed in tension or suspension. This sticking may also lead to hesitation, an occupation of the adherent ground between oppositions. In fact, in "Prufrock" and *The Waste Land*, it is this condition of hesitation that is the "whole of feeling." In a letter to Richard Aldington on the eve of his journey to Margate, Lausanne, and the completion of the poem, Eliot writes, "I am satisfied, since being here, that my 'nerves' are a very mild affair, due not to overwork but to an aboulie and emotional derangement which has been a lifelong affliction. Nothing wrong with my mind" (WLFS, xxii). *Aboulie* is a variant of *abulia*, a psychiatric term for the loss or impairment of the ability to decide or act independently. This emotional state pervades and unites the poem, though ironically, for it is a unity of inability, indeterminacy, indecision. Overcompensating, Eliot fills his poem with a clutter of "objective correlatives" for the state of feeling first dramatized by *Hamlet*. Eliot's spelling also significantly recalls his citation of Nerval's "la tour abolie" from "The Disinherited," in which the tower also figures in an Orphic tale that condenses the lover's and the artist's inconsolable fates in a shuttling between two worlds. Orpheus and Eurydice, by way of Hades and Persephone, cast a dark shadow across the mythic revivification of unity presided over by the poet-priest.

According to Eliot, the disinheritance of the modern poets occurred when feeling and intellect split, as they do in the "ordinary" mind. "When a poet's mind is perfectly equipped for its work, it is constantly amalgamating disparate experience; the ordinary man's experience is chaotic, irregular, fragmentary. The latter falls in love, or reads Spinoza, and these two experiences have nothing to do with each other, or with the noise of the typewriter or the smell of cooking: in the mind of the poet these experiences are always forming new wholes" (SE, 247). J. Hillis Miller observes that these "*are* a miscellaneous lot," betraying Eliot's "feeling that experience is in fact chaotic" and harmonized only by "ironic conjunction."[11] This miscellany, however, is no random choice, for it represents just those experiences that *The Waste Land* tries to set in order. In his essays on Leibniz (1916), Eliot's passing references to Spinoza are in the context of debates over the connections between mind and matter or body and soul. "Spinoza represents a definite emotional attitude," he asserts, leaving this attitude undefined, though we may infer a reference again to "Spinoza's naturalism . . . his disbelief in free-will and immortality" and the "materialistic epiphenomenalism" of his "view of the relation of mind and body" (KE, 198, 194). Reading Spinoza plunges one into a deterministic "naturalism" that leaves little room for the soul to govern its responses to sensory influences. The doctrines of this heretical, exiled philosopher question the modality of a soul that would transcend, yet still involve, sensation—a doubt Eliot attempts to resolve by recourse to Aristotle and Bradley (KE, 194–95, 205–206). Falling in love and the smell of cooking awaken the natural emotions and senses that lead to these dilemmas. From the "Preludes" to "Burbank with a Baedeker" and "Gerontion," Eliot explores the disturbing effects of sensory life on the orders of consciousness. Of course, it is up to the "noise of the typewriter" to write these feelings into a satisfying accord.

In *The Waste Land*, "whole of feeling" turns out to be an oxymoron since the emotions stirred in the various scenes of sterility, adultery, rape, lust, and purgation are decidedly unwholesome and destructive of harmony or coherence. When we examine the published poem alongside the manuscript drafts, such as the dirges and the portraits of ladies like Fresca and the duchess, we see more clearly than ever that the poem's many voices speak obsessively of the feelings inspired by sex and death, those two main enemies of the fortress of identity. As in Eliot's previous poetry, speakers and readers are made to suffer a morbid acuteness of the senses in scene after scene—the lilacs "breeding . . . out of the dead land"; "the brown fog of a winter dawn"; "her strange synthetic perfumes, / Unguent, powdered, or liquid—troubled, confused / And drowned the sense in odours"; "It's them pills I took, to bring it off"; "Silk handkerchiefs, carboard boxes, cigarette ends / Or other testimony of summer nights"; "White bodies naked on the low damp ground"; "And bats with baby faces in the violet light." Eliot's fragments cohere chiefly in their physicality, in the music of their borrowed sounds and in the kinds of sensual experiences they represent. *The Waste Land*'s "symbols are not mystical, but emotional," wrote I. A. Richards, who called the poem "radically

11 J. Hillis Miller, *Poets of Reality* (New York, 1969), 155.

naturalistic."[12] It composes a body, we might say, of sensory and poetic life, if indeed the two can be distinguished. The fragmentation of parts reenacts the *sparagmos* of the physical body of desire, torn by its conflicting responses to the excitements it tries to lift into the wholeness of meaning. Corresponding to these fractures is the poetic *sparagmos* of the body of the literary fathers— "And other withered stumps of time . . . told upon the walls"—toward whose sounds and feelings the poet reacts with a neurosis of the poetic libido, so to speak. Philomel's rape and dismemberment are supplemented by their change into "inviolable voice," but that sublation is now "'Jug Jug' to dirty ears." Were we to clean up our response, what would we hear but the painful truth that her voice sings of the violence at its origin? Philomel's change and the metamorphosis of the father in Ariel's song figure the work of art as a transformation of loss into something rich and strange. While it seems to lament our incapacity to realize again such sublimations of the material into the spiritual, Eliot's poem also demonstrates that no "voice" is "inviolable." Even the play of syllables between those two words articulates the work of difference and interpenetration in language, and the location of identity in the rupture between things.

The "dissociation of sensibility" cataloged by Eliot's imagery traces the dissociation of individual senses from each other in the absence of any intellectual *Aufhebung* into a logos. There is a great irony, for example, in Eliot's assertion that "what Tiresias *sees*, in fact, is the substance of the poem." Tiresias' blindness should, according to myth, grant him a vision of the truth. What he "sees" in Eliot's poem is a troping of the primal scene in the mechanical copulation of the typist and the young man carbuncular. The metric, the rhyme scheme, and the ending sight of the "automatic hand" that "puts a record on the gramophone" enforce a feeling of remorseless repetition of a scene "foresuffered" a thousand times in memory and desire. Tiresias endlessly sees the scene of the crime, the origin of his own "blinding" or castration in witnessing the difference between men and women. What Tiresias sees is "substance" itself, physical life (or signifiers) unredeemed by spirit (or a transcendental signified). Eliot's note plays on the philosophic sense of "substance" as essence and tacitly reminds us of its declension into mere matter (see KE, 182–88). In some legends, Tiresias loses his eyes in retaliation for looking upon the naked body of the bathing Athena, goddess of wisdom. In the version from Ovid that Eliot quotes as "of great anthropological interest," we have the tale of the coupling snakes, Tiresias' bisexuality, and his blinding by Hera / Juno for answering that women enjoy sex nine times more

12 I. A. Richards, *Principles of Literary Criticism* (New York, 1928), 292.

than men. Of course, he is also the prophet of the dead in Hades, guide to sailors like Odysseus and Aeneas, and the seer who knows the fatal story of Oedipus. According to Eliot, he is "the most important personage in the poem, uniting all the rest." This unity will not cohere, however; Tiresias figures the mobility of sexual identity and the negative relation of what we see to what we know. To know the body of truth repeats the crime. Tiresias stands for the dissociation of sensibility in "all the rest" and everyone's participation in his pagan version of negative theology. What we see through his eyes is the involvement of transgression in the genesis of the logos. (Eliot's gramma-phone replays the old song recently rewritten by Derrida's grammatology.) A dissociation of sensibility sets in as the new prophet's "inviolable voice" sings out its reading of the writing of the oracular dead.

If we switch from mythological to other allegorical registers or codes of reference, we note that erection and resurrection also figure the *Aufhebung*, or blindness-made-vision, that achieves the "relevé," the raising of the dead or the return of what was invested in a threatening abyss. A castration logic, whereby loss is made the agency or origin of the logos, is the "system" that arranges Eliot's "bits of information." The dissemination of any single lyric speaker amid these babbling tongues seems to denote the final demise of the Romantic subject, but in fact the ventriloquial appropriation of dismembered parts remembered from other authors composes the new poet as an intertextual force. In these acts of loving violence toward the body of tradition, the poet resurfaces not as the origin of the poem but as the poetic principle (principal), the deconstructed genius loci of a textual waste land. The *sparagmos* as theme and method both expresses his dissociation by the daemons inhabiting his poetic landscape and exorcises those daemons by a ritual incorporation of their torn parts. Resemblance, correspondence, and other modes of identification predominate in the "cohesion" of the fragments, and they follow the practice of Lacan's "imaginary," or "mirror stage," discourse. The Father's No, Name, and Law have not been acceded to, the Oedipus complex (as the structure or language of the unconscious) has not dissolved, and a regression to the strategy of narcissism, doubling, identification, competition, and aggression has taken place. *The Waste Land* exhausts, and then will relinquish, the conceptual responses to sexual, philosophical, and poetic indeterminacy already introduced in "Prufrock," "Narcissus," and "Gerontion."

Translating Lacan's terms into poetics, we find that the "specific prematurity of birth," the child's "primordial Discord" and "motor-unco-ordination" become the young poet's incoherence. The mirror stage next provides cohesion through speculation. Recognizing his own image in that of others, the subject enters a drama "which manufactures for the subject, caught up in the lure of spatial identification, the succession of fantasies that extends from a fragmented body-image to a form of its totality." Images of the fragmented body recur when the symbolic systems of totalization give way, opening up a return to aggressive rivalry with the other for what both, because of their similarity, desire, so that such images connote at once a violence toward the other and a disintegration of self-identity: "These are the images of castration, mutilation, dismemberment, dislocation, evisceration, devouring, bursting open the body, in short, the *imagos* that I have grouped together under the apparently structural term of *imagos of the fragmented body*." In contrast, "the formation of the *I* is symbolized in dreams by a fortress, or a stadium— its inner arena and enclosure, surrounded by marshes and rubbish-tips, dividing it into two opposed fields of contest where the subject flounders in quest of the lofty, remote inner castle whose form . . . symbolizes the id in a quite startling way."[13] The Quester's journey to the Chapel Perilous marks the transition from the *sparagmos* of the God/king to the ritual decipherment of original mysteries, worked out by Eliot in his commentaries on the "Da" of the thunder.

The vocations of the Quester, detective, and critic merge in the attempt to solve once more the riddle of the sphinx or to recapture the sibyl's power to gather the scattering leaves into a logos—a power denied to Dante as he sought to express the vision of the Eternal Light and compared himself to the sibyl. The poem hesitates, like Hamlet, in the face of re-membering, torn between the idea of logos as the recollection of a lost absolute and logos as the emergence, in unauthorized directions, of beings gathered in their difference. The Heideggerian sense comes closer, I think, to Dante's single volume bound by love than Eliot's search for the Word of the Father, as a comparison to the end of "Little Gidding" will suggest. Love, as the call of being, remains open to the life that logocentrism forecloses. What we see with Tiresias throughout the poem is dead people, like scattered leaves, whirled beyond the bounds of love.

For the reader, the question becomes that of whether any interpretative ritual can, or should, reunite the leaves of this *sparagmos* in a transcendental image of harmony. The trace of guilt that marks Oedipus and the Quester suggests that acts of interpretation or divination are also acts of violence, that transgression may not be fully integrated when the truth is finally told. Unless we repeat it word for word, our critical account of the poem must always

13 Jacques Lacan, *Ecrits: A Selection*, trans. Alan Sheridan (New York, 1977), 4, 11, 5. The fragmentation in modern art can also be read according to the theory of reification developed by George Lukács in *History and Class Consciousness*, trans. Rodney Livingstone (Cambridge, Mass., 1971), 83–222. See also Fredric Jameson, *The Political Unconscious: Narrative as a Socially Symbolic Act* (Ithaca, 1981), 206–57.

leave out something, must choose and select to form our solution to its riddle. Reading *The Waste Land* requires an interpretation that will also figure the tension between the desire to totalize and the need to criticize. One figure for the poem, then, is that of a corpus. The various definitions of *corpus* include 1) a physical body, especially when dead; 2) a structure constituting the main part of an organ; 3) the principal, or capital, as distinguished from the interest, or income, of a fund, estate, investment, or the like; 4) a large collection of writings of a specific kind or on a specific subject. As a critical metaphor, corpus makes the connection between a body of writing and a writing of or about the body. The representations of literature and sexuality in *The Waste Land* join in overdetermined settings, as Eliot draws upon the capital of a certain body of texts for his poetic treatment of failed passions, violent conquests, mechanical copulations, and purgative fires. In the strange logic of condensation, literary potency and sexual potency become a single problem, their result a common issue. The literary surrender of self that negatively produces an authorizing tradition coincides with images of emasculation that negatively body forth a sensation of the sexual sublime. In the metaphor of the corpus we may avoid imposing an a priori discrimination between sexuality and textuality, resist totalizing the poem's vital differences of detail in some metacritical order, and point toward the relations of crisis— between the body and writing, nature and culture, women and men, sons and fathers, talents and traditions—that sound throughout *The Waste Land*.

The critical detective discovers, then, that the corpus itself is a sphinx, an enigmatic collection of texts whose particular puzzle is the bond that joins the animal and the human and by extension the human and the divine. When we look into the corpus of *The Waste Land*, we do not find the identity of its owner, but instead the bric-a-brac from other writers' estates, or from the poet's past texts and memories. And the question those purloined letters pose is most often a variant of the sphinx's: what is man, if he should have such animal desires? What is the logos, that it can raise man's nature to its truth? What is a poet, that he presumes to place himself at such crossroads? The lines that open "The Burial of the Dead" place us before such oracular mysteries.

> April is the cruellest month, breeding
> Lilacs out of the dead land, mixing
> Memory and desire, stirring
> Dull roots with spring rain.

We can sketch with little difficulty the "self-reflexive" allegory of poetic beginnings in this overture. Though Eliot first intended a now-excised Boston night-town scene for his opener, the poem as published fortuitously contrasts with the beginning of Chaucer's *Canterbury Tales*, thus making English poetry new by turning the original celebration of fertility into an ode to dejection. "After great pain, a formal feeling comes," wrote Emily Dickinson, and in Eliot's lines a similar necessity of hurt seems involved in committing his feelings to form. "Winter kept us warm, covering / Earth in forgetful snow," a secure oblivion that seduces and comforts those who do not presume to begin writing again, who do not dare force the moment to its crisis. The meager quantity and the sorrowful content of so much of Eliot's poetry testify, as do his critical statements on daemonic possession, that writing was for him an anguish second only to the "acute discomfort" of feeling like a haunted house. Certainly one of the strongest of the obscure impulses behind *The Waste Land* is Eliot's recurring dread that his poetic springs have run dry. April stands for a new season of poetic creation, "breeding" poems out of the detritus of his literary inheritance and notebook drafts. His memory of past glories (his own and others, for as signs of poetic achievement they come to the same thing) obsesses him, cruelly blocking his desire to engender some new flowering. As a rendition of the Anglican burial service, Eliot's opening inters the corpus of the fathers, buries them to sprout according to his own pronouncements. While it tropes against the poets and metaphors of natural regeneration, it also laments (and so in a sense denies) its own impotence. "Dull roots" characterizes the literary ancestry and the poet's own instrument of creation.

In these lines and throughout the poem, we encounter the same overdetermination of Eliot's rhetoric seen in his critical accounts of poetic genesis. The foregoing poetic allegory already employs terms that lead into an interpretation of the passage as an allegory of sexuality. April denotes the awakening of passion, the surge of desire to break out of the cold forgetfulness of repression. Memories cruelly block the fulfillment of desire, as the dead hand of past experiences—formed by the history of the unconscious—reaches out to obstruct present feelings. Prufrock had invoked the figure of Lazarus, come back from the dead to tell us all, to signify an intercourse he never dares begin. In *The Waste Land*, resurre(re)ction is no "friend to men," since it draws them out of the winter warmth of indifference and into the world of nature, woman, and history. Corresponding with the refinement of the poet's nature by his surrender to the voices of the dead, desire seeks a fiery sublimation that also takes its cue from the figure of Arnaut Daniel, one of Dante's tongues of flame who undergoes a transfiguration into Buddha and Saint Augustine at the end of "The Fire Sermon."

The analysis could be further extended, with appropriate precautions, by invoking the Dantean model, explicated in the letter to Can Grande, of the "polysemous" text so influential in Eliot's method. At the literal level is the poetic exodus from anxiety; at the moral level is the salvation from the death of the soul in lust; at the allegorical level is the soul's ascension from earth to heaven; at the anagogical level is the union of logos and nature in the Corpus Mysticum, or celestial church body, that regathers the saved in the volume of the Word. If there has been a murder here, if author, reader, and Quester join in a single detective adventure, it concerns the discovery of a Corpus Mysticum resolving these various levels in a single thunderous apocalypse that crosses the aporia between nature and the logos.

Eliot's attraction to Catholicism as it emerges in the poem may well turn on the transcendental poetics its theology offers. In contrast to the iconoclasm of Hebrew, Protestant, and Puritan theories of the sign, Catholicism reunites the letter and the spirit, signifier and signified, nature and culture, human and divine in the dogmas of the Incarnation, Passion, and Resurrection. The fertility rituals would be a type to the antitype of the Sacrament, as indeed the Grail legends imply. Following traditional theological exegesis, the waters of *The Waste Land* are both the baptismal river and the blood of the Eucharist. Echoing Dante, these waters mark the entrance to a regenerated Earthly Paradise at the end of purgatory. The first three sections of the poem constitute a kind of preparation of the soul and heart for reception of the Word, adopting from mystic literature their climactic call for a prerequisite purification or celibacy before the final approach to the mystery. The final two sections, written at the last and chiefly at Lausanne, move away from the vegetation ritual schema into two related models—those of the quest and the elegy—to resolve the puzzle. What is achieved thereby is a powerful revision of the precursors as Eliot thinks poetically through the structures of negative theology, but he never finds his Beatrice. The poem leaves us at the edge of purgatory but still far distant from paradise, lacking that loving logos that moved the constellations of Dante and that returns in the brightest moments of the *Quartets*.

CHAPTER 10

THE CASE OF THE ELEGY
Milton, Shelley, and Whitman

"That corpse you planted last year in your garden,
"Has it begun to sprout? Will it bloom this year?"

The Waste Land

The corpus of the elegy lies buried in *The Waste Land*. In detecting the significance of its "presence" there, it would be tempting to declare the poem's case solved at last, the truth finally risen after so many grave diggings. Such generic labeling could fix the poem in a formulated phrase, leave it sprawling, like Prufrock, on a pin. This is always a danger when we put our words of understanding in the place of those we have read. I will argue, however, that the elegy figures a poetic crisis, questions the poet's ability to re-collect wholeness, and thus appropriately forestalls its own employment in any totalizing interpretation of Eliot's fragments. The reader will not be forced to endure here another line-by-line *explication de texte* resulting in a paraphrase of the poem's "meaning." My purpose is rather to demonstrate the correspondence, in the sense of a dialogue or exchange of letters, between Eliot's poem and its most illustrious forebears: Milton's "Lycidas," Shelley's "Adonais," and Whitman's "When Lilacs Last in the Dooryard Bloom'd." All of these poems concern (at least) three "resurrections": of the dead hero, of the elegy as a poetic vehicle, and of the poet's own powers. Thus, when Eliot eventually turns to Frazer and Weston for a unifying mythic schema, he focuses on the ritual vegetation deities that also underlie the elegy.

Frazer himself never speculated on the connection of Adonis, Osiris, and Tammuz with the subject of the elegy, but scholars were quick (after Eliot's example perhaps) to see in myth and anthropology an explanation of its sources. Northrop Frye, writing on "Lycidas," surmises that "Milton knew at least as much about the symbolism of the 'dying god' as any modern student could get out of *The Golden Bough*. . . . The notion that twentieth century poets differ from their predecessors in their understanding or use of myth will not bear much scrutiny." In his analysis of "Adonais," Earl Wasserman likewise notes that "the conventions of the pastoral elegy originally grew out of the structure of such fertility myths as that of Adonis." And in his essay on Whitman and the tradition, Richard P. Adams repeats the essential plot: "In the fertility cults, comfort was found in the faith that the demigod would be reborn or revived, that the goddess of fertility would rejoice, and that the earth would be replenished in the spring." Finally, a recent history of the elegiac mode calls the theory of descent from ancient vegetation rites "still probably the most widely accepted view of the origins of the convention."[1] This critical tradition seems to owe much to Eliot's use of Frazer, but there has been no extended discussion (to my knowledge) of *The Waste Land's* elegiac roots and devices, though many have noted the relation in passing.

As a genre the elegy is by definition an art of intertextuality. Each new work deliberately refashions the resources and conventions of the pastoral elegy from Theocritus, Bion, Moschus, and Virgil. "Lycidas" synthesizes, annotates, and revolutionizes this history, becoming the encyclopedia of elegy for modern practitioners. The elegy is reborn when the poet achieves an identity for his work, and himself, by making the old song new. This structure, common to all genres, is thematized in the case of the elegy through the narrative of death and its transfiguration and in the special relation of the poet to the elegized one. The subject of the poem, therefore—whether Edward King or the Fisher King—stands also for the corpus of a poetic mode once more brought to life. A mystery surrounds this corpus, since it may simultaneously embody a poetic style, a philosophy, a particular presursor or poem, or even the new poet himself. Indeed, the elegy involves a complex dissociation and identification in its relation to the identities of the corpus and the author. In his account of "Lycidas" and the pastoral elegy, James Hanford notes how early in the tradition this condensation takes place. Many classical elegies open with a poetic contest or agon between pastoral figures. "This character of the shepherd as a poet gives rise to another common motive: namely, the fiction that the writer of the elegy is himself the poetical successor of the dead shepherd. . . . This sense of personal relation as a poet to the subject of his song justifies the writer in allowing himself digressions concerning his own poetic achievements and aspirations."[2] A

1 Northrop Frye, "Literature as Context: Milton's 'Lycidas,'" in C. A. Patrides (ed.), *Milton's "Lycidas": The Tradition and the Poem* (New York, 1961), 201; Earl Wasserman, *Shelley: A Critical Reading* (Baltimore, 1971), 403; Richard P. Adams, "Whitman's 'Lilacs' and the Tradition of the Pastoral Elegy," *PMLA*, LXXII (1957), 484; Ellen Z. Lambert, *Placing Sorrow: A Study of the Pastoral Elegy Convention from Theocritus to Milton* (Chapel Hill, 1976), xxix.

2 James H. Hanford, "The Pastoral Elegy and Milton's 'Lycidas,'" in Patrides (ed.), *Milton's "Lycidas,"* 34–35.

kind of "mirror stage" occurs in the elegiac process, making the new poem a way for the poet to write himself into literary history. He seeks by poem's end to have composed a tropological transcendence, successfully completing the challenging quest for an answer to the riddles of death, silence, and non-identity. To use a foreign name I have already enlisted to tie together a number of tendencies in Eliot's poetic thinking, the ideal structure of the elegy is that of the *Aufhebung*. Eliot appropriates the elegiac tradition in *The Waste Land*, using it to give coherence to a decade of his life in writing, and turning against it as the son will repudiate his fathers. His poem engages in the elegy's formal convention of stealing from the precursors: he enters into an agon with these ancestors over the issue of poetic salvation, troping their narratives and their figural language in what one might in the end call an elegy for the elegy.

My investigation will include empirical evidence substantiating the roles played by this genre and these poems in *The Waste Land*; at the same time, the inquiry will treat the problems (poetic and otherwise) such performances raise. Before these proceedings, some theoretical objections need to be sworn in. First, does not Eliot's poem violate, beyond any hope of restitution, what Derrida calls "the law of genre"?[3] Precisely so, which underscores the relevance of the elegy, for its operations (as Eliot's poem will disclose them) retrace the lawlessness inherent to the establishment of a generic logos. The elegy is a self-consuming or self-deconstructing genre, slaying and reviving the logos simultaneously, dictating the genealogy of this mode as a sequence of supplements. Within that lineage *The Waste Land* cancels the achievements of its predecessors, reduces the poetic terrain to ruin again, drowns the hero once more, and substitutes its own negation of transcendence as a species of prophecy.

For many years, baffled and outraged adjudicators of the poem's claims either denied its literary identity altogether or took refuge in the hope that it was all a "hoax" or a parody excludable from the canon of authorized forms it seemed to subvert. What confuses any taxonomic placement of *The Waste Land* in a literary class is not the absence of identifiable and conventional traits, but their proliferation. We detect a text's genre by noting the recurrence in it of some trait that the law of that genre has deemed the token of membership. These traits, as Derrida argues, are thereby always "re-markable": they must be repetitions in order to constitute a genealogy and so be re-markable by readers as kinds of citations. The allusiveness of *The Waste Land* leads us astray by reiterating traits from the crime novel, Ar-

---

3 Jacques Derrida, "The Law of Genre," *Critical Inquiry*, VII (Autumn, 1980), 55–82.

thurian romance, pagan myth, Christian Scripture, Romantic lyric, dramatic monologue, Wagnerian opera, Elizabethan theater, Hebrew prophetic books, national epic, spiritual autobiography, and music-hall vaudeville, to name just the more prominent genres. With archaeological care Eliot preserves his shards so that they may indicate their genesis, their genre, even in its *sparagmos*. What occurs, then, is both a dissemination and a coherence, since all the disparate re-marks from different genres belong nevertheless to their own corporate genre, that of those textual indicators that signal the presence of a genre and its historical corpus. The uncanny quality of a trait that characterizes a genre is that of belonging to two genres at once: it participates both in the genre it indites (poem, play, novel, etc.) and in the genre of genre indicators.

Double in its function, the sign of genre mixes two genres even as it delimits the presence of one. In the trait by which we would recognize the nature of a genre ("Those are pearls that were his eyes"), by which its history would repeat itself in a restricted genealogical economy ("To Carthage then I came"), the trace of another genre is legible ("Old man with wrinkled female breasts"). In *The Waste Land*, the *sparagmos* of the corpus and of the Name of the Father corresponds with the violation of the law of genre. The logos that would both belong to and transcend creation is always a law of genre, genesis, and gender. Tiresias embodies the play of genres as the oscillation of gender, his punishment for separating the coupling in genesis. The poem engenders itself by a rehearing of the differences within and between genres and genders. In choosing the elegy as precursor, however, it identifies with a homoerotic genre that invokes the law of the same. It mourns the necessary passing of life through time and elegizes all desires. Although negative theology certainly undergoes its most coherent transfiguration in the poetics of the elegy, it cannot reimpose the law except as an interpretation of differences. When the paternal "DA" resounds near the end, each repetition signifies differently and takes its meaning only in the gloss it receives in its particular intersections with human nature and history.

A second objection to reading *The Waste Land* as a descendant of the elegy could seek support in Eliot's well-known protest against "explanation by origins" in "The Frontiers of Criticism" (1956). The essay is a locus classicus of the old New Criticism, emphasizing "poetry as poetry" in contrast to source study of the kind that "sent so many enquirers off on a wild goose chase after Tarot cards and the Holy Grail" (OPP, 122). Using the examples of Joyce and Coleridge as stand-ins for the Eliot of *The Waste Land*, he reaffirms his thesis that "poetic originality is largely an original way of assembling the most disparate and unlikely material to make a new whole." Yet, he quickly calls this originality unfathomable: "How such material as those scraps of Coleridge's reading became transmuted into great poetry remains as much of a mystery as ever" (OPP, 119–20). It would indeed remain a mystery were we barred from setting Coleridge among the dead for contrast and comparison. Eliot assimilates poetic originality to the mystery of the Incarnation and the transmutation of fallen materials into purified identities. Here is a reincarnation of the Paterian figure within Eliot, who had chided Arnold in *The Sacred Wood* for hunting outside the literary preserve and instead advocated an analysis of the work of art qua art: "the illusion that in poetry we come nearer to a purely aesthetic experience makes poetry the most convenient *genre* of literature to keep in mind when we are discussing literary criticism itself" (OPP, 118). The law of poetry's genre is Roderick Usher's: to bury the body of the Other out of sight beneath the house of art. Likewise, the critic is enjoined not to disinter what art has laid to rest. But ten pages later, as an example of poetry understood without explanation, he cites Ariel's song beginning "Full fathom five thy father lies."

Of course, another part of Eliot knew of how Usher and his rational narrator, while they read a quest romance, listened in horror to the return of the repressed. "And keep within thy charnel vault!" cries the speaker of Eliot's unpublished "Elegy" (circa 1917–1919), "as in a tale by Poe" (WLFS, 117). Comparing "the various *genres* of literature," Eliot notes that their indicators are "formal qualities": "In poetry, it might seem that style is everything" (OPP, 118). The qualifications notwithstanding, the generic indicators of poetry are stylistic differences, dependent on the materiality and sensual qualities of signifiers. Nor can traits be properly registered without putting them into relation with other genres or without unearthing the figures of precursors.[4] The difference between the poem-as-aesthetic whole and everything outside of poetry is none other than a displaced idealization of the difference within the poem between itself and its predecessors. This law of poetry's genre establishes its authority on an aesthetic ground that collapses into the corpora it entombs.

Eliot presents his alternative for criticism when he abruptly turns from discussing *The Waste Land*'s source hunters to quote from Father Victor White, O.P., whose *God and the Unconscious* exposes a "radical difference" between the methods of Freud and Jung, aligning the former with causal explanation by origins and the latter with an "energic viewpoint," or what today we would call a structural or economic account. Eliot credits both methods with

---

4 See A. Walton Litz, "'The Waste Land' Fifty Years After," in Litz (ed.), *Eliot in His Time* (Princeton, 1973), 12–13.

understanding, but urges us toward the latter, so "that we should endeavour to grasp what the poetry is aiming to be; one might say—though it is long since I have employed such terms with any assurance—endeavouring to grasp its entelechy" (OPP, 122). The parenthetical allusion sends source hunters back forty years to "Leibniz' Monads and Bradley's Finite Centres." There the attempt to discriminate between personality, self, center, and soul comes down to two "points of view" toward the soul. It would be "untrue" to "declare that the soul 'bears traces' of everything that happens to it," making soul thus "only the function of a physical organism, a unity perhaps only partial, capable of alteration, development, having a history and a structure, a beginning and apparently an end" (KE, 205–206). That would be the Freudian soul as it appears in *Beyond the Pleasure Principle*. But from another point of view the soul is impenetrable, "a universe in itself. . . . not identical with its states . . . a whole world, to which nothing comes except as its own attribute and adjective" (KE, 205). The first point of view represents the belated, influenced soul; the second images a solipsism so original that all the world is its emanation. Though "irreconcilable," these viewpoints "melt into each other by a process which we cannot grasp," through a transition Bradley calls "transcendence": "We thus pass to the point of view from which the soul is the entelechy of the body" (KE, 206). Philosophy and poetry share, across a forty-year divide, a mode of transcendence in which the soul mysteriously fulfills and passes beyond the telos of the body that engendered it. But origins in this scheme become the effects of the (poetic) soul, products of a *Nachträglichkeit*, or retrospective interpretation, that grasps the entelechy and puts the origin in its place. The "aiming to be" of the poem reaims the body of signifiers, adopts a transcendent point of view toward them that re-collects memories according to a telos the new work projects into the past. Poetry takes aim at its being by resighting/re-citing the materials of others. Every poem writes literary history, a hypothesis formally highlighted by the genre of the elegy and ostentatiously performed by *The Waste Land*.

A third and final objection could point to Eliot's canonical list of sources for his poetry and to the largely negative presence of Milton, Shelley, and Whitman in his criticism. I do not think that these three are more *important* influences in the poem than the generally accepted ones, but that their influence operates in a different register, telling us something about the poem's buried life. Between intended references and unconscious echoes lies a rich spectrum of re-sounding degrees, and it is never an easy matter to say why or how a particular note is struck. In an erudite study of English poetic intertextuality, John Hollander distinguishes theoretically between actual "*quotation*, the literal presence of a body of text," *allusion*, the intentional and playful (*ludus*) troping that the audience is meant to recognize, and *echo*, "which represents or substitutes for allusion as allusion does for quotation" and which "may be unconscious or inadvertent." With echo, "a pointing to, or figuration of, a text recognized by the audience is not the point," but it may well enrich the poem's resonance if we attempt to account for it in a reading.[5] In practice, particular re-citations may move among these three points on the scale, so that fixing the genealogy of an intertextual trace is never a certain enterprise. Most of the borrowings discussed herein have been noted before in scattered places, but with little speculation as to the coherent rationale that may guide their joint appearances in the poem. Taking account of them as an elegiac group means interpreting such scholarly facts according to the peculiar logics of denial, revision, and intertextuality. These strategies can easily be seen at work in Eliot's confusing and contradictory critical statements about his predecessors.

It took him two infamous essays to explain his animosity toward Milton, to the satisfaction of almost no one.[6] In the first he declares, for different reasons, the thesis that will be the cornerstone of Harold Bloom's history of poetic anxiety. "Milton's poetry could only be an influence for the worse, upon any poet whatever. It is more serious, also, if we affirm that Milton's bad influence may be traced much further than the eighteenth century, and much further than upon bad poets: if we say that it was an influence against which we still have to struggle" (OPP, 157). The second essay, purportedly written to correct the abuses in the first, continues the attack on Milton's "bad influence." Eliot's question is, "Of what *use* is the poetry of this poet to poets writing to-day"? (OPP, 166). He once more details Milton's "unwholesome influence" on the Romantics, but his real concern is with Milton's "peculiarity of *diction*," his "perverse and pedantic principle" of using English words with a foreign idiom, in sum his "eccentric" and "*Babylonish dialect*." Milton's "personal style" is "a perpetual sequence of original acts of lawlessness" (OPP, 174–75). Milton is the Individual Talent unbound. He represents a transumptive appropriation of literary history so powerful that it blocks the way for other poets, who cannot (or should not) be so original.

In contrast Eliot advocates the "common style" in "Johnson as Critic and Poet" (1944), written between the times of the two Milton pieces. Here the

---

5 John Hollander, *The Figure of Echo: A Mode of Allusion in Milton and After* (Berkeley, 1981), 64.

6 For a comprehensive review of Eliot's writings on Milton, see E. P. Bollier, "T. S. Eliot and John Milton: A Problem in Criticism," *Tulane Studies in English*, VIII (1958), 165–92. See also Herbert Howarth, "Eliot and Milton: The American Aspect," *University of Toronto Quarterly*, XXX (January, 1961), 150–62.

poet is valued "not for his invention of an original form of speech, but by his contribution to a common language" (OPP, 188). Defending Johnson's strictures against "Lycidas," Eliot charts a kind of map of mishearing: "The deafness of Johnson's ear to some kinds of melody was the necessary condition for his sharpness of sensibility to verbal beauty of another kind" (OPP, 192). No devotee of "sound for sound's sake" or "melodious raving," Johnson is "contented with intelligence set forth in pedestrian measures" (OPP, 193). The Arnold in Eliot will not stay still, and Johnson becomes a way of refiguring again poetry's relation to society, culture, belief, morality, and politics. The principle of poetry as "edification" is put forward: "certainly from great poetry, we must derive some benefit as well as pleasure" (OPP, 211). To practice the "common style" is to work on behalf of unity and order and tradition. "To be original within definite limits of propriety may require greater talent and labour, than when every man may write as he pleases, and when the first thing expected of him is to be different" (OPP, 216). The "common style" is another of Eliot's ingenious critical fictions, one that allows the author, by recourse to an intertextuality that is both submissive and revisionary, a way out of the struggle for identity. This issue of keeping "purely literary values" separate from those of other discourses put Eliot off balance throughout his career and nearly ruined parts of *Four Quartets* with "pedestrian measures" like those that doomed the "common style" of his plays. Such an isolation of sound from sense turns out to be paradise lost: "It is simply that the conditions under which literature is judged simply and naturally as literature and not another thing, no longer prevail." That would require "a society which believed in itself, a society in which the differences of religious and political views are not extreme" (OPP, 221).

The second Milton essay (1947) begins with the words "Samuel Johnson," and Eliot confesses to share Johnson's "antipathy towards Milton the man." "Of no other poet is it so difficult to consider the poetry simply as poetry, without our theological and political dispositions, conscious and unconscious, inherited or acquired, making an unlawful entry" (OPP, 168). Eliot cannot help but commit the crime, for the "law" that separates the "man" from the "poet" is as arbitrary and misleading as the one that tries to separate poetry from other genres of writing. We are put on notice to look for the "other" and "unlawful" malefactors that enter into Eliot's discussions of poets and technique. In the case of Milton and "Lycidas," the culprit's act may be discerned. We are told that Milton's loss of sight is the "most important fact" for Eliot, that it supposedly "withered" the poet's "sensuousness" to leave only "a blind alley for the future development of language" (OPP, 162). Eliot's insight about the auditory imagination or overbearing voice of

Milton exacts the cost of blindness from the critic: "in the Garden of Eden
. . . I for one can get pleasure from the verse only by the deliberate effort not
to visualize Adam and Eve and their surroundings. . . . So far as I perceive
anything, it is a glimpse of a theology that I find in large part repellant, expressed through a mythology which would have better been left in the Book
of *Genesis*, upon which Milton has not improved" (OPP, 162–63). The problem is indeed to fashion something that improves on one's genesis, as the
quotations that follow show. Eliot gives two examples of Milton's use of
nominative litanies, the first of which he calls a kind of "solemn game" that
demonstrates the "division, in Milton, between the philosopher or theo-
logian and the poet" (OPP, 163). The second is from "Lycidas":

> Whether beyond the stormy Hebrides,
> Where thou perhaps under the whelming tide
> Visit'st the bottom of the monstrous world;
> Or whether thou to our moist vows deny'd
> Sleep'st by the fable of Bellerus old,
> Where the great vision of the guarded Mount
> Looks toward Namancos and Bayona's hold . . .

"For the single effect of grandeur of sound," says Eliot, "there is nothing
finer in poetry" than these lines (OPP, 164).

But are we dealing only with sound, and not with sense? It is hard to see the
answer, since Eliot leaves out of his quotation the two preceding lines, which
begin Milton's sentence: "Ay me! Whilst thee the shores and sounding Seas /
Wash far away, where'er thy bones are hurl'd . . ." Blinded, we still may hear

> Phlebas the Phoenician, a fortnight dead,
> Forgot the cry of gulls, and the deep sea swell
> And the profit and loss.
>   A current under sea
> Picked his bones in whispers. As he rose and fell
> He passed the stages of his age and youth
> Entering the whirlpool.

Eliot's excision is explained by his interest in names, but it also functions
to obscure the view of Milton's role in the genesis of his own boats and
drowned bodies. "Sunk though he be beneath the wat'ry floor," Lycidas offers a more sanguine fate than the figure of the father in Ariel's song. The
quoted lines immediately precede the final movement of Milton's poem into
a dialectical recuperation of natural death "Through the dear might of him
that walk'd the waves." Eliot's Phlebas continues to sink into chaos. The passage tropes against the strength of Milton's resurrections (poetic and reli-

gious), supplementing the precursor's vision with the hard Metaphysical image of "Picked his bones in whispers." This reincarnating of Milton's aural style raises Eliot and his poem from shipwreck and provides a transition into part 5, where the concluding Miltonic transfiguration of pastoral suffers desiccation as Eliot tests the alternatives offered by Shelley and Whitman.

The vexing corruption of poetry by belief, and vice versa, cripples Eliot's 1933 lecture on Shelley and Keats, forming a sequence with the 1929 essays on Dante and with the next American lectures, *After Strange Gods: A Primer of Modern Heresy.* Shelley ranks among "the great heretics," his ideas even more "repellent" in their Protestant, individualistic, and Romantic skepticism than were Milton's. Eliot does not deign to specify these ideas, though one can surmise that they had to do with religion, politics, poetry, and sex, with Shelley playing the "blackguard" of otherness in each arena. Eliot is "confounded by the philosophy of *Epipsychidion*" and quotes with particular repugnance its famous lines rejecting monogamous attachments. Any enthusiasm for such writing, as in the case of Poe and others in Eliot's limbo, is "an affair of adolescence" outgrown in "maturity" (UPUC, 89). George Bornstein has already made an acute study of Shelley's effects on Eliot, noting how the latter's personal fears and emotional projections determine most of his critical accusations. Examining the ambivalence that characterizes the use of Shelley in Eliot's poetry and prose, Bornstein finds "a kind of schizophrenia. . . . a mind divided against itself, at once enormously susceptible to Shelley and distrustful of that very susceptibility."[7]

Only "The Triumph of Life" earns Eliot's consistent praise, for its revision of Dante seems to prefigure an exorcism of the ghost of Rousseau and Romanticism and a submission to a very different tradition of ideas and styles. Shelley, Eliot said in 1929, was "the one English poet of the nineteenth century who could even have begun to follow those footsteps of Dante" (SE, 225).[8] In 1950, when Eliot recounts how he set out to "imitate" Dante in the "compound ghost" scene of "Little Gidding," he acknowledges Shelley's "better" transumption by quoting thirty lines from "The Triumph of Life," an extraordinary tribute considering the steep decline in the number of quotations in Eliot's later prose. It also helps us see that Shelley is one of the major precursors "Little Gidding" hopes to exorcise. Shelley's passage (quoted in part in 1933 and echoed in the fourth stanza of "Sweeney Erect") is of course the one in which the shade of Rousseau appears, a guilty ghost sum-

7 George Bornstein, *Transformations of Romanticism in Yeats, Eliot, and Stevens* (Chicago, 1976), 124.
8 See Glenn O'Malley, "Dante, Shelley, and T. S. Eliot," in George Bornstein (ed.), *Romantic and Modern: Revaluations of a Literary Tradition* (Pittsburgh, 1977), 165–76.

moned from among the "deluded crew." He confesses the "corruption" of his spirit's spark by a misplaced passion for the things of nature. For Eliot the lines emblematically signify the late "wisdom" of Shelley's skepticism toward his own youthful ideas and exhibit a Dantean power to put one's origins—personal and poetic—in their purgatorial place.

Before quoting the passage in 1950, Eliot says that it "made an indelible impression upon me over forty-five years ago," or in about 1905 at the age of seventeen. Eliot's reiterated thesis of youthful poetic incarnation as a kind of "daemonic possession" by the overwhelming precursor refers pointedly to Shelley: "It is not from rules, or by cold-blooded imitation of style, that we learn to write: we learn by imitation indeed, but by a deeper imitation than is achieved by analysis of style. When we imitated Shelley, it was not so much from a desire to write as he did, as from an invasion of the adolescent self by Shelley, which made Shelley's way, for the time, the only way in which to write" (OPP, 19). The disparity between Shelley's style and Eliot's means little, then, and is no index to the depth of their relation. We may justly doubt Eliot's assertion that his quarrel with the Romantics or with Milton was simply over technique. The "deeper imitation" of Shelley is precisely what readers of *The Waste Land* will find when they compare that poem to "Adonais."

He had been "intoxicated by Shelley's poetry at the age of fifteen" during that legendary seizure of his soul by Romanticism. Laying such influences to rest or casting them, as it does Rousseau, in purgatorial figures, *The Waste Land* combines an elegy for youth's passions with a quest for "mature" wisdom. Eliot calls the ghosts of the Elizabethans and the French to his aid, sculpting an anti-Romantic surface that persists in treating the problems of self, recollection, death, and sublime recovery ingested from the intoxicants of the Romantics. Eliot's prim delectation of the sordid turns his own Romantic tendency into manageable caricature, and his cultivation of classicism clamps a lid on the transcendental liftings of Romantic verse. But the Romantic "raid on the Absolute" that Eliot sneered at was not an absolute in *The Prelude*, in Shelley's quest poems, or in Keats's odes of negative capability.

The role played by "Adonais" in *The Waste Land* stems from the way Shelley's poem positions its tentative conclusions in relation to Milton's ascension to sublimity. The sinking of Lycidas' craft leads, through the power of the Resurrection, upward into the "blest Kingdoms" where he is received by singing "Saints," much as Dante is welcomed into poetic heaven by the "bella scuola" of his precursors. Milton dubs Lycidas "the Genius of the shore," the spirit of the place between land and sea, an inspiration "To all that wander in that perilous flood" (compare DS, parts 1 and 2). Troping Milton's argument and imagery, Shelley closes "Adonais" otherwise.

> The breath whose might I have invoked in song
> Descends on me; my spirit's bark is driven,
> Far from shore, far from the trembling throng
> Whose sails were never to the tempest given;
> The massy earth and sphered skies are riven!
> I am borne darkly, fearfully, afar:
> Whilst burning through the inmost veil of Heaven,
> The soul of Adonais, like a star,
> Beacons from the abode where the Eternal are.

Whose "breath," or poetic spirit, drives Shelley's craft so far from shore? It could be Dante's, who addresses his readers on the brink of paradise (*Paradiso*, canto 2) in just such navigational metaphors. But it is the attempted recovery of Milton's paradise that is more immediately at stake. Throughout "Adonais" the dead Keats has been a double of Milton, "Who was the Sire of an immortal strain" (l. 30). Shelley feels the "strain" of Milton's "Lycidas," as he too makes the hero's death an occasion to test the powers of his own poetry. It is Shelley, the "frail Form. . . . Who in another's fate now wept his own" (ll. 271, 300). The corpus of Keats raises for him the central question of poetic immortality and thus as a figure condenses Dante, Milton, and other stars of the literary pantheon. At the risk of all credibility, I shall suggest that the agon with Milton also informs the poem's oddest element, its inclusion of the incredible tale of how a "viperous murderer" and "nameless worm" killed Keats with a review of *Endymion*. Behind this fable's intense representation lies Shelley's own creative insecurities and his displaced anxiety about re-viewing Milton's elegiac achievement with his own.

Thus that "breath" is a figure of influence itself. By opening himself to the words of Dante, Milton, and Keats, Shelley turns indebtedness into transumption. His poetic craft thus escapes "the trembling throng / Whose sails were never to the tempest given." This imagery of the "bark," "shore," and "sails" connects Shelley's figurations of the poetic quest back to Dante and Milton and forward to Tennyson and Eliot. Shelley tropes the vertical salvation in "Lycidas" into a horizontal drifting, thus challenging Milton's confidence about resurrections while simultaneously expressing his own fear of being forever "borne" in belatedness. Yet, above gleams the star of Adonais/Keats, promise of the Eternal Paradise. The two sets of figures, nautical and astral, form a catachresis of an interesting sort. In accepting his driven fate, as the genius of tempests rather than of shores, Shelley implicitly becomes a poet of negative capability and so achieves what Keats represents. But he remains at a calculated distance from the poets' Olympus, and it is in that oceanic space that Shelley's own bark sails. The dead masters guide from on high, while the new poet charts his own course by interpreting his spirit's response to them. Shelley ends adrift beneath the Eternal and so figures a skeptical stance toward poetic transcendence that Eliot's closing boat imagery will echo.

On native grounds, the American successor to Romantic explorations of personal genius and poetic immortality is Walt Whitman. His Lucretian dissemination of resurrection into the processes of compost heaps and scattered eidolons would be only one of many elements in Whitman that Eliot could find repellent. His example single-handedly disproved all the lamentations about America's impoverished resources for the creation of great art, while his innovations made it difficult to go on writing "traditional" poetry in English, though both these facts were denied well into the twentieth century and obscured by their repetition and transformation in Eliot's and Pound's hands. The audacious scope of Whitman's stylistic experiments prompted a constraining reaction from his heirs, as did the outrageous content of his verse. The narcissism and homoeroticism, the celebration of nature and the body electric, and the expansion of the individual into "kosmos" and poet into seer made *Leaves of Grass* a summa of the inheritance Eliot struggled to revise. Whitman's democratic vistas leveled the order of differences Eliot sought to revive with his triple allegiance to the logocentrisms of classicism, royalism, and Catholicism. Even when Eliot turned abroad, Whitman came back to him secondhand. The youthful Swinburne was set afire by his discovery of *Leaves of Grass*, and he wrote a passionate tribute to Whitman at the close of his Blake study (1868). Despite later recantations, Swinburne wrote in response to Whitman's Eros and passed the legacy on to the young Eliot. The same can be said for Laforgue, who was translating *Leaves of Grass* as he wrote *Dernier Vers*, working out in his lower key Whitman's thematics of the city and its sexual unconscious. But the amply recognized Eliot-Whitman connection has not generally taken hold in the critical community for lack of a convincing theoretical perspective that can maintain their dissimilarity while joining them in a single intertextual framework.[9]

Of course, Eliot's comments on Whitman have not been much help. In his 1928 introduction to Pound's *Selected Poems*, Eliot takes the time to differentiate his "own type of verse, that of Pound, and that of the disciples of Whitman."[10] He is "here speaking of origins," fabulating the now canonical story of his discipleship to "Laforgue together with Elizabethan drama," putting the maximum distance between himself and Whitman's "barbaric yawp." The

9 The most thorough study is still Sydney Musgrove, *T. S. Eliot and Walt Whitman* (Wellington, New Zealand, 1952). See also Philip Hobsbaum, "Eliot, Whitman, and the American Tradition," *Journal of American Studies*, III (1969), 239–64; and James E. Miller, Jr., *The American Quest for a Supreme Fiction* (Chicago, 1979).

10 Introduction to *The Selected Poems of Ezra Pound* (London, 1928), vii.

chosen exile from the burdens of his American legacy is exposed in this genealogy of origins, framed as it is by a second exclusion of Whitman: "I did
not read Whitman until much later in life, and had to conquer an aversion to
his form, as well as to much of his matter, in order to do so. I am equally
certain—it is indeed obvious—that Pound owes nothing to Whitman."
What is "indeed obvious" to the reader of this edition of Pound's poetry,
selected by the wily Possum himself, is the inclusion of Pound's "A Pact," his
declared truce with Walt Whitman the "pig-headed father." How can we explain Eliot's obtuseness or deliberate misstatement of the facts except as a
displacement of his own unresolved "commerce" with the paternal force who
"broke the new wood"? As for his claim that he "did not read Whitman until
much later in life," the rhetoric implies a time span of decades the evidence
belies. Even if Eliot managed to miss Whitman, as he claims to have missed
Twain, throughout school and college in America, he was by 1919 competent
to review a new history of American literature and to center his discussion on
Poe, Hawthorne, and Whitman. The derogatory statements about American
literature in this review have been overemphasized to produce a simplistic
view of Eliot's feeling toward his national forebears. Their flaws are analyzed
in terms justifying Eliot's exile, but not to the extent that England's virtues
are entirely victorious: "Compare 'Leaves of Grass' with 'Dramatic Monologues,'" Eliot observes, "and you see that Whitman is more creative, more
original, more 'shocking' in single lines than Browning."[11]

A year later, the essay on Blake focuses on the "naked man," his individual
power and correspondent need for tradition. The article reads like a covert
tribute and corrective to Whitman (perhaps due to Swinburne's comparison
of Blake and Whitman).[12] Eliot's Blake is "honest," and his "poetry has the
unpleasantness of great poetry" (SE, 275). He is not distracted by "the ambitions of parents or wife, nor the standards of society, nor the temptations of
success" (SE, 275–76). (The compounding of Whitman, Blake, and Eliot begins.) Blake has "a profound interest in human emotions, and a profound
knowledge of them" (SE, 277). Blake's great flaw, yet also what makes him
"terrifying," is the personal, individual nature of his philosophy ("an ingenious piece of home-made furniture"). The infamous judgment that Blake
lacked traditional ideas would astonish Blake scholars who spend their lives
documenting his sources in biblical, Gnostic, and Miltonic traditions. The
description and charge suit Whitman better.

Whitman was the real "naked man" (or, in his own words, "hankering,

---

11 "American Literature," *Athenaeum*, No. 4643 (25 April 1919), 237.

12 Eliot's "Swinburne as Critic," a review of Swinburne's *Contemporaries of Shakespeare*,
appeared five months before the Blake essay, but neither mentions Swinburne's study of
Blake or the Whitman connection.

gross, mystical, nude"). His celebrations of the flesh, of "robust American love," fascinate and repel the prurient Possum, whose juvenilia and unpublished fragments teem with sensual and sexual excess. "Whitman," Eliot later wrote, "had the ordinary desires of the flesh; for him there was no chasm between the real and the ideal, such as opened before the horrified eyes of Baudelaire." And, presumably, before the horror-struck eyes of the Tiresian Eliot. The degree to which Eliot may have shared Whitman's tumultuous engagement with the body, and even its unsanctioned desires, is measurable by the incredible assertion, passed off in the lowest key, that Whitman's were "the ordinary desires of the flesh." For Eliot, Whitman remains "a great representative of America, but emphatically of an America that no longer exists."[13] America, nakedness, sexuality, and idiosyncratic philosophical poetics fuse in Eliot's mind with Whitman, as adolescence was identified with Shelley. Through creative repression they now no longer exist, and Eliot seeks England, askesis, and maturity as his salvation and self-humiliating song. His antipathy toward Whitman tempers, as does his hostility toward the Romantics, when the solid accomplishments of his own poetic career are behind him. In 1948 he admits to "having frequently re-read Whitman," discovering him now "not in the least provincial" (CC, 30, 29). But indebtedness is still a sore subject: "To Walt Whitman . . . a great influence on modern poetry has been attributed. I wonder if this has not been exaggerated" (CC, 53). Certainly in Eliot's case it has been underestimated, if one sees influence in less intentional terms. The elegiac effort to reach the heavenly spheres comes down to Eliot from Dante through Milton, Shelley, and Whitman. Theirs is the eccentricity and lawlessness his adopted "minor" precursors help him to control. Whitman is a difficult ancestor, however, since he writes a post-Romantic elegy for Romantic solipsism.

The "powerful western fallen star" serves as only one aspect of Whitman's symbolic trinity in "When Lilacs Last in the Dooryard Bloom'd." Adonais/ Keats, "robed in dazzling immortality," was transfigured into the genius of the third sphere, the heavenly place of Lucifer and Venus, morning and evening star. In his section 8, Whitman recalls nights of wandering with that star, seeing its woe as an image of his own: "As my soul in its trouble dissatisfied sank, as where you sad orb, / Concluded, dropt in the night, and was gone." Prefiguring Lincoln's death without a morning resurrection, the scene already inscribes the narcissistic structure of identification in mourning and melancholia outlined by Freud.[14] Long before his death, Lincoln has be-

---

13 "Whitman and Tennyson," *Nation and Athenaeum*, XL (December 18, 1926), 426. Eliot accuses Whitman and Tennyson of idealizing sex.
14 Freud, "Mourning and Melancholia," *Works*, XIV, 243–58.

come Whitman's ego ideal and representative American, standing for his logos and thus for the source of a new poetic voice.[15] The historical trauma of the assassination, however real in itself, takes on meaning from its place in a recurrent structure of losses—personal, poetic, and political. Like all elegies, Whitman's poem is about getting the power of his voice back, here imaged by the death-singing thrush. The way to such "retrievements out of the night" involves the sinking of Shelley's star and a further distancing from the elegiac quest for a traditionally conceived immortality of identity, for what "Adonais" envisions as Keats's return to "the Eternal, which must glow / Through time and change, unquenchably the same" (ll. 340–41). The narcissistic dream undergoes a severe askesis in Whitman's poem when death is embraced as the ultimate trope of creation.

On his quest for a "sane and sacred" intimacy with death, Whitman is repeatedly "detain'd" by the "lustrous star" and by the "mastering odor" of the lilacs. These are the tempting signs of immortality and love that he must forsake before reaching his Chapel Perilous, "the fragrant cedars and the ghostly pines so still." Only when he contemplates the "unconscious scenery" of life's onward flowing, "the ships how they sail'd / And the summer approaching with richness, and the fields all busy with labor, / And the infinite separate houses, how they all went on," does he finally join hands with the "thought of death" and the "knowledge of death" to hear the thrush's carol. There is an infinite horizontal dissemination of life here and no resolvent end to the spectacle save death. The passing of the father figure and the relinquishment of narcissistic identification with him precedes, then, the erotic chant by the "ocean shore" to the "Dark mother" who contains the voices of the dead. At one level an Oedipal fantasy is fulfilled, while at the same time the fathers live again in this son's knowledge of the source. But in Whitman's troping, this origin has become the difference that death makes, that sex repeats, that appears in the condensed image of the thrush's "bleeding throat," or organ of parturition and creation. Words are wombs and wounds, singing of time the "strong deliveress" and "flood of thy bliss O death," maternal and fatal. Whitman's Lincoln does not rise, nor does Whitman continue to lie against time, though by incorporating his poetic origins his song becomes one of the "retrievements out of the night." An unexpected "impersonality" overtakes the author of "Song of Myself" when he gives voice to the "Victorious song, death's outlet song, yet varying ever-altering song." The appearance of the hermit thrush in part 5 of *The Waste Land* will measure out another poet's strength in such singing.

15 See Harold Bloom's reading of the poem in *Agon: Towards a Theory of Revisionism* (New York, 1982), 186–95.

CHAPTER II

READING THE VOICES OF THUNDER

I should myself be glad to know whether the primal scene in my present patient's case was a phantasy or a real experience; but, taking other similar cases into account, I must admit that the answer to this question is not in fact a matter of very great importance. These scenes of observing parental intercourse, of being seduced in childhood, and of being threatened with castration are unquestionably an inherited endowment, a phylogenetic heritage, but they may just as easily be acquired by personal experience. . . . All that we find in the prehistory of neuroses is that a child catches hold of his phylogenetic experience where his own experience fails him. He fills in the gaps in individual truth with prehistoric truth; he replaces occurrences in his own life by occurrences in the life of his ancestors.

Freud, "From the History of an Infantile Neurosis"

It would be a mistake to make the death of Jean Verdenal or Henry Ware Eliot, Sr., the objective referent of Eliot's elegiac mood in *The Waste Land*. No doubt these wrenching experiences, Eliot's own death-in-life in marriage, and the catastrophe of the war played a part in the poem's composition, but as with Whitman's response to Lincoln's murder these losses were felt through a structure already largely in place and found their interpretation when Eliot looked to literary history (the poet's "phylogenetic heritage") for ancestral, even prehistoric, truths to supplement a contemporary anguish. In the archaeological and allusive method of *The Waste Land*, Eliot "replaces occurrences in his own life by occurrences in the life of his ancestors." Childhood memories, adolescent fevers, and adult failures correspond with scenes out of the written past, and each domain exchanges meanings with the other. An incessant interchange of meanings goes on between personal and literary history when we try to decipher Eliot's representations of fathers, mothers, writers, lovers, kings, queens, saints, sinners, cultures, and natures. Everyone authors his or her past in memory; for the writer, the mediation is redoubled by this process of remembering representations. The coincidence of personal and poetic structures in Eliot's work confounds or compounds literary and familial anxieties of genealogy. Personal relations may be lived out according to poetic concerns about influence, genesis, intercourse, inspiration, and identity; poetic theories, such as that of tradition and the individual talent, may be translations of sexual and familial ambivalences. The vast ambiguity of Eliot's work arises from this compounding, wherein poetic theory interprets personal history and personal history supplies poetic theory with its terms. No original incident appears to start the process. The two separate discourses seem offshoots of a single conceptual structure, are inextricable from the start, and have their coincidence as the very inspiration of Eliot's writing.

Shipwrecks and drowned bodies, for example, are figures that appear from the inception of Eliot's career. A year after taking sailing lessons from a re-tired mariner in Gloucester, the sixteen-year-old Eliot wrote two short sto-ries about whalers and ocean adventures, borrowing some of his lore from the tales he eagerly heard told by Gloucester's voluble old salts.[1] His Harvard *Advocate* essay of 1909, "Gentlemen and Seamen," portrays Cape Ann's cap-tains and sailors as ego ideals, worthy ancestors comparable to, though more daring than, Hawthorne's "steeple-crowned" progenitors. Nautical figures accumulate more and more resonance during the coming decades. Tennyson, Dante, Conrad, Milton, Shelley, and others provide variations on the *topos* of the voyage as literary quest. The personal delights of sailing off Cape Ann are retrospectively invested with values, feelings, and references carried over from literature, a transfiguration that seeks to provide present emotions (in response, say, to marital strife, a father's death, or spiritual doubt) with inter-pretative scaffolds. At the same time, Eliot's reading of these past literary fig-ures is caught up in his ambivalent feelings toward America, nature, and adolescence.

"Prufrock," "Rhapsody on a Windy Night," "Morning at the Window," "Mr. Apollinax," "The Death of Saint Narcissus," "Burbank with a Baedeker," "Sweeney Erect," and "Dans le Restaurant" all utilize imagery of the seashore or drowning. The importance of this motif increases during the four years before publication of *The Waste Land*. Though the dating of the manuscripts remains uncertain, the evidence points to a recurrent fascination with watery death from 1918 to 1921, as in the versions of "Dirge" that grotesquely parody Ariel's song from *The Tempest* (WLFS, 119–23).[2] "Elegy" and "Exequy" also

---

1 Neville Braybrooke, "T. S. Eliot in the South Seas," in Allen Tate (ed.), *T. S. Eliot: The Man and His Work* (New York, 1966), 382–88; Lyndall Gordon, *Eliot's Early Years* (New York, 1977), 6–8.

2 Though great progress has been made, we shall probably never know the whole story of *The Waste Land*'s sequence of composition. On this, and the limitations of Valerie Eliot's published edition of the poem's drafts, see Grover Smith, *T. S. Eliot's Poetry and Plays: A Study in Sources and Meaning* (2nd ed.; Chicago, 1974), 300–14; Gordon, *Eliot's Early Years*,

date from this period. We have already seen the first culmination of this thematic in the Tennysonian echoes of "Gerontion" (1919). Over the next two years, Eliot searches for the subject of his long poem, trying to balance the satiric verse of social and urban apocalypse with symbolic allegories of the poet's spiritual condition. "Prufrock" juxtaposed these realms in dramatizing a speaker whose voyage to love ends in the drowning voices of the cultural and personal unconscious. "Gerontion" repeats the maneuver in its concluding image of the "whirled" socialites and "old man driven by the Trades." Had Eliot gone ahead with his intention of fixing "Gerontion" as a prelude to *The Waste Land*, he would have strengthened our sense of the latter's place in the traditions of voyage and elegy that combine in Tennyson's "Ulysses." As the poem progressed, Eliot adopted Frazer's vegetation deities, at least one of whom (Osiris) is ritually drowned in a river, in order to fuse the story of a culture's crisis with that of its representative spirit.

Readers generally see the first half of the poem as depicting cultural, personal, and poetic crises in a common context of the failure of love to regenerate wholeness and identity. Religion, sex, and poetics inhabit the same drowning corpus. Eliot's mariners suffer romantic shipwrecks as they crash against "Belladonna, the Lady of the Rocks," or founder in an impotence linked to mourning of a dead father. Across their visionary seas these sailors spy a homecoming to the embrace of a saving logos in woman's form, but she turns out to be the prophetess of one more lesson in the limits of what Eros can offer in the way of metaphysical comforts. We should recall here Eliot's judgment that in Baudelaire the "Romantic idea of Love is never quite exorcised, but never quite surrendered to. . . . There is all the romantic idea, but something more: the reaching out towards something which cannot be had *in*, but which may be had partly *through*, personal relations. Indeed, in much romantic poetry the sadness is due to the exploitation of the fact that no human relations are adequate to human desires, but also to the disbelief in any further object for human desires than that which, being human, fails to satisfy them" (SE, 379). The obscure object of Eliot's desire might be clarified by recalling Laplanche's thesis, after Lacan, that sexuality is inherently metaphorical, a "clinamen," or swerve, from the instinctual or biological activities upon which it props itself in its genesis. This means that "on the one hand there is from the beginning an object, but that on the other hand sexuality does not have, from the beginning, a real object." The real object would be, say, the mother's milk demanded for nutrition, which gives way in the sym-

---

143–46; and Hugh Kenner, "The Urban Apocalypse," in A. Walton Litz (ed.), *Eliot in His Time* (Princeton, 1973), 23–49.

bolic register of sexuality to the desire for the breast as object of the sexual drive: "From this, of course, arises the impossibility of ultimately ever rediscovering the object, since the object which has been lost *is not the same* as that which is to be rediscovered. Therein lies the key to the essential 'duplicity' situated at the very beginning of the sexual quest."[3] Although a physical demand may be satisfied, desire seeks its pleasures in experiences that are representational and whose images are derived from the realities of the biological order. Always a writing, desire is an endless voyaging in the signifier toward the horizon of the signified. Eliot resists the decentering of desire, as found in Freud and the Romantics, by negative restitutions of transcendental objects (the Father, the Phallus, the Word). The askesis of a sexual desire aims to return to the truth itself.

Keeping in mind previous cautionary notes about psychoanalytic criticism, we can suggest that a myth of the textual psychology behind Eliot's poem might go something like this. The rejection of endless desire and linguistic dissemination constitutes a refusal to dissolve the Oedipal structure. Rather than accept a series of loves in place of those of the father and the mother, the subject enters into a family romance with multiple contradictions. He refuses the possibility of his own "castration" or belatedness and goes on desiring the prohibited maternal muse. At the same time, he hallucinates images of emasculation that represent both his Oedipal aggression and guilt. Requiring the father's love to kindle the spark of his own sense of self, he must also identify with the receiving mother and so desire his own castration as the cost of the father's embrace. Desiring above all, according to Lacan, the desire of the mother, desiring to be the object of her desire, he figures himself as the phallus. Thus, in their mutual love he may restore to her the imaginary phallus he thinks she has lost and so undo the threat of castration in a final phantasm of (re)union. This "restoration" of the phallus denies the difference between men and women and so completes the quest for a metaphysical and phallogocentric identity. The *sparagmos* of the father's body has been ritually made into the law of the signifier as the phallic son returns the truth to its proper place, sublating the murder of the father. Although the journey began as a flight from the difference of woman and made its descent into the other world of ghosts and memories, it ends (as *Ash Wednesday* would later have it) in the harbor of a beatified lady. But it is Belladonna, not Beatrice, who guides *The Waste Land*'s seamen. She leads them, like Whitman's "Dark Mother," the ocean, to a death both feared and de-

3 Jean Laplanche, *Life and Death in Psychoanalysis*, trans. Jeffrey Mehlman (Baltimore, 1976), 19–20.

sired. It is she whom the son accuses of inspiring the father's murder, she who tempts others to desire the rivalry, and she who urges him to repression. In this reading the modernist tropes against the Romantic's Beatrice, since her perfections excited the new poet to seek in "human relations" (and poetry) a Truth they could not provide.

"The Fire Sermon" brings the poem's first three parts to their negative epiphany: "Burning burning burning burning / O Lord Thou pluckest me out." To use the phrase Eliot notes from Saint Augustine, the poem's focus has been on "unholy loves" and on protagonists doomed because of their "Romantic" quest to satisfy desire in personal or human relations. Thus, the "collocation" of Buddha and Augustine, Eliot tells us, "of eastern and western asceticism, as the culmination of this part of the poem, is not an accident." To the compound must be added Arnaut Daniel, whose willing submission to the fiery refinement of his faith in another Passion combines the lover's askesis with the poet's and the Christian's. Figuratively, it is the Quester's vow of celibacy that the conclusion signals, the sublimation of corrupting lust into a Higher Love. This prepares for the spiritual voyage of part 4 and the approach to the chapel in part 5. The elements of the elegy and the quest emerge most intensely in these parts, apparently the final ones set down by Eliot at Lausanne during what he later called the "illumination" that often follows illness (SE, 358). The juncture between "The Fire Sermon" and "Death by Water" marks the poem's pivotal crisis, its attempted crossing from *sparagmos* and askesis to cohesion and transumption. In this final effort to regenerate poetry and spirit out of allusion and impotence, Eliot returns again to Tennyson's "Ulysses" as his chief antagonist, whose moaning sea voices he again consciously echoes. Though he tropes against that sorrowful tale of a "self-conscious poet" eloquently and vainly trying to begin again, he remains daemonically possessed by the strength Ulysses exhibits in renouncing wife and family for a knowledge of the beyond. "Ulysses" (along with *Hamlet*) supplies *The Waste Land* with an influential figure of the "aboulie" resulting from the impasse between memory and desire, human relations and eternal longings. The weakness of the longer "Death by Water," aside from questions of technique, stems from its irresolution of that impasse, though by the end, and in the Phlebas lyric, a partial victory is won. Eliot will at once criticize the Tennysonian hero for his sublime posturings and himself adopt a position of higher knowledge to keep the critique afloat. He does it by invoking the figure of Dante's Ulysses (*Inferno*, canto 26) as an authorized corrective to Tennyson's.[4]

4 Sister M. Christopher Pecheux, "In Defense of 'Death by Water,'" *Contemporary Literature*, XX (Summer, 1979), 339–53.

In one sense, then, the voyage sets sail for the logos and for the restitution of poetic divination. It journeys away from carnal knowledge and its woundings and back toward a knowledge of (re)union with paternal and maternal sources. The ascetic discipline of sailing with male comrades appears in the "sailor, attentive to the chart or to the sheets / A concentrated will against the tempest and the tide" (WLFS, 55). The mariner's life also promises to refine even a drunken mate, "limping with a comic gonorrhea," symbolically castrated for his foolish attempt to satiate desire in earthly ports. The allusion in the third stanza to the opening of Homer's *Odyssey*, where Odysseus is distinguished from his wild companions destroyed by their own recklessness, picks up the tension between passionate hubris and saving restraint in "The Fire Sermon" and prefigures the allusion to Dante's account of Ulysses' own tragic arrogance. Dante innovatively assimilates Ulysses to the guilt of lawless desire and places him in the circle of frauds and verbal tricksters. Eliot adopts that reading and turns it on Tennyson, who becomes a mellifluous but dangerously wily sophist leading others in a futile quest for knowledge (or poetic power) beyond their capacities and in violation of divine will. Dante's figuration of Ulysses allows Eliot 1) to negate his own sense of belatedness and impotence by judging Ulysses' aspiration (and that of Tennyson as a figure of poetic desire) as misdirected and fatal, a sin and not sublimity; and 2) to achieve an authority for transumption by identifying with the higher logos, the "Another" who punishes Dante's Ulysses for his pride. Like Milton's Satan, Dante's Ulysses is a usurper plotting against the throne of knowledge and the law. "Some work of noble note," says Tennyson's Ulysses, "may yet be done, / Not unbecoming men that strove with Gods" (ll. 52–53). The irony or aporia of Eliot's scheme is that he, too, must play the rebellious angel toward the figures of previous poets.

The anomalous character of Eliot's narrator underscores the section's divided allegiances. He is a Tiresian observer of the ship's mundane castings for cod, a somewhat odd allegory of the folly of loving created things. He does not celebrate when the nets are full or join in laughing thoughts of money, brothels, and gin. His self-conscious eye looks out for a bigger Fish, and so he repeats the alienated condition of Prufrock, Narcissus, and Gerontion in the midst of common life. When the storm comes up, he has a nightmare vision of sirens singing to charm his senses, evidently the kind of catch his shipmates are so fatally pursuing. The voices try to lure him as well, in fear and horror, back to a love for human relations, meaning now both women and Romantic love poets insofar as their songs tempt or challenge the strength of desire. The critique of past voyagers is largely displaced onto the other sailors, while the narrator assumes a transfigured, but not entirely glorious, role as seeker for the true Apocalypse. This makes him perilously like the ambitious Ulysses of Dante and kin in spirit to Tennyson's restless king. But this sailor is not a leader of men; indeed, there seems to be no captain aboard this driven vessel, his absence being part of the structure borrowed from the myth of the Fisher King and Quester. The narrator's passivity exculpates him from Ulysses' or Oedipus' guilt as the will of "Another" carries him submissively toward revelation.

As the ship goes down, they glimpse "a dawn— / A different darkness" above the clouds—and "A line, a white line, a long white line, / A wall, a barrier" dead ahead (WLFS, 61). Eliot combines the apparition of the purgatorial mountain in Dante with the white mystery at the end of Poe's *Narrative of Arthur Gordon Pym*, where, as the boat rushes into the "embraces of the cataract" and the chasm opens to receive them, a titanic white human figure rises to block the way. Eliot's sailors go under thinking of "Home and mother" even as they descend into the dark, maternal sea. In the holograph copy an unidentified voice speaks a last "Remember me," echoing the parting and essential words of Hamlet's ghostly father when the morning drew near (I, v, 92). The ship's noiseless submergence before the whiteness recalls further the sailor-framed scene of the hyacinth garden and its "heart of light, the silence." Fitful annunciations of the characters of family romance appear in this apocalypse. A return home to identity with the Eternal Feminine is consistent with the passivity of the narrator, continuing in spirit the strategy of Eliot's narcissistic martyrs. The Father, Dante's "Another," returns to block the way and insist upon even greater sacrifices. The shipwreck of carnal desire, Romantic love, and precursor poets is turned, via the elegiac quest, into the resurrection of a paternal logos whose punishment of the usurping son replays an internalized, masochistic conflict. Women and mothers undergo a further repression, linked as they now are to death and nonidentity, in contrast to the received imago of the Father's Law.

The figure of the poet who might achieve satisfaction of desire in human relations and creations is sent to the bottom of the sea, and the present poet assumes the voice of Dante's divine will. It is that voice that then pronounces the transumptive elegy for Phlebas in a tone of confident judgment: "Consider Phlebas, who was once handsome and tall as you." It was the sailors' folly, we are told, to believe in themselves, to sail against fate or divine law, or to take satisfaction narcissistically in their own and others' charms. But of course all of this is what the poem required of Eliot. As an elegy for Romantic philosophy, the lyric both buries mistaken hopes and redeems them for another cause. Redemption, however, remains in the key of an admonition, a rhetorical stance of warning that continues the poem's evocation of uncertain prophecies. The contrast to "Lycidas" set in motion by imagistic echoes reminds us of the distance between this negative annunciation and Milton's apotheosis of Lycidas as the "Genius of the shore." With Romantic love and poetry seemingly behind him now, the poet-quester is ready to confront what for him is an even more sublime precursor, the Christian schema of resurrection itself, with its identification of Father and Son with the Holy Spirit of the creative logos. Having rejected a vision of poetic voyaging as an infinite series of mutabilities, of poets torn between belatedness and heresy, he joins Milton, Dante, and others "to look to *death* for what life cannot give" (SE, 235).

The death alluded to in the opening lines of "What the Thunder Said" is explicitly and first of all Christ's, carrying over from Phlebas' lyric the question of His power to raise dead men and their elegists above the waters of time. Thus, despite the history of its composition and the poem's own unsettling of literary foundations, it would be erroneous to characterize it as a kind of dadaist montage arbitrarily jumbled together. Critics who seek to establish either the presence or the absence of a narrative, plot, central character, chronology, biographical referent, mythical unity, or other technique for closure in the poem fail to appreciate that it is the impossibility of just such decisions, grounded as they are in binary oppositions of identity and difference, that the text explores in its methods and themes. The poem utilizes all the means of literary order to gain quite powerful effects, as in its imitations of the elegy, but does so in a way that reopens those structures of the other they would waste, exclude, master, and subl(im)ate. If for some reason one wanted to call this a "deconstructive" poem, it would not be because it somehow signifies in a naïve utopia of free play outside any logocentrism.[5] Rather, within the inheritance of literary thought, *The Waste Land* exemplifies the Derridean argument that deconstruction takes place genealogically within structures, "inhabiting them *in a certain way*, because one always inhabits, and all the more when one does not suspect it. Operating necessarily from the inside, borrowing all the strategic and economic resources of subversion from the old structure, borrowing them structurally," a deconstruction does not merely redouble error by privileging absence or any other negative half of a dualism.[6] It locates within a structure the aporia (or what Derrida calls the "hymen") that both joins and separates conceived opposi-

5 Such a misunderstanding and misapplication of Derrida may be witnessed in Ruth Nevo, "The Waste Land: Ur-Text of Deconstruction," *New Literary History*, XIII (1982), 453–62. Although many of her observations about the poem are accurate, Nevo wrongly conflates literary experimentalism with philosophical deconstruction.

6 Jacques Derrida, *Of Grammatology*, trans. Gayatri Spivak (Baltimore, 1976), 24.

tions. The narrative structure of *The Waste Land*, for example, cannot be merely affirmed or dismissed, for its calculated intermittence is crucial to the poem's effects. Parts 4 and 5 clearly exhibit an increase of narrative expanse and control, intermixed with lyric reflections, as the quest for the logos culminates. We have come ashore here from an ambiguous baptism to the drought of a Sinai landscape. The poem refers back to the rain and desert of part 1, framing the prophet's emergence from the modern Babylons of parts 1 through 3. In the manner of his biblical forerunners, this bitter soul leaves behind the worshipers of man-made icons to seek a rendezvous with an unknowable transcendence.

The structure of the narrative, however, is neither progressive nor circular. The beginning of the poem's end narrates Christ's death, which was the end figured in the poem's cruel April beginning. Have we come full circle or to a dead end? An exorcism of Romantic love separates these two moments of epitaph and joins them in the cause of the poet's identity. The poem's first three parts write an elegy for Romantic love's power to save mankind from time and its differences, while the last two parts write an elegy for the Higher Love of Christian death and for the salvation of Son and Father in each other's image. Romantic love could not satisfy because its objects were but metaphors of the thing itself. A narrative or relation, the story of Christ's death and resurrection replaces those imperfect vehicles with a supplement on the conquest of time; moreover, everyone is asked to identify with this hero's corpus. Yet, what enables the narrative to draw us forward, what elicits desire, is the deferral of divinity and the reiteration of the aporia between human and divine. While Christ stands for the perfect poet and poem, the present poet's *imitatio christi* consists of a self-crucifixion that will once more delimit the difference between body and soul or signifier and signified. Negative theology and castration psychology continue to structure an approach to the *Aufhebung*. When "What the Thunder Said" opens with another dirge for belatedness, we see that the April desire for passionate love has become a desire to participate in the Passion.

> After the torchlight red on sweaty faces
> After the frosty silence in the gardens
> After the agony in stony places
> The shouting and the crying
> Prison and palace and reverberation
> Of thunder of spring over distant mountains
> He who was living is now dead
> We who were living are now dying
> With a little patience.

On one level the passage describes a modern age come too late for salvation, Christ's resurrected living truth "now dead" to those diminished people who are "dying / With a little patience." Their impatience to die, to be free of imperfect satisfactions and reach eternal happiness, is checked by a self-deprecating irresolution that measures their nonidentity with the Risen One. For the poet the crossing to transumption here leads back to the scene of a crime, to the mystery of incarnation, and to the puzzle of how the *figura* of each new poet can both cancel and preserve the Word. He has come too late on the primal scene and can only elegize what is lost there: a power to possess the immortal, the sublime, and one's self. On the other hand, he is burying his precursor's victory over the unoriginality that is poetic death, pronouncing their imperfect transumptions "now dead," and straining to die into the image of the Son who is his own Father. But this voice is not steadfast for death, does not welcome it confidently. It is overshadowed by other voices, by an *apophrades* or unlucky return of the dead who seemed to succeed in the poetics of elegiac resurrection. Whereas "Lycidas" was the touchstone for the limits of the Phlebas lyric, Whitman's "When Lilacs Last in the Dooryard Bloom'd" haunts the opening of "What the Thunder Said," where the word of the father is never quite what was expected.

The description of the mourning land as Lincoln's coffin passes utilizes the convention of the "pathetic fallacy" standard to the vegetation myths, Fisher King legends, the elegiac songs. Although clearly a version of Christ's agony in Gethsemane, his imprisonment, trial, and Crucifixion, Eliot's lines also re-read Whitman's account of a nation lamenting its native son and representative man.

> With the show of the States themselves as of crape-veil'd women
>   standing,
> With processions long and winding and the flambeaus of the night,
> With the countless torches lit, with the silent sea of faces and the unbared
>   heads,
> With the waiting depot, the arriving coffin, and the sombre faces,
> With dirges through the night, with the thousand voices rising strong
>   and solemn,
> With all the mournful voices of the dirges pour'd around the coffin,
> The dim-lit churches and the shuddering organs—where amid these you
>   journey,
> With the tolling tolling bells' perpetual clang,
> Here, coffin that slowly passes,
> I give you my sprig of lilac.

Of course, it will be said that the similarities are owing to the two poets' common source in the gospel accounts of Christ's last days. To stop there, however, would be naïve in light of the way poems project their origins, of *The Waste Land*'s massive intertextuality, and of the fact that the following lines go on to a Whitmanian song of the hermit thrush. For Eliot, Whitman's elegy would represent a heretical usurpation of the Christian schema. Whitman's strength in welcoming death, his tallying of love, immortality, and relinquishment as his soul's song, presents a formidable challenge to someone who would resurrect the elegy for more traditionally metaphysical purposes. One might just as validly argue that Christ's death provides Eliot with metaphors of his relations to other poets and poems as vice versa. The threatening elements of Whitman's dirge—in addition to its magnificent beauty—are its askesis of narcissism in the communion of grief, its stubborn philosophical naturalism, and the uncanny insight of the hermit thrush's song into the human relations linking Eros, death, and poetry. Prospects for personal immortality are unabashedly transfigured into the poet's capacity to tally the father's death with his own and so to receive the embrace and recognition of the oceanic maternal muse. Read as wish fulfillment, "When Lilacs Last in the Dooryard Bloom'd" happily completes the family romances of both Freud and Bloom.[7] Such a triumph of the individual talent was precisely the Romantic and American legacy Eliot imitated through denial.

Lilacs have long since disappeared from *The Waste Land* by the time we reach part 5. As the American genius loci, Whitman tallies his love for the American body in his complete consort of lilac, star, and bird. In the deserts of "What the Thunder Said," nature undergoes a severe askesis, a mortification of landscape itself, exorcising the disseminative naturalism of Whitman. Eliot's tropes of desiccation, his "dry sterile thunder without rain," condense in a single problematic image the son's emasculation by the father and the father's infertility as seen by the son, who seeks to be the author of his own emotional springs. As Eliot's Quester journeys into the mountains, he seeks solitude for his confrontation with divine mysteries. Yet, like Whitman's isolation in "Lilacs," his isolation yields an agon with a spirit of place, the thrush, whose birdsong is conventionally speaking every past poet's immortality ode. Whitman:

> In a swamp in secluded recesses,
> A shy and hidden bird is warbling a song.
>
> Solitary the thrush,
> The hermit withdrawn to himself, avoiding the settlements,
> Sings by himself a song.

7 For very different conclusions see Stephen A. Black, *Whitman's Journeys into Chaos: A Psychoanalytic Study of the Poetic Process* (Princeton, 1975), 234–44.

Song of the bleeding throat,
Death's outlet song of life, (for well dear brother I know,
If thou wast not granted to sing thou would'st surely die.)

Eliot:

        If there were water
And no rock
If there were rock
And also water
And water
A spring
A pool among the rock
If there were sound of water only
Not the cicada
And dry grass singing
But sound of water over a rock
Where the hermit-thrush sings in the pine trees
Drip drop drip drop drop drop drop
But there is no water

Eliot wrote in 1923 to Bertrand Russell that part 5 was the poem's strongest and to Ford Madox Ford that the twenty-nine lines of the water-dripping song were the best (WLFS, 129). The "bogus scholarship" of his notes includes one quoting Chapman's *Handbook of Birds in Eastern North America* (which he received as a present on his fourteenth birthday) detailing the characteristics of the *Turdus aonalaschkae pallasii*. The note both gives a clue to the bird's significance as the voice of Eliot's native ground and decoys critical detectives with its references to ornithology and Quebec province. Thrush songs will reappear at crucial moments of "Marina" and "Burnt Norton," and, as Musgrove speculates, as "the song of one bird" in Eliot's list of obsessive personal memories (UPUC, 148).[8] A deep investment has been made in this thrush's song. For Eliot it is the melody of "the past recaptured," of a song that truly fills the solitude with "inviolable voice." His appreciation for the lines seems to be for their marvelous technical virtuosity in imitating the water-dripping sounds and rhythms of the bird. The oddity comes in the final line: "But there is no water." There is certainly a liquidity in the verse that belies this statement of sterility.

What has been emptied out is Whitman's content, his "Loud human song, with uttermost woe," and his thrush's erotic "chant of fullest welcome" for the "bliss" of death. "When Whitman speaks of the lilacs or of the mocking-

8 Sydney T. Musgrove, *T. S. Eliot and Walt Whitman* (Wellington, New Zealand, 1952), 67–69.

bird," wrote Eliot in 1926, "his theories and beliefs drop away like a needless pretext."[9] The mockingbird refers to "Out of the Cradle Endlessly Rocking," where it sings the aria of unsatisfied love to the daemonized boy who then becomes the "outsetting bard" of Eros. Eliot's hermit thrush distills the song of the beloved's death into the absence of water, figuring abstractly in that element a host of losses now made into a single tune of the Fall: "Drip drop drip drop drop drop drop." The love of created things, of fathers and women and past poems, suffers its sea change through askesis and so points toward a new transcendental infusion. In rehearing Whitman's birdsongs of erotic death, Eliot withdraws his affections from them in search of his own poetic identity and salvation and does so by redoubling the mode of narcissism. Fixing on the death of Christ, as Whitman had on Lincoln, for that elegiac identification that saves, Eliot supplements his kinship to a pagan precursor by substituting Christ's ghost for Walt's. Whitman:

> Then with the knowledge of death as walking one side of me,
> And the thought of death close-walking the other side of me,
> And I in the middle as with companions, and as holding the hands of
>   companions,
> I fled forth to the hiding receiving night that talks not,
> Down to the shores of the water, the path by the swamp in the dimness,
> To the solemn shadowy cedars and ghostly pines so still.

And there he hears the bird's carol of death. Eliot:

> Who is the third who walks always beside you?
> When I count, there are only you and I together
> But when I look ahead up the white road
> There is always another one walking beside you
> Gliding wrapt in a brown mantle, hooded
> I do not know whether a man or a woman
> —But who is that on the other side of you?

Whitman's companions are the "thought" and the "sacred knowledge" of death, its mortal terror balanced against the affirmation chanted by the thrush. This latter is the key to Whitman's mystery and to that of "the third" who walks beside Eliot's wanderer and is elusive to his apprehension.

Substituting the figure of Christ appearing to the disciples on the road to Emmaus for that of Whitman appearing to Eliot, the poem defends against Whitman's "sacred knowledge" of disseminative death with a recuperative vision of the logos of the Resurrection. Neither kind of knowledge, however,

9 "Whitman and Tennyson," *Nation and Athenaeum*, XL (December 18, 1926), 426.

is revealed to Eliot's Quester. The Borgesian note Eliot supplied for this passage adds considerable diabolical irony to the Whitman-Christ intersection: "The following lines were stimulated by the account of one of the Antarctic expeditions (I forget which, but I think one of Shackleton's): it was related that the party of explorers, at the extremity of their strength, had the constant delusion that there was *one more member* than could actually be counted" (italics Eliot's). The apparition of a saving dialectical third may be a "delusion," depending on the explorer's strength. At the extremity of his powers, the poet hallucinates, or receives in vision, the ghostly presence of another, someone who has also made the journey. In straining toward a centering point at the world's upside-down apex, the poem resurrects the logos only to find a delusion and the specter of a precursor's more powerful and less reassuring knowledge of death. To recognize the uncanny companion would be "death" for the poem's identity quest.

The frozen Antarctic desert of frightening incertitude dramatically revisions the "shores of water" to which Whitman's companions led him to hear "the carol of death, and a verse for him I love." Whitman's thrush welcomes "The night in silence under many a star, / The ocean shore and the husky whispering wave whose voice I know." He knows the voice of the waves that drowned Lycidas, the voice of Christ, who walked upon them, and the voice of Shelley, who drifted over them while Keats's star beckoned. Now there is "many a star," an unnumbered, perhaps innumerable scattering of prophets and losses. Echoing proleptically the doomed voices of *The Waste Land*, the thrush sings of death "Over the dense-pack'd cities all and the teeming wharves and ways." Unlike Eliot, it exults: "I float this carol with joy to thee O death." That "bliss" in Whitman results from the association of death with the sea and "Dark mother," joyfully available in the wake of the father's demise. A narcissistic economy allows Whitman to play all the parts—son, father, and mother—and so to author his own voice. Yet, one might argue that such narcissism is at least partially left behind with the lilacs and star as the voice in Whitman is a "tallying chant," an "echo arous'd" in his soul. It is a paratactic song that differs from the origin it commemorates.

Whereas Whitman's "Dark mother" whispers death to her grateful child, Eliot's mothers bewail the slaughter of sons: "What is that sound high in the air / Murmur of maternal lamentation." From the allusion to Christ the narrative moves, via the cries of Jerusalem's daughters and the mourning of Mary before the cross, to the contemporary butchering of the "hooded hordes" in war, a multiplication of the previous "hooded" walker into a swarm of sacrificial victims whose resurrection is not as certain as that of the armies of Israel in Ezekiel. (Whitman had also turned from his thrush's song to "panoramas of visions" of "armies" and "battle-corpses".) The poet-Quester reassumes the martyr's cross, the negative theology of Saint Narcissus and Saint Sebastian, and elicits from the mother a lament that also punishes her. Whereas Whitman identifies with the mother on his way to a non-Platonic Eros of death, Eliot's protagonist redoubles his identification with son and father and exhibits his pain in such a way as to inflict it on the mother. She is to replace the threatening women of previous sections, offering a Virgin Mother who is the agency of the Son's return to his Identity in the Father. Resentment of woman's failure to bring man to the sublime leads to her division into fair and dark ladies and to man's regression back to the son whose mother first taught him the virtues of virginity. This division of emotions appears in the myths behind the poem. The legends of Daphnis and Adonis tell of men doomed by love's conflicts. Frazer, in the volumes cited by Eliot, recounts it: "The dispute between the two goddesses of love and death was settled by Zeus, who decreed that Adonis should abide with Persephone in the under world for one part of the year, and with Aphrodite in the upper world for another part."[10] Eliot reintroduces this tragic shuttling in his poem, which becomes a lament for the torn male whose ritual deaths reenact a romantic and sexual allegory. Woman is divided between Aphrodite, Venus, the Muse of creation, and the hyacinth girl, on the one hand, and on the other, Persephone, Belladonna, and the lady of mortal situations. The Virgin Mother saves the Son from this living death-in-love by recalling him to his higher duty to the Father. The Quester to the Perilous Chapel was supposed to revive the king and the land by, among other things, his intercourse with a queenly lady. He was also required to puzzle out a riddle, thus linking in Eliot's synthesizing mind the potency of love and the power to make the fragments cohere. The Christian Mother ascends to her throne by promising access to the divine and protection from its paternal anger. She represents a spiritual regeneration that does not require investment in the physical female Other. She is Union without previous violation, creation without disturbance of identity. The orthodox Virgin lures the man whose powers fail him and who sees his impotence as the wound inflicted by mortal woman.

The Virgin Mary (and later, Dante's Beatrice) transfigures the ancient Mother Goddess whom Frazer treats in his survey of the dying and reviving gods. As Cybele she figures in the myths of Attis, "a fair young shepherd" alternately described as Cybele's lover and her son. The priests of Attis were self-emasculated, ritually repeating their god's mutilation—again alternately

10 Sir James Frazer, *The New Golden Bough*, ed. Theodor H. Gaster (New York, 1959), 342.

described as the result of a boar's attack and as a self-inflicted wound. The goddess' month of arrival was April, commemorated in a spring festival. Attis' flower was the violet, sprung from his blood as were anemones from Adonis and hyacinths from Hyacinthus (all flowers repeatedly mentioned in Eliot's poems). The priests of Attis underwent a gruesome ceremony that could not have escaped Eliot's Jacobean eye: "Wrought up to the highest pitch of religious excitement they dashed the severed portions of themselves against the image of the cruel goddess. These broken instruments of fertility were afterwards reverently wrapt up and buried in the earth or in subterranean chambers sacred to Cybele, where, like the offering of blood, they may have been deemed instrumental in recalling Attis to life and hastening the general resurrection of nature, which was then bursting into leaf and blossom in the vernal sunshine."[11] A crueler April is scarcely to be imagined. The ambiguous kinship of Cybele and her son-lover, the ascetic mutilation of the priests, the idea that the painful rending of the creative instrument is instrumental to a resurrection—these have their corollaries in Eliot's poetics of dismemberment. The Hanged God to whom Eliot alludes early in the poem was in fact played by one of Attis' priests at his springtime rite. Eliot's notes associate this god explicitly with the tarot's Hanged Man and with the hooded figure of Christ in the passage on the journey to Emmaus.

The uncanny "third" who always walks beside, tracing the path of displacement, is therefore also a castration figure, imaging the poet's delusion of "one more member" both lost and restored. The preoccupation in Eliot's verse through *The Waste Land* with castration and other forms of impotence and sterility is necessarily matched by a quest for the logos, for a revealed truth, as the renunciation of woman for the Virgin cuts man off from the mundane in hopes of the divine. As the rituals of Attis attest, castration operates strategically to reaffirm the authority of what is lamented. It is a recuperative strategy, the antidotal gathering of the text's *sparagmos*, the re-memberment of Osiris' limbs. The argument has been made by Derrida in his dispute with phallogocentrism.

> The determination of the proper, of the law of the proper and of *economy* leads back, therefore, to castration as truth, to the figure of woman as a figure of castration *and* of truth. Of castration as truth, which does not at all mean, as one might tend to believe, that we are led back to truth as essential dislocation and irreducible parcelling. On the contrary, castration is what contracts . . . to bring the phallus, the signifier, the letter of the fetish back to their oikos, their familiar dwelling, their proper place. In this

11 *Ibid.*

sense castration-truth is the opposite, the very antidote, of parcelling. . . . Because of castration, the phallus always remains in place in the transcendental topology we spoke of above, where it is indivisible and thus indestructible, like the letter which *takes its place*. . . . The difference I am interested in here is that the lack has no place in dissemination—a formula to be understood however you will.[12]

The economies of castration and elegy coincide in their affirmation by dislocation, their centering through lament. Always in place when eulogized, the missing truth has the letter (as the precursor has the new poet) take its place, usurps it in a way that confirms it, and supplants it without changing the metaphysical security of its site.

Formally, *The Waste Land* parcels, divides, and scatters, but it does so according to the elegiac economy, remembering at the level of its "transcendental topology," in "the heart of light, the silence," the unities it laments: father, god, mother, lover, poet, phallus, language, civilization, self. Each is parceled out in the poem as if in a self-inflicted ritual wounding that hopes to turn this blood, like Whitman's, into "Death's outlet song of life." With every slash of the pen the priest-poet "murders" and exalts his signifying deities, placing himself upon the altar where both he and his text are dismembered. As sacred dismemberment the text burns to recover its loss and is thus not to be categorized by Derrida's "dissemination," which continues its dispersions of meaning beyond the boundaries set by rituals of recovery. There is no Neitzschean pleasure in the scattering of truth that Eliot feels and that he must repeat in his criticism of the words he inherits. Eliot's elegy participates in the dialectical scheme, though it fails, in the end, to produce a star. Dissemination is the fate it courts and resists, negative capability the final stance to which it falteringly aspires.

The "maternal lamentation" sounds as the cry of the Source for this *sparagmos* of the son. It bewails the loss of authority and order in their historical, social, and material incarnations, the "Falling towers" of the self-wounded city-centers of Western civilization. Their destruction merges with the crucifixion of the martyr, and negative theology extends its logic to the catastrophic purgation now visited on what culture has erected. If the son's masochism means to punish the mother, it is for urging him to sublimation, to the route of metaphorical substitution that ends with taking self-inflicted pain for the love of another. From the image of the maternal voice that is made to weep for the wounded sons, we shift in the following stanza to the

12 Jacques Derrida, "The Purveyor of Truth," *Yale French Studies*, No. 52 (1975), 52, 62–63.

last of the poem's dark ladies. She is woman in her place as lover and wife, the son's supposed opportunity for new life. She is a nightmare, whose most ordinary acts inspire terror and despair.

> A woman drew her long black hair out tight
> And fiddled whisper music on those strings
> And bats with baby faces in the violet light
> Whistled, and beat their wings
> And crawled head downward down a blackened wall
> And upside down in air were towers
> Tolling reminiscent bells that kept the hours
> And voices singing out of empty cisterns and exhausted wells.

These lines were reworked from manuscript material dating back at least to 1914. The source fragment, included in the now published drafts of the poem, has its narrator undertake a quest through night and "violet air," seeking a saving "word" (WLFS, 112–15). Suddenly, among his "Gathered strange images" he encounters a woman combing and fiddling complacently. Afflicted "by some mental blight / Yet of abnormal powers," a man appears creeping "down a wall," searching either to find or escape the depth of his relation to women. The narrator gathers one last image of a "deaf mute swimming deep below the surface / Knowing neither up nor down," "deaf mute" having been substituted for a deleted "blind man." This man's quest for meaning takes him through a spiritual dark night in which women induce fear rather than beatitude, drowning him in a "fixed confusion" of solipsism. The handling of this scenario in "What the Thunder Said" obscures the presence of the man, but retains the "towers," "reminiscent bells," and "empty cisterns and exhausted wells" that begin to stir recollections of Browning's "'Childe Roland to the Dark Tower Came,'" important to the poem's next stanza. It is as if Eliot drew all his dark ladies out tight into an ultimate nightmare condensation and then bade them farewell.

Having passed this trial, the Quester finds himself "In this decayed hole among the mountains" (perhaps Lausanne), where rises the Chapel Perilous, bathed in a "faint moonlight" amidst "tumbled graves." Like Browning's "squat turret, blind as the fool's heart," it is empty, "has no windows, and the door swings"—the phallogocentric tower drained of its inseminating core. With this chapel and Browning, Eliot marks the fusion of the quest poem and the elegy. By this superimposition of poetic stances Eliot detects the quest within the elegy and the elegy within the quest. With Milton's "uncouth Swain," each seeks to go "Tomorrow to fresh Woods, and Pastures new." This final pastoral bliss eventually ends up as Browning's "stubbed ground, once a wood, / Next a marsh, it would seem, and now mere earth / Desperate and done with," and Eliot's waterless mountain desert. Childe Roland, too, crosses a fearful land with bats, a river, and a baby's shriek.[13] Like the protagonist of *The Waste Land* he quests in repetition, retracing the precursors.

> "The Band"—to wit,
> The knights who to the Dark Tower's search addressed
> Their steps—that just to fail as they, seemed best,
> And all the doubt was now—should I be fit?

Roland's plain also gives way "All round to mountains," where the tower sits. Eliot's "towers, / Tolling reminiscent bells" retoll Browning's: "it tolled / Increasing like a bell. Names in my ears / Of all the lost adventurers my peers." These dead men do tell tales. Bloom reads this moment as Roland/ Browning's climactic *apophrades*: "What he *sees* is the place of trial, scene of his true ordeal, which is not by landscape, but by the return of his precursors."[14] So Eliot has *his* fathers ranged round in his ascetic's Sinai—Milton, Shelley, Whitman, and Browning playing the band to his own Childe Roland. "Tolling reminiscent bells" becomes a metaphor of intertextual retuning. The graves of Eliot's elegiac predecessors tumble around him, and their voices sing from the empty spaces of time. Roland sees his band "in a sheet of flame," as Dante had seen Arnaut Daniel. "Dauntless," Roland raises horn to lips to blow his own belated trumpeting: "'Childe Roland to the Dark Tower Came.'" For Eliot "Only a cock stood on the roof tree / Co co rico co co rico," hoping to announce the departure of night's evil spirits and the coming of day. Bloom eloquently tries to convince us that Browning achieves a transumptive prophecy that turns belatedness into strength and vision. Eliot's cock cry mocks this prophecy, repeating a meaningless sound of time's measure. No more than the hermit thrush can it sing a natural song that will harmonize the unnatural relations of people or language.

In its quest, the poem reads the leaves of its predecessors and finds an insoluble riddle: the apparenlty successful agon of a previous writer with (poetic) death spells doom for the anxious new poet, while a liberating critique of a past master's mode of transcendence likewise ends in "dry sterile thunder without rain." But if we invoke here, as before, the gap that separates the figure of the poet from the poet's figures—his assemblage of different

---

13 See Martin Puhvel, "Reminiscent Bells in *The Waste Land*," *English Language Notes*, II (1965), 286–87.

14 Harold Bloom, *A Map of Misreading* (New York, 1975), 114. Bloom's essay on Browning's "Childe Roland" reads like a displaced commentary on *The Waste Land*.

voices—then we may read of an intertextual identity that offsets the lament for original life. *The Waste Land* would exorcise the metaphysics of a recuperated poetic identity that it finds in Milton, Shelley, and Whitman. It does so, however, precisely by reading them romantically: they turn out to be the kinds of created things that can never satisfy human desire, although desire goes on looking to human relations or poetry for a life they cannot give.

The last rejoinder to those siren songs "singing out of empty cisterns and exhausted wells" comes in the word of the thunder, a primal image of voice that might resolve the cacophony of belated and mutilated tongues by returning to the originating Word. Elegies conventionally turn upon the disparity between the metaphors of natural regeneration and the untimely lives led by people, and here we once more leave behind the model of seasonal rejuvenation. The "damp gust" may or may not bring rain, and it ceases to matter, since the genealogy of the soul knows no such mechanical covenant. A life lived in representation "dies" and "grows" otherwise. Lycidas must be raised by Christ, and Shelley bitterly observes that, while the idealized Keats may be "unquenchably the same,"

> *We* decay
> Like corpses in a charnel: fear and grief
> Convulse us and consume us day by day,
> And cold hopes swarm like worms within our living clay.
>
> (ll. 348–51).

Substituting thunder for Shelley's projected star, Eliot leads us into the strange temporality of reinterpretation. Each time the thunder speaks its identical word, it receives a reading as an echo aroused in the poet's soul. The father's logos becomes the occasion of the son's introspection, and these lines of the poem speak in a lyric and dramatic voice virtually unheard in the previous sections. A poetic gathering of repressed materials occurs following the encounter with Romanticism. The voices of "Prufrock" and "Gerontion" resemble the form of address here, as the passing beyond the logocentric quest is glimpsed when the words of the father and son participate in a revisionary dialogue that opens the way to other explorations.

The thunder would seem at first to be the essential sign of metaphysical and anthropological nostalgia. *Da* is a primary term in the hypothetical root diction of Indo-European. Hugh Kenner has written an excellent account of the philological impetus to this maneuver and of its dependence on two centuries of scholarship and philosophical speculation.[15] A former student of

---

15 Hugh Kenner, *The Pound Era* (Berkeley, 1971), 109–10.

Sanskrit, Eliot replays the scholar's quest for an original speech. With this assimilation of the ancestral voice, *The Waste Land* emerges as not only what Pound called the longest poem in English, but also the oldest, reversing the temporality that had defined it as either belated or radically modern. It now appears to be the earliest poem of the first authoritative voice. The words and names of fathers (Da-da?) have been ingathered and here counsel the son who has fled from both mother and lover-wife. In these thundering annunciations the elegized dead, now innumerable compound ghosts, answer the Quester's plea. Even in this oracular origin, though, revelation remains of language and within its disturbing genealogical economy. The voice of the thunder, enunciated from an invisible source in the night, echoes at the threshold separating nature and culture, involving the human and mutable in the divine and eternal. The Origin speaks in code, a word single yet disseminated, requiring the supplementary interpretative gloss of philologist, poet, and person.

"DA / *Datta*: what have we given?" Data and inherited artifacts, certainly, but what actual self-sacrifice has there been in this *sparagmos* of culture? Identity has been held in reserve throughout the poem, shored up by ruins: it could well be said that it is the fear of radically surrendering oneself to the other that paralyzes the poem in its antiromanticism. Eliot had written in "Tradition and the Individual Talent" of the poet's need to "surrender of himself as he is at the moment to something which is more valuable," the procurement of the "consciousness of the past" (SE, 6–7). Much of the time what Eliot surrenders is parts of himself—unlawful desires—whose exclusion would shore up the logos. In the following lines a more authentic self-dissemination is figured.

> The awful daring of a moment's surrender
> Which an age of prudence can never retract
> By this, and this only, we have existed

This reimagination of the Fall exhibits the paradox that the timeless moment is the beginning of history, an origin of existence in a difference that can never be retracted. Eliot will come back to this scene, already an advance on the nostalgia of the hyacinth garden, when he returns to the garden in "Burnt Norton." The language is also reminiscent of the phrase "In memory only, reconsidered passion," from "Gerontion," only now the poet begins to move, however unwillingly, away from this projection of Eden into the past, looking to the life such surrenders of identity enable. Such moments are "not to be found in our obituaries" or in last wills and testaments "broken by the lean solicitor." Those three forms parallel the elegy as texts of loss and inade-

quate retrieval; they stand for the kind of text *The Waste Land* has, ambivalently, been—a memorial to absent life—and point the way toward a reconciliation with language's entombment of any logocentrism. *Four Quartets*
will find "Every poem an epitaph."

Of course, it is a very fine line that tries to separate nostalgia for a figural
origin from a use of representation that works from the knowledge that writing requires "death" or from a textual practice that explores the possibilities
time and mutability offer. Readers will recognize in Eliot's lines a Romantic
theory of language. While deriding Shelley's "Defence of Poetry," Eliot sin-
gles out for praise "the magnificent image" of the imagination as a "fading
coal" (UPUC, 93). Shelley's poet awaits the annunciation of "some invisible
influence, like an inconstant wind," to awaken him from forgetfulness and
poetic death. All poetry then becomes elegy: "Could this influence be dura-
ble in its original purity and force, it is impossible to predict the greatness of
the results; but when composition begins, inspiration is already on the decline, and the most glorious poetry that has ever been communicated to the
world is probably a feeble shadow of the original conception of the poet. . . .
For Milton conceived the Paradise Lost as a whole before he executed it in
portions."[16] Surrender to the influence of precursors results in an ecstasy and
then a paradise lost, the poet's analogue to the lovers' moment in the garden.
Defense against such surrender only leads to a repression that reinscribes the
returned tropes of the repressed in displacements of representation that are
symptoms of daemonic possession. To dare a radical surrender means aban-
doning romantic nostalgia and negative theology for explorations of what
human relations and the mind's imaginings can beautifully, though not metaphysically, provide. Whom was Eliot addressing, after all, in his continual
insistence that art could not be a substitute for religion, if not himself?

"DA / *Dayadhvam*." This stanza on the necessity of sympathy presents that
emotion as a key to unlocking the prison of solipsistic identity and alienation, as Eliot's note referring to F. H. Bradley shows. Sympathy demands a
putting of oneself in the other's place—a surrender of perspective and an extension of imagination. (*Sympathy* is also the word Hawthorne reiterates as
the key to his critique of the New England mind in *The Scarlet Letter*.) Each
of the thunder's articulations receives its significance from a "personal" interpretation that supplements it with the context of a particular life, as well as
with the shards retrieved from culture's storehouse. Here the brief hope for
"a broken Coriolanus" offers another figure of the poet's exile from his

---

16 Percy Bysshe Shelley, "A Defence of Poetry," in Donald H. Reiman and Sharon B.
Powers (eds.), *Shelley's Poetry and Prose* (New York, 1977), 504.

homeland and of his family drama with a weak wife and a dominating widowed mother who eventually bends the traitorous son to her will. The loneliness, estrangement, and domestic strife of Coriolanus—along with his "royalist" disregard for common people—provide Eliot another transfiguration of his own condition, as we sympathize with (and thus revive) Coriolanus and the poet at the moment they themselves learn compassion's value. "The creation of a work of art," Eliot wrote in 1919, "consists in the process of transfusion of the personality, or in a deeper sense, the life, of the author into the character. This is a very different matter from the orthodox creation in one's own image. The ways in which the passions and desires of the creator may be satisfied in the work of art are complex and devious" (SE, 137). "Complex and devious" is the allusion to Coriolanus, and the "transfusion" runs from the character through the poet as well as vice versa. It reintroduces the agon with the mother, restaged in "Difficulties of a Statesman" (1931; "Mother / May we not be some time, almost now, together") and *The Family Reunion* (1937–1939). (Eliot's mother died in 1930.) A "broken Coriolanus" may be a humble martyr to duty, nation, and family, brought down from his isolate pride. Yet, we may also hear an accusation of lack of sympathy against the demanding mother, who wants to keep the son in her prison of sublimated love as she practices her own version of the rose garden strategy. Sympathy from her, a giving that frees man from the law, might revive him. The burial of the father only intensifies the unresolved struggle for understanding between son and mother, as the poet's desire for an independent identity clashes with his need for a loving recognition of himself.

"DA / *Damyata*." The final admonition to "control" evokes a return of nautical imagery, a highly charged condensation of voyages poetic and erotic. From the figure of son and mother we move to the new worlds aspired to by sons and lovers.

> The boat responded
> Gaily, to the hand expert with sail and oar
> The sea was calm, your heart would have responded
> Gaily, when invited, beating obedient
> To controlling hands

The manuscript shows this "would have" as an addition, edging through grammar into lament. This heart, the friend of the moment's surrender, the lady of so many situations, the poet himself, would have responded to controlling hands. Or the roles can be reversed, and the figures extended. There is a fault in the hands that create, the hands that choose, build, direct, the hands that write for the silent heart. The blame falls on the uncontrolled responses of souls who drown each other, unable to give the sympathy that keeps wrecked hearts afloat. Mere circumstance and accident are not sufficient explanations for the disaster. Milton had similarly absolved Neptune's sea from guilt for Lycidas' shipwreck.

> The air was calm, and on the level brine,
> Sleek Panope with all her sisters played.
> It was that fatal and perfidious Bark
> Built in th'eclipse, and rigg'd with curses dark,
> That sunk so low that sacred head of thine.

Shelley places the poet himself on the driven bark, emblem of the inadequacy of all human vehicles, including language, as transportation to eternity. They are "Built in th'eclipse," when the sun that stands for Truth, Presence, Vision, and God has been suddenly obscured, as if all linguistic constructions took place in the night of absences and blindness.[17] The vision of Eliot's seers has been eclipsed throughout the poem; if all Eliot's protagonists are one Quester for the Word, then what Tiresias *hears* in the thunder's "DA" is the substance of his own guilt in the darkening of language and love.

Attending to the task of interpreting the father's word in time and through himself, the narrator manages to steer to shore, still seeking his own "Genius." Deleted in the manuscript are indications that he has also left his loved one behind (WLFS, 79). The method of the final stanza of the poem breaks abruptly from that of the personal meditation spurred by the thunder, where allusion blended less obtrusively as lyric and elegy predominated. The poems to follow, such as *Ash Wednesday*, the Ariel poems, and the *Quartets*, will in fact develop the style explored in "What the Thunder Said." These last lines, however, circle back to the earlier style of startling *bricolage*. Once more the poet sets artifacts together in dazzling array, as if both to mock and to culminate his strategy. The archaeological poet returns, back from a lyrical death supervised by the thunder and with the accompaniment of Milton, Shelley, Whitman, and Browning. The poem has itself undergone an askesis, momentarily surrendering its earlier juxtaposition of references, leaving behind most of the texts and authors it had conspicuously relied upon. *The Waste Land* most often described is represented in the final stanza by characteristic fragments that echo the first sections of the poem, while the corpus of the elegy is buried again.

Yet, this discovery of the corpus yields no ultimate solution to the murder mystery. The poem ends in a flurry of multiplicity, torn between the ascen-

---

17 On the metaphor of the sun see Jacques Derrida, "White Mythology: Metaphor in the Text of Philosophy," *New Literary History*, XI (Autumn, 1974), 7–74.

sion from mortal ruin and the necessity of madness, death, and disorder. Eliot's poetic soul yearns to rise as far as those of his star-struck predecessors, while his heart recalls the failings that shadow this quest for the eternal. He would "at least set" his "lands in order," but this order turns out to be not that of a transcendental logos but that of the belated bricoleur's shoring of quotes against chaos, albeit performed with genius. Civilization continues to crash in a nursery rhyme tune, Arnaut Daniel burns in a sexual and poetic purgatory, Philomela longs for a metamorphosis into beauty, and Nerval's prince slumps lamentably at the broken tower of poetic tradition and potency. "Why then Ile fit you. Hieronymo's mad againe." Eliot, too, fits us into his revenge play of alien voices, inscribing a madness all the more disturbing because we cannot, any more than in *Hamlet*, separate actual dementia from demented playacting. The three "shantih" at the end tell us only that this has been a "piece" that passeth understanding.

Eliot concludes with what he elsewhere called the "oscillation . . . of secular philosophies between antithetical extremes." *Secular* means for Eliot a discourse without any Center to gather its broken images into Incarnate Truth. The passing away of that focal power of halting and evaluating oscillations initiates the elegy, a dirge for authority, love, and immortality. It will be the task of the *Quartets* to explore the Incarnation as metaphor of what empowers the reconciliation of "antithetical extremes," though the result will transfigure the intention. In the meantime, in the secular world of self, history, and writing, warring oppositions preside over Eliot's view of the poetic mind: "The human mind is perpetually driven between two desires, between two dreams each of which may be either a vision or a nightmare: the vision and nightmare of the material world, and the vision and nightmare of the immaterial. Each may be in turn, or for different minds, a refuge to which to fly, or a horror from which to escape. We desire and fear both sleep and waking; the day brings relief from the night, and the night brings relief from the day; we go to sleep as to death, and we wake to damnation." [18]

---

18 Quoted in John Baille and Hugh Martin (eds.), *Revelation* (London, 1937), 31–32.

PART FOUR

"EVERY POEM AN EPITAPH"
Transfiguration in *Four Quartets*

When you have the words for it, the "thing" for which the words had to be found has disappeared, replaced by a poem. What you start from is nothing so definite as an emotion, in any ordinary sense; it is still more certainly not an idea. . . . [The poet] is oppressed by a burden which he must bring to birth in order to obtain relief. Or, to change the figure of speech, he is haunted by a demon, a demon against which he feels powerless, because in its first manifestation it has no face, no name, nothing; and the words, the poem he makes, are a kind of form of exorcism of this demon. In other words again, he is going to all that trouble, not in order to communicate with anyone, but to gain relief from acute discomfort; and when the words are finally arranged in the right way—or in what he comes to accept as the best arrangement he can find—he may experience a moment of exhaustion, of appeasement, of absolution, and of something very near annihilation, which is in itself indescribable. . . . I don't believe that the relation of a poem to its origins is capable of being more clearly traced.

"The Three Voices of Poetry"

CHAPTER 12

ENTRE DEUX GUERRES

Twenty years and the spring is over;
To-day grieves, to-morrow grieves,
Cover me over, light-in-leaves;
Golden head, black wing,
Cling, swing,
Spring, sing,
Swing up into the apple-tree.

"New Hampshire"

In the concluding confessional section of "East Coker," Eliot looks back at "the years of *l'entre deux guerres*," and finds them "Twenty years largely wasted." The failure to produce a work of satisfying coherence has plainly discouraged the poet in Eliot. The effort to control language falters for two reasons. First, because the poet's identity changes through time, as do his words, and every attempt

> Is a wholly new start, and a different kind of failure
> Because one has only learnt to get the better of words
> For the thing one no longer has to say, or the way in which
> One is no longer disposed to say it.

Second, because this stuttering intensifies as the years complicate the emotions. "All poetry," wrote Eliot, "may be said to start from the emotions" (CC, 38). Time adds connotations to emotions through the context of their involvement, until emotions become a sedimented, overdetermined vocabulary of recollection, encumbering present speech and present emotion with the influences of other strains. Thinking of *Ash Wednesday*'s dream language, of the awkward formalities of *Murder in the Cathedral*, of the clumsy mixture of prophecy, lyric, and satire in *The Family Reunion*, Eliot sees that each venture

> Is a new beginning, a raid on the inarticulate
> With shabby equipment always deteriorating
> In the general mess of imprecision of feeling,
> Undisciplined squads of emotion.

The *Four Quartets* are made from the emotions generated by Eliot's experiences "entre deux guerres," though the roots run deep past *The Waste Land* and back to childhood's waters. An awareness of the ventures of those middle years, and the effect they had on Eliot's recalling of his roots, is central to comprehending the pattern of his career. This is not the place for a comprehensive review, which has been performed by many critics. But on the way to a close look at the transfigurational poetics of the *Quartets*, these years can be scanned for evidence of the stream, emotional and poetic, that runs through the geography of his work.

A fair estimate would be that they were years of great achievement. Editing the *Criterion*, Eliot involved himself in the affairs of the age.[1] His quarterly was a forum for Communists and Anglicans, poets and critics, artists, philosophers, and economists. As an editor at the Faber publishing house, he aided authors old and new. He continued to write reviews for numerous periodicals and began to lecture frequently. During this time Eliot wrote many of his finest essays: over a dozen on the English dramatists; studies of artists from Dante to Baudelaire, Pound, and Yeats; books on the literary criticism of English poets and on the "strange gods" of modern literature; and numerous reflections on education, the classics, and religion. This output startles when we remember the personal distress of those years: the ruinous marriage Eliot finally ended with a telegram across the Atlantic to his solicitor; the conversion to Anglicanism that cost him friends and aggravated his obsession with guilt and suffering; the estrangement from Pound; and of course, the sorrow of a poet unable, for whatever reasons, to practice his craft regularly and successfully. The *Quartets* transfigure those years, finding in their accumulated emotional disturbance the only inspiration Eliot could count on for writing poetry. In his effort at comprehension he reaches back farther into the past, to America, his childhood, to remembrances of native shores and promises. These reflections, in "Animula," "New Hampshire," "Cape Ann," "Burnt Norton," *The Family Reunion*, and "The Dry Salvages," were occasioned by a train of events.

His mother's death in 1930 formally closed one stage of Eliot's family drama. *Ash Wednesday* (1928–1930) is dedicated "To My Wife," but its disturbed prayer to the Lady and the Virgin Mother mixes confusedly the emotions of the son, the lover, and the husband. It announces the Eliotic quest to restore "With a new verse the ancient rhyme. Redeem / The time. Redeem / The unread vision in the higher dream." The poem's turning from "The in-

---

1 On the *Criterion* years see the essential study by John Margolis, *T. S. Eliot's Intellectual Development* (Chicago, 1972).

firm glory of the positive hour" leads to an ambiguous dismemberment and to a troubled reconciliation through the "Lady of silences," ending strangely with "Grace to the Mother / For the Garden / Where all love ends." Turning now from, now toward, his ladies, the speaker whirls in the silence of the lost Word and speaks the word only. Excessive self-concern corrupts the askesis of this willing martyr. He is too quick to renounce the sensuous vision of the "slotted window bellied like the fig's fruit." Love of the Lady takes the poet not just upward to the divine, as Beatrice had guided Dante, but to other earthly ladies, maternal and marital, the lower dream shadowing the higher. Though he clings to Augustine's example and does not "wish to wish these things," the speaker's desiring memory recalls in Romantic fashion the images of childhood on the coast Gloucester and the thoughts of a love somewhere lost.

> And the lost heart stiffens and rejoices
> In the lost lilac and the lost sea voices
> And the weak spirit quickens to rebel
> For the bent golden-rod and the lost sea smell
> Quickens to recover
> The cry of quail and the whirling plover
> And the blind eye creates
> The empty forms between the ivory gates
> And smell renews the salt savour of the sandy earth

After this powerful, beautiful outburst comes an almost whining prayer, a liturgical invocation that passively seeks annunciation. The concern with the speaker's own agony grates, and he reaches a stillness more of exhaustion than beatitude. Encounter with the agony of others, and an active reformation of the self's character, are missing, still a decade away.

In 1932 Eliot goes to America for the first time since 1915. There he resolves to separate from his wife and visits New Hampshire, probably with Emily Hale, the mystery lady of his middle years who will later accompany him to the rose garden at Burnt Norton.[2] The anguish of those months can be read throughout *After Strange Gods*, especially in the choice of texts by Mansfield, Joyce, and Lawrence. "All turn on the same theme of disillusion. In Miss Mansfield's story a wife is disillusioned about her relations with her husband; in the others a husband is disillusioned about his relations with his wife"

---

2 Helen Gardner, *The Composition of "Four Quartets"* (New York, 1978), 35–36. Evidently Eliot met Emily Hale in 1913 in Boston. They exchanged some two thousand letters, now sequestered at Princeton University until the year 2020. See also Lyndall Gordon, *Eliot's Early Years* (New York, 1977), 55–56.

(ASG, 35).[3] As he had found it two years earlier in Dante's *Vita Nuova*, so Eliot now finds the "philosophy of disillusion" in modern treatments of love's failed sublimity. Always attracted and repulsed by Lawrence's "sexual morbidity" and his diagnosis of "the living death of modern material civilization," Eliot breaks down in face of *Lady Chatterly's Lover*, a book he would later defend in court. "The author of that book seems to me to have been a very sick man indeed" (ASG, 61). Later, he recanted that opinion and his book, turning the adjective "sick" upon his own condition at that time.

Back in England, Eliot began his career as a dramatist with *The Rock*. Its choruses rehearse Eliot's late poetic voice, the phrases and themes that will be repeated through "Little Gidding." Eliot returns from the personal turnings of *Ash Wednesday* to the turnings of the world, adopting once again the prophet's stance, exhibiting however ineptly that concern with worldly affairs evident in *The Waste Land*. Here is London again, where "The desert is in the heart of your brother." History and inheritance are a burden, "And all that is ill you may repair if you walk together in humble repentance, expiating the sins of your fathers." The prophet Nehemiah appears to rebuild wasted Jerusalem, where "Usury, Lust and Power" reign, having forgotten the timeless moment of the Incarnation. And askesis is reminded that

> Man is joined spirit and body
> And therefore must serve as spirit and body.
> Visible and invisible, two worlds meet in Man;
> Visible and invisible must meet in His Temple;
> You must not deny the body.

Eliot ends with a prayer to the Greater Light that will shine once more at the beginning of "Burnt Norton," to be later merged into the fire that refines.

Murder in the Cathedral (1935) puts the speaker of *Ash Wednesday* and the chorus of *The Rock* in a drama that further tests their souls' worth. Here Eliot analyzes that penchant for martyrdom apparent from his earliest poems. The problem Becket faces replays the ambivalence in *The Waste Land* over guilt for the Fisher King's death. Again a figure of real authority dies, and from one perspective he is said to be guilty of his own fall. It is a murder mystery, according to the Fourth Knight: "What I have to say may be put in the form of a question: *Who killed the Archbishop?*" He answers himself in a mockery of courtroom rhetoric. "Need I say more? I think, with these facts before you, you will unhesitatingly render a verdict of Suicide while of Unsound Mind."

---

3 Samuel Hynes notes this autobiographical disturbance of the moralist's objectivity in "The Trials of a Christian Critic," in David Newton-De Molina (ed.), *The Literary Criticism of T. S. Eliot* (London, 1977), 64–88.

Eliot's Becket joins the fraternal order of the priests of Attis. At stake is the ascetic imperative itself, the self-murdering in dialectical service of the good. The play questions the saint's search for martyrdom, implying that dialectical recovery may be thwarted by its own desires. This is Becket's new, unexpected fourth temptation. The First Tempter lures with the bait of past pleasures, friendship with the king, flutes, viols, appleblossoms, "wit and wine and wisdom." Becket dismisses this "springtime fancy," though "The impossible is still temptation . . . walking a dead world, / So that the mind may not be whole in the present." The Second Tempter urges him to grasp the presence of power by submission to the king: "Power is present. Holiness hereafter." With temporal power Becket could "arrest disorder" and guide a secular reformation. Becket rejects this (in words that recall Eliot's critique of Irving Babbitt's humanitarian liberalism), demanding a center in the timeless as foundation for temporal change. The Third Tempter, who would have Becket join a conspiracy against the king, offers the future: "We expect the rise of a new constellation." Past, present, and future have all had their try at Becket's soul, but his victory turns into another temptation, out of time: "Who are you? I expected Three visitors, not four."

The Fourth Tempter urges him to use eternity for himself, to make of his death an immortality of his desires.

> You hold the skein: wind, Thomas, wind
> The thread of eternal life and death . . .
> Saint and Martyr rule from the tomb . . .
> Seek the way of martyrdom, make yourself the lowest
> On earth, to be high in heaven.

Thomas mourns, "Is there no enduring crown to be won?" He wants to control time and his image in it. He resists and delivers a speech that begins the process toward *Four Quartets*.

> The last temptation is the greatest treason:
> To do the right deed for the wrong reason.
> The natural vigour in the venial sin
> Is the way in which our lives begin.
> Thirty years ago, I searched all the ways
> That lead to pleasure, advancement and praise.
> Delight in sense, in learning and in thought,
> Music and philosophy, curiosity,
> The purple bullfinch in the lilac tree,
> The tiltyard skill, the strategy of chess,
> Love in the garden, singing to the instrument,

Were all the things equally desirable.
Ambition comes when early force is spent
And when we find no longer all things possible.
Ambition comes behind and unobservable.
Sin grows with doing good.

Becket has known them all already, known them all. The autobiographical cast of this remembrance is unmistakable, as it gathers previous symbols from Eliot's poetry in the retrospective mode that dominates the *Quartets*. Eliot discovers the gap between intention and act, creator and artifact, which he will accept when he retires from the "occupation" of "the saint" at the end of "The Dry Salvages." His self-martyrdom has been self-willed for self's sake; the submission to impersonal orders has been a strategy of resurrection, even perverse glorification. Becket must know if his martyrdom is self-willed or God's will. His dilemma repeats in different terms that of *The Waste Land* and the criticism. Is the tradition or authority submitted to really an autonomous, transcendent one or only the make-believe god of a pagan ritual?

The archbishop follows his resolution with a Christmas sermon. The saint's martyrdom adheres to the figural scheme as a type of Christ's suffering. Becket's exegesis of the Incarnation and Resurrection will be a gloss on his own death, doubling Eliot's reading of himself through Becket. The lesson is that "a Christian martyrdom is no accident. . . . A martyrdom is never the design of man; for the true martyr is he who has become the instrument of God, who has lost his will in the will of God, not lost it but found it, for he has found the freedom in submission to God." The martyr becomes the transparence of God's word, reversing the Fall into representation. He is the perfect poet. God writes history with his instruments; martyrs and poets act through submission to the tradition. Becket makes the most extreme argument for a unification with the Logos, picturing an ideal impersonality (or emasculation) raised into identity with the Transcendent Will. Unfortunately, the procedure works poorly for poets, as literature follows representation's errancies instead of Providence, and tradition is a pale imitation of divine authority.[4] The martyr suffers but one death, but the poet dies in every line. "Every phrase and every sentence is an end and a beginning, / Every poem an epitaph" (LG, V). Becket's philosophy rephrases the line from Dante that Eliot often quoted: "E'n la sua volontade è nostra pace" ("And in his will is our peace"; *Paradiso*, canto 3).

4 The point is made by Michael T. Beehler, in "*Murder in the Cathedral*: The Counter-sacramental Play of Signs," *Genre*, X (Fall, 1977), 329–35. Despite my sympathy with Beehler's perspective in his essays on Eliot's dramas, it must be said that they often reduce deconstruction to a formula for finding "absence" and are not the best examples of poststructuralist prose style.

As Becket represents the ideal dialectical hero, so the chorus speaks for humankind, who can bear only so much reality. They, too, borrow emotions and images from Eliot's repertoire and provide the counterpoint to Becket's grandeur. They "wander in a land of barren boughs" and cry out for a cleansing of "the world that is wholly foul." Between Becket and the chorus plays the oscillation of a negative ascension to Eternity and a wandering in exile from God's presence. The knights and priests act a comic denouement that falls back into Eliot's social satire once Becket's tale has been told. There is nowhere to go after this saint's apotheosis, except back into a world where such intersections are rare and where the resolution of Becket's dilemma remains inconclusive. The plays and poetry to follow gradually descend from Becket's height, further humiliating the pretension to oneness with God's will and looking sharply at the pattern of human wills.

The *Four Quartets* are sometimes discussed as if they were written as a whole, despite the fact that "Burnt Norton" was made from excised portions of *Murder in the Cathedral* and followed by *The Family Reunion*. There was no intention in Eliot's mind of writing three more corresponding poems until the war made theater impossible.[5] "Burnt Norton" moves through the illusions of lost presence.

> Quick now, here, now, always—
> Ridiculous the waste sad time
> Stretching before and after.
>
> (BN, V)

The emotion exorcised here is nostalgia for "our first world" of innocence, as children's laughter and visiting lovers refill the drained pool "with water out of sunlight." In section 2 the theophilosophical analogue to this vision is imaged by "the still point of the turning world." It is a mistake, I think, to read this passage as simply a mystical account of metaphysical vision in the Christian sense. In a commentary on the fragments of Heraclitus from which Eliot draws his first epigraph for "Burnt Norton" ("But although the logos is common to all, the majority of people live as though they had an understanding peculiarly their own"), Heidegger argues that the logos of Heraclitus names the gathering of being in emergence, not an unchanging Center or mimesis of the Same.[6] It is not logic or a truth beyond nature or thought as opposed to existence or an *Aufhebung* of differences. This logos in its emergence (and this is the act of the poetic logos as well) produces being as the

5 Gardner, *The Composition of "Four Quartets,"* 15, 18n.
6 For background see Merrell D. Clubb, "The Heraclitean Element in Eliot's *Four Quartets*," *Philological Quarterly*, XL (January, 1961), 19–33.

thoughtful gathering into appearance of relations within nature and its history.

> *Physis* and *logos* are the same. . . . If we take the basic meaning of *logos* as gathering and togetherness, we must note the following:
>   Gathering is never a mere driving-together and heaping-up. It maintains in a common bond the conflicting and that which tends apart. It does not let them fall into haphazard dispersion. In thus maintaining a bond, the *logos* has the character of permeating power, of *physis*. It does not let what it holds in its power dissolve into an empty freedom from opposition, but by uniting the opposites maintains the full sharpness of their tension. . . . *Logos* in the New Testament does not, as in Heraclitus, mean the being of the essent, the gathering together of the conflicting; it means *one* particular essent, namely the son of God.

Christ as logos, he goes on to say, is "the herald, the messenger, who hands down commands and commandments. . . . He is the logos of redemption, of eternal life. . . . A whole world separates all this from Heraclitus."[7]

Eliot's attempt to identify the Heraclitean logos of of his epiphanic moments and of his poetic gatherings with the Logos of Christianity does not work: "And do not call it fixity, / Where past and future are gathered." An agon takes place in these moments between a desire for fixity and the recognition of the gathering differences that precede and exceed it. His invocation of a Christian Word cannot prevent the poem from continuing to follow the processes of gathering and emergence and not of the law.[8] Even Dante's vision at the end of the *Paradiso* becomes assimilated in Eliot to a Heraclitean reading that accentuates desiring motion rather than the unmoved mover. The rhetorical obeisance to the Christian logos misreads it to stand for an activity of thinking, writing, and representation inimical to it, borrowing its authority for an antithetical purpose. The gatherings of the figural imagination in *Four Quartets* accord more with Heraclitus and Heidegger than with the Gospel of John. But Eliot seems unable to accept this realization of an unlawful logos and so misreads Christianity and its mystical tradition as espousing in authorized form a logos peculiarly his own.

The corresponding sections of the other *Quartets* all move steadily away from orthodox revelation, into time, loss, and the human world of limits:

---

7 Martin Heidegger, *Introduction to Metaphysics*, trans. Ralph Manheim (New Haven, 1959), 130–31, 134–35.

8 Morris Weitz concludes otherwise, thinking that Eliot succeeds in transforming Heraclitus into Christian dogma. See Weitz, "T. S. Eliot: Time as a Mode of Salvation," in Bernard Bergonzi (ed.), *"Four Quartets": A Casebook* (London, 1969), 138–52. Weitz's Eliot is a Neoplatonist.

"For the pattern is new in every moment / And every moment is a new and shocking / Valuation of all we have been" (EC, II). "The Dry Salvages" echoes "the sudden illumination," only to realize that

> We had the experience but missed the meaning,
> And approach to the meaning restores the experience
> In a different form, beyond any meaning
> We can assign to happiness.

(DS, II)

This restoration is not of sameness, not an approach to eternal presence, but a re-storing and re-calling that alters form and grants unforeseen meanings transfiguring happiness. "Now we discover that the moments of agony . . . are likewise permanent," known best not in self-flagellation but "In the agony of others, nearly experienced, / Involving ourselves," the agony of families, lovers, wives, and husbands (DS, II). As we shall see later on, the sudden illumination of presence becomes in section 2 of "Little Gidding" the "compound ghost" fashioned of pentecostal fire, figure of the end of a history (poetic and otherwise) thought in a sequence of isolable identities.

These variations on the recapture of the past that came after "Burnt Norton" go by way of the intervening work, *The Family Reunion*, which tells the story of Harry's homecoming to the family at Wishwood.[9] This Jamesian play of Freudian traumas and wish fulfillments seeks a cause for the fall from the rose garden. Aided by Greek tragedy and the doctrine of Original Sin, Eliot shifts the blame unconvincingly to the parents. It is hard to make sense of the play or to fathom its place in Eliot's career without asking to what degree it serves as a talking cure for the poet, an exorcism of his daemons. The undisciplined emotions of the dramatist disjoint the play's argument and inform its elements. Harry had married against his family's wishes and gone into an eight-year exile with a nervous wife of suicidal tendencies. Loyal and miserable, he "Suffered from what they call a kind of repression." On a sea voyage his wife disappears overboard. Accident, suicide, or murder, the mystery is sustained, though Harry's words and those of his valet implicate him. The uncertainty of this guilt over the jettisoning of a wife inspires the play's action, yet seems obviously psychological and in excess of the play's facts. As early as the period 1917 through 1919, Eliot hallucinated through Poe the death of a woman who will not, in the realm of moral consciousness, lie still.

---

9 My reading of the play is indebted to C. L. Barber's ground-breaking essay, "Strange Gods at T. S. Eliot's *The Family Reunion*," in Leonard Unger (ed.), *T. S. Eliot: A Selected Critique* (New York, 1948), 415–43. See also Michael T. Beehler, "Troping the Topic: Disclosing the Circle of *The Family Reunion*," *Boundary 2*, VIII (Spring, 1980), 19–42.

> How steadfastly I should have mourned
> The sinking of so dear a head!
> Wer't not for dreams: a dream restores
> The always inconvenient dead.

(WLFS, 117)

More jovial, Sweeney in "Fragment of an Agon" merrily confides that

> Any man might do a girl in
> Any man has to, needs to, wants to
> Once in a lifetime, do a girl in.

At home Harry's mother, Amy, tries to reverse time and restore the past: "Please behave only / As if nothing had happened in the last eight years." Against her is set Aunt Agatha, the prophetess of the play, who asserts:

> everything is irrevocable.
> Because the past is irremediable,
> Because the future can only be built
> Upon the real past.

The Family Reunion moves away from redemption toward expiation, an active living in relationship to the past and loss that defers redemption as the choice of Another while the soul shoulders the burdens of temporality. As Harry puts it, echoing the first lines of "Burnt Norton," which are a gateway to the Light:

> I am the old house
> With the noxious smell and the sorrow before morning,
> In which all past is present, all degradation
> Is unredeemable.

These lines lead to the discovery that the children were not always laughing in the leaves, that "all seemed to be imposed upon us" by mother Amy. Harry had come home with "The instinct to return to the point of departure / And start again as if nothing had happened." He expresses the characteristic American innocence that believes in fresh beginnings and is haunted by ghosts. Eliot drew upon James's "The Jolly Corner" and Hawthorne's *The House of the Seven Gables* to strengthen his sense of the past, that ambivalence between new beginnings and inherited burdens that propels one in both exile and homecoming. Eliot had jettisoned his own wife during his homecoming to America, and his subsequent poems reveal an effort to make a new start and forge a reconciliation with the past.

A Mary awaits Harry, a childhood friend his mother had kept around in case Harry shook his wife. Mary's intuition tells him:

> You attach yourself to loathing
> As others do to loving: an infatuation
> That's wrong, a good that's misdirected. You deceive yourself
> Like the man convinced that he is paralyzed
> Or like the man who believes that he is blind
> While he still sees sunlight.

(We think of the deceptive status of blindness, and what it signifies, in *The Waste Land.*) She represents a fresh start and a new love, perhaps as Emily Hale did for Eliot. For Harry, though, spring is cold, "an evil time, that excites us with lying voices," as this debate repeats the opening paradoxes of *The Waste Land*. To Harry spring means blood sacrifices.

> Returning the ghosts of the dead
> Those whom the winter drowned
> Do not the ghosts of the drowned
> Return to land in the spring?
> Do the dead want to return?

The drowned male bodies of Lycidas and Phlebas symbolized the poet's troubled hopes of identity's resurrection. The drowned female body symbolizes a complicated twist on the first model of revival. Whereas woman had once taken the blame for the sailor-lover-poet's drowning (and language, too, was thus blamed for its seductions from propriety), her murder seeming then a salvation, she now becomes the floating signifier of the male's guilt. Her resurrection, unwanted, recalls the self that had loved her, the truth about that love, and the joint responsibility for the destruction of its promise. Through the identification of woman with language and the investment of writing, the return of the female body becomes the return of writing as risk, impropriety, wandering from home, the drifting of identities. In the character of loss the life of writing returns. Harry's love for Mary would be haunted by his dead wife, as each fresh start is haunted by what it repeats in the very act of erasure. Harry is tempted by Mary's faith, but the Eumenides intervene, halting this resolution of love and Christian philosophy. They are Harry's reality principles, demanding that he sublimate his pleasure in quest of a Higher Love—another way of fleeing the ghosts. The awful daring of a moment's surrender fades: "It was only a moment, it was only one moment / That I stood in sunlight and thought I might stay there." The narrowness, as well as the depth, of Eliot's poetry stems from this consistent conviction that joy always betrays us and that disillusionment yields a satisfaction "beyond any meaning / We can assign to happiness" (DS, III).

Seeking the source of unhappiness beyond him in the past, Harry asks "to know more about my father," who separated from an unhappy marriage to live abroad. We are told that Harry looks much like his father, that he resembles him in expression and gesture when he refuses to talk the family language to Amy. This identification moves Harry closer to the origin of his secret destiny, or so he believes. There he discovers his father's early adultery with Agatha. So passionate had that affair been that his father considered murdering Amy and was stopped only by Agatha's pleading for the yet unborn Harry. Harry has repeated his father in his relation to his own wife and become his father as the intimacy between himself and Agatha deepens. Now Harry's fate appears predetermined, "just part of some huge disaster, / Some monstrous mistake and aberration / Of all men, of the world, which I cannot put in order." The echo of Hamlet connects Eliot's work again with Shakespeare's drama of a living-dead father, adulterous queen, crazy mistress, and mad son. In response to what he saw as the lack of objective correlatives for Hamlet's emotions, Eliot provides the figures of the Eumenides to represent Harry's haunted soul. But the attempt ludicrously fails to divert our attention from the confusion of Harry's characterization. Eliot betrays his play, and himself, by insisting on the visible reality of the Eumenides. They are no more or less "real" than the ghost of Hamlet's father or the ghosts in James's *The Turn of the Screw*; yet, Eliot strives to give them a supernatural weight that would hold down the story's implications about the origin of Harry's obsessions. The return of the dead exceeds objective representation and is the ironic sign of objectivity's limits. Harry's mind is a continual family reunion of the living and dead, his "private puzzle" neither "simply outside" nor "simply inside." He berates language as inadequate, for language, too, has the original sin of falling from presence and authority at its source, where spoken intercourse adulterates visible partners.

The Eumenides had first stood for Harry's guilt. Now they remind him of deeper, repetitive stains.

> The shadow of something behind our meagre childhood,
> Some origin of wretchedness. Is that what they would show me?
> And now I want you to tell me about my father.

"There was no ecstasy" in his parents' marriage, but with Agatha, Harry's father surrendered to Edenic temptations. He stands for those who seek transcendence romantically, among hyacinths and roses. Agatha confesses, "There are hours when there seems to be no past or future, / Only a present moment of pointed light / When you want to burn." Sexual sublimity fades, no better a means of holding on to the eternal than writing. Saving Harry's life, Agatha becomes his "mother." Harry's sins are muted by the Original Sin that both extends and lightens his guilt. He has only repeated his father's crime and been an ignorant participant in a story written by others. "One had that part to play. . . . The book laid out, lines underscored, and the costume / Ready to be put on." Accepting the "burden of all the family," Harry enters with Agatha into a kind of trance as they walk into the timeless past together. He is and is not his father as times collapse in a knot of guilts, desires, and expiations.

> I was not there, you were not there, only our phantasms
> And what did not happen is as true as what did happen,
> O my dear, and you walked through the little door
> And I ran to meet you in the rose-garden.

Eliot and Freud agree that in the wish-strewn mind of the neurotic "what did not happen is as true as what did happen." Again, in Freud's words, Harry "fills in the gaps in individual truth with prehistoric truth; he replaces occurrences in his own life by occurrences in the life of his ancestors."[10]

In this phantasmal replay of the origin, Harry becomes his father, unites with his ideal mother, and experiences in imagination the bliss he will pay for forever in the economy of his psyche. He goes off to the Eliotic desert, a negative experience of divinity Agatha had counterposed to her experience of the "pointed light": "perhaps there is another kind, / I believe, across a whole Tibet of broken stones / That lie, fang up, a lifetime's march. I have believed this." Harry goes off to "worship in the desert" at a "stony sanctuary and a primitive altar." This vision works in the symbolic contexts of a poem like *The Waste Land*; it is pretentious as the serious climax to a manor-house drama of English aristocrats.

Harry's exit precipitates the death of his actual mother, Amy, fulfilling yet another wish. The play reads like a wishful dream, the justification of a murder and a martyrdom that condemns one set of parents and exalts another. The way of redemption is a strange recollection of family history that exposes corruption at the source as a salvation from personal doubt and sin. Harry has merged with God's will, or Freud's, in the form of a relentless family neurosis. His final wish is granted: departure from the family, model of genealogical anxiety and of temporalities contaminating each other. Agatha has the last word, chanting the validity of the pilgrimage.

> So the knot be unknotted
> The cross be uncrossed
> The crooked made straight
> And the curse be ended.

10 Freud, "From the History of an Infantile Neurosis," *Works*, XVII, 97.

Her faith commands little credence, for we have seen how deeply Harry's life roots down in the family, seen that one more exile may be only a repetition of his father's life abroad. His expiation seems a contrived escape from the play's supposed lesson: that the burdens of the past are inescapable. The desert is in his own heart; the waste land is here and in England. Eliot's poetic protagonist will return from this wishful thinking to the further homecomings of the last three *Quartets*.

CHAPTER 13

AT SEA

There is no relief but in grief.
O when will the creaking heart cease?
When will the broken chair give ease?
Why will the summer day delay?
When will Time flow away?

"Lines to a Persian Cat"

Expiation yields to exploration as the *Quartets* proceed. The quest for the chapel of Highest Being, a redemption from temporal loss, undergoes recalcitrantly a transformation into interminable, endless voyaging. Sea adventures, which had always held a special place in Eliot's memory, become the dominant philosophical metaphors of survival and writing. In the earlier poems the emphasis had been on shipwrecks and drownings, deep sinkings that dragged down (though they negatively affirmed) the hopes of ascension. At the end of *The Waste Land* we briefly glimpse another possibility, a boat responding gaily to "the hand expert with sail and oar," the poet riding his vehicle through the churning surfaces of things. In the development of the metaphor the horizontal will replace the vertical: the voyager sails forward toward the unknown rather than upward toward the Absolute. In *Ash Wednesday* the penitent speaker of part 6 experiences this new possibility intensely, though still reading it as a temptation to be renounced.

> (Bless me father) though I do not wish to wish these things
> From the wide window towards the granite shore
> The white sails still fly seaward, seaward flying
> Unbroken wings

The worlds of sensory pleasure, Romantic aspiration, and American childhood memories make a transfigured, if brief, return, in defiance of the Father's law. "Marina" (1930) combines the motif of the drowned soul with that of the poet who has built and sailed the ship. "What seas what shores what grey rocks and what islands" the poet has known return like the daughter of Pericles, unexpectedly grown into a maturity that discomforts and discovers.

In Shakespeare's later plays the shift to the father-daughter relationship dramatizes a conception of memory, repetition, and genealogy apart from the patriarchal models of the early and middle plays. The line from father to son repeats identities: the son reincarnates and immortalizes the father.[1] Authority passes ideally from king to prince in the metaphysics of political kinship systems. Of course, the plays show this system foundering in usurpations, mistaken identities, and stubborn individualities. Bastards and ghosts upset the order, representing (paradoxically) the unrepresented, the dispossessed traces of what exceeds the structure yet always plays within it. Macbeth cannot control the lineage of his power and authority in time. Lear tries to control daughters, those who by their very sex limit his ability to reproduce himself exactly. Goneril and Regan turn monstrous when they enact male roles in a patriarchal system, while Cordelia is banished for her refusal to repeat the words Lear would have her say, words that would mark her submission to the father at the expense of a future love in a different genealogy. The fathers' reconciliations with daughters in *Pericles* and *The Winter's Tale* in particular present a dawning of otherness and of the limits of repetition. In the latter play King Leontes hopes to reconcile Bohemia and Sicilia by reestablishing a boyhood friendship with King Polixenes. This desire to return to the past, and to a narcissistic love of the Same, precipitates his jealousy over Polixenes' attentions to the queen. The result estranges the two kingdoms. Leontes' daughter Perdita is born and is mistakenly rejected as a bastard; the tumult causes the death of his male heir, Mamillius. The recovery of Perdita after sixteen years and her betrothal to the heir of Sicilia signals the beginning of a new genealogy of differences. Recovery requires the rejected other, the bastard that is also our own interior exile, whose repression makes possible the order that excludes it. The daughter's return is the father's transformation, the shipwreck of his desire for absolute authority, the promise of a new life open to the miracle that disturbs settled preconceptions about the living, the dead, and the loved. The daughter is the father's horizon, the unsettled end of the Same.

So in "Marina" the daughter's return occasions the poet's questioning of his desire and vehicle.

> Bowsprit cracked with ice and paint cracked with heat.
> I made this, I have forgotten
> And remember.
> The rigging weak and the canvas rotten

---

1 On this topic see Herbert Schneidau's chapter on "The Paradigms of History and Paternity" in his *Sacred Discontent: The Bible and Western Tradition* (Berkeley, 1976).

Between one June and another September.
Made this unknowing, half conscious, unknown, my own.
The garboard strake leaks, the seams need caulking.
This form, this face, this life
Living to live in a world of time beyond me; let me
Resign my life for this life, my speech for that unspoken,
The awakened, lips parted, the hope, the new ships.

The speaker's ill-made ship is the schooner of remembrance.[2] Remembrance is here remembered like Marina's return, a metamorphic recovery and initiation of the differences time makes: time recovered not as the Same, but as "The awakened, lips parted, the hope, the new ships." What comes back comes back in another meaning, retrospection altered into projection. The poem ends repeating its beginning.

What seas what shores what granite islands towards my timbers
And woodthrush calling through the fog
My daughter.

The daughter comes last, supplementing the repetition, for circling back initiates a journey forward toward another. The recollected images are the timbers that the poet builds his poem with; the poem becomes a new ship, a daughter rather than a son, a creation other than its origin. The identity of the remembered sets sail into the manifold seas of other readings. There beyond the horizon of the Same, poet, reader, and text make unknowing their own, resign this life and speech "for that unspoken" language of the future.

"East Coker" follows "Marina" and *The Family Reunion* by returning to the Eliot ancestral home from which the voyagers set out for the New World. The awakening acceptance of nonidentical repetition, in metaphysics and poetics, parallels Eliot's rapprochement with his homeland. He had joined other American writers in pretending that the new nation was an empty and even degenerate simulacrum of the European original. Or it was a devolution toward barbarity. Either way the recalcitrant futurity and feverish modernism of America were conceptually obliterated. Europe becomes for certain Americans at the end of the nineteenth century a metaphysical fabulation of beauty and order, a nearly theological realm of reassuring meanings and unaltered traditions. Europe had an archive of history in the old sense. By that standard America, self-constituted and declared independent without an origin beyond its performance, had no history. The paradoxes of self-naming and

2 Martin Scofield has a particularly fine reading of the poem in his "T. S. Eliot's Images of Love," *Critical Quarterly*, XVIII (Autumn, 1976), 5–26.

self-reliance unsettle the concept of history as a genealogical unity. America's ground was its only grounds. Europe becomes a revitalizing sameness, a dialectical corrective to America's deviation. Of course, for the American, Europe is actually the revitalizing Other, while America is the entropic Same. Same and Other are binary accomplices in every revisionary work. Overcoming this dualism, and its metaphysics of Identity, will change Eliot's poetry and his attitude toward new worlds. America was made as a rereading of Europe and is in essence a revisionary nation. In its beginnings it reinterpreted the Bible, set up its own constitutional document as the center for the discourse that would sustain the society, and glossed nature for the laws and principles human creation required as aid. The adoption and adaptation of Europe by James, Eliot, and Pound was part of a long American tradition, one that has an initial exile built into its structure before the possibility of transfigured return can be imagined. In his late poetics, as in his mature attention to his American roots, Eliot confirms the American character of his project from the start and at its end.

The return of "East Coker" does not redeem time; it repeats it, with Thomas Elyot's quotations meticulously reproduced (though he was no "real" family relation), as the poet fares forward in retrospection. He comes home, yet is not at home, and starts up again from this land of recurrences, "Feet rising and falling. / Eating and drinking. Dung and Death." He looks to the sea and the uncertainties it symbolizes.

> Dawn points, and another day
> Prepares for heat and silence. Out at sea the dawn wind
> Wrinkles and slides. I am here
> Or there, or elsewhere. In my beginning.
>
> (EC, I)

On the shore the paths lead not to Paradise, but further into the "selva oscura," to a mire or "grimpen" borrowed from the detective adventures of Sherlock Holmes.

> In the middle, not only in the middle of the way
> But all the way, in a dark wood, in a bramble,
> On the edge of a grimpen, where is no secure foothold,
> And menaced by monsters, fancy lights,
> Risking enchantment.
>
> (EC, II)

The voyage out to sea and the adventure to the edge of a grimpen are also the reader's travels through this poem. The *Quartets* usually produce interpretations that imitate the homecoming to truth rather than the voyaging to uncertainty, though in recent years the tide has turned. Joseph Riddel finds that "the absence of presence" characterizes Eliot's rhetoric and that the signs of the timeless "repeatedly become comments on themselves, and point to the silence at their own center." Eliot's effort "to reconstitute a lost whole, to recover a lost origin," is the nostalgic "exploration" shipwrecked by the deconstruction at play in all acts of writing. William Spanos goes further and attributes that "deconstruction" of metaphysics to the poem, if not the poet, insisting that "the poem, whatever its overt intention, is not ultimately a logocentric poem, a poem of presence." Spanos' reading is more sensitive to the poem's complexities than any other since Helen Gardner pioneered the canonical view in her essays of 1942 through 1950. He focuses on the poem's projective rhetoric to refute critics who find the poem a closed circle of total recuperation, invoking for his purposes Kierkegaard's key distinction between backward-looking Recollection and forward-projecting Repetition: "Repetition deconstructs the circle of Recollection and, in so doing, remembers the difference." Spanos' Eliot also "discloses absence rather than presence at the center of the turning world," and there begins the adventure of putting his beliefs at risk.[3]

These are useful correctives to readings that might dismiss the poem as dogma or euphonious wool-gathering, but they also are in danger of turning deconstruction, along with the *Quartets*, back into negative theology. The poem does undergo a philosophical askesis that opens the way to the exploratory and provisional. Spanos rightly judges this adjustment to indeterminacy an influential model for "postmoderns," citing Williams, Olson, Creeley, Barth, Barthelme, and Pynchon as fellow travelers in the "deconstructive strategies." Yet, with the exception of Pynchon, who consciously joins Hawthorne, Henry Adams, and Eliot in the Puritan suffering of the guilts of history, this grouping seems mostly predicated on an abstract collocation of positions vis-à-vis "presence" that would hold true for most post-Enlightenment literature and that reaches back to the beginnings of writing. Though all these modernists might be classified as metaphysical skeptics, their individual reactions to disillusionment vary enormously. One is uncomfortable with Spanos'

---

3 Joseph N. Riddel, *The Inverted Bell: Modernism and the Counterpoetics of William Carlos Williams* (Baton Rouge, 1974), 265–66, 268; Helen Gardner, *The Art of T. S. Eliot* (New York, 1959); William V. Spanos, "Hermeneutics and Memory: Destroying T. S. Eliot's *Four Quartets*," *Genre*, XI (1978), 526, 534. See also Sören Kierkegaard, *Repetition: An Essay in Experimental Psychology*, trans. Walter Lowrie (New York, 1941). Spanos underestimates, I think, the pathos and irony of Kierkegaard's position. Jacques Lacan discusses the new and playful differing of meaning in both Kierkegaard's and Freud's notions of repetition. See Lacan, *The Four Fundamental Concepts of Psycho-Analysis*, trans. Alan Sheridan (New York, 1978), 61–64.

assimilation of their positions to each other because it fails to comprehend emotion, tone, and attitude, the elements Eliot insisted were the fundamentals of poetry. Eliot's exploration supplements the absences at the center of the turning world, exorcising those ghostly daemons by poetically transfiguring the emotions their figures inspire.

The poem discloses not simply the idea of the end of a certain metaphysics (a disclosure philosophy and literature had already made), but the delicate fabric of feelings that this disclosure occasions in a particular imagination, in a particular place, at key moments in that imagination's life. The idea alone is common. The subjective stance alone is parochial. Their interaction turns the poem into the expression of both a character and a time, each with an individual history and archive of emotions and images. The poet of the *Quartets* becomes the genius loci of landscapes both physical and metaphysical, the spirit who haunts the intersection time of memory and desire, who identifies himself with the processes of representation rather than with any of its incarnations, though he stops, like Whitman in his elegy for Lincoln, to bestow signs of affection on each as they pass into time, death, history, and eternity. Eliot takes his disillusioned or deconstructed retrospect and, as he said of Yeats, "out of intense and personal experience, is able to express a general truth; retaining all the particularity of his experience, to make of it a general symbol" (OPP, 299). In subjecting his recollections to repetitions, Eliot frees himself to feel and express their new possibilities, to inhabit and orchestrate the coexistence of nostalgia, despair, faith, and skepticism in the unfolding remembrance that is his present. A pathos qualifies Eliot's poem and makes it an unlikely candidate for enrollment in a school of celebratory deconstruction.

When Eliot challenges the authorities in "East Coker," his voice is not Pound's or Barth's or Barthelme's or Olson's. Not shrill, sarcastic, silly, or oracular, it simply questions, including itself in a bitter, puzzled, sad, and compassionate review of elderly wisdoms.

> What was to be the value of the long looked forward to,
> Long hoped for calm, the autumnal serenity
> And the wisdom of age? Had they deceived us
> Or deceived themselves, the quiet-voiced elders,
> Bequeathing us merely a receipt for deceit?
> The serenity only a deliberate hebetude,
> The wisdom only the knowledge of dead secrets
> Useless in the darkness into which they peered
> Or from which they turned their eyes.

(EC, II)

This leads the poet to the grimpen, to the undoing and unknowing of the serenities. The critique is not an accusation, nor does it partake of the satirist's implied superiority. The longing for wisdom, which some would erase by dividing the poem into logocentric and deconstructive tendencies and then nominating the latter as authoritative, survives. It endures the shipwreck of other "dead secrets" and enters the darkness of another knowledge: "The only wisdom we can hope to acquire / Is the wisdom of humility: humility is endless." This endless humility of the philosophical imagination repeats Keats, marking Eliot's own long-awaited arrival at negative capability. Negative capability may be distinguished from negative theology as an askesis of the latter, for in it what returns is the ability to take satisfaction in the transient truths and beauties of time, to regather human relations in a logos that does not sacrifice their nature in the name of a forbidding law. The humility of negative theology looks to an end in philosophical martyrdom; the humility of negative capability undertakes the task of endlessly rebeginning the nature of our history. Yet, Eliot does speak in the language of the elders. One traditional definition of wisdom, as complete knowledge, meets its ancient foe and accomplice, wisdom as the continuing discovery of ignorance. The distinction between recollection and repetition falters, then, as do all simple oppositions in Eliot's poem. The repetition that alters the retrieved moment by its replacement in a new discourse does not re-present a former experience of presence, but a feeling or spirit of place that was already an interpretation. What repetition repeats, in fact, is a recollection, transfiguring one interpretation by another. Eliot recollects his own and others' desires for wisdom, and in repeating that cherished memory, he both humiliates and exalts it.

In "Burnt Norton," for example, the moment in the rose garden, of "our first world," is a retrospective interpretation (*Nachträglichkeit* in Freud's sense) that figures the origin, "Down the passage we did not take, / Towards the door we never opened." In the garden the roses have "the look of flowers that are looked at." Burnt Norton is a ruin, a haunted house, but those spectral "guests" are "accepted and accepting."[4] This scene is actually an opening revision and transfiguration of the nostalgia that permeates Eliot's early verse. We read a repetition that deconstructs a recollection, exorcising nostalgia and redeeming desire. We watch as representation produces a moment of presence in a speculation on an empty pool: "And the lotos rose, quietly,

4 See Barbara Everett, "A Visit to Burnt Norton," *Critical Quarterly*, XVI (Autumn, 1974), 199–224.

quietly, / The surface glittered out of heart of light." Whereas *The Waste Land*'s hyacinth-garden scene elegized the loss of love and the empty, desolate sea, "Burnt Norton" affirms that moments of presence are imaginary, and does not lament the fact. Eliot tropes against his own earlier poetics of belatedness by viewing the ground of the logos not in past time or distant eternity, but in what human relations, including poetry, can figuratively create. The human origin of such knowledge does not detract from its reality or value, though it does lack the secure foothold of the Absolute that haunts metaphysical epistemologies.. What is "always present" here is the mind's power to represent, and so "Burnt Norton" introduces us to a post-Romantic and post-Freudian poetics, however reluctantly: "Go, go, go, said the bird: Human kind / Cannot bear very much reality."

If recollection is defined as the memorial system that recovers the metaphysical truth, or the true reality, of a past moment, then repetition is the re-presenting of such a recollection in a way that appreciates its inspiration while altering its direction and meaning. The reinscription of the recollected moment in another time, place, or text alters the matrix of signifying differences and so reinterprets the feelings and ideas that are recalled. What occurs is a new feeling—an "exhaustion . . . appeasement . . . absolution . . . and . . . annihilation" of old emotions. Yet, to these negatives must be added an affection for memorial traces, whose interpretation establishes the being and resource of the new. Repetition, even as a projective differing of a thing from itself, carries the mark of remembrance, a gleam attracting and motivating the repetition that will change it. Thus, the poet will recall

> Whisper of running streams, and winter lightning.
> The wild thyme unseen and the wild strawberry,
> The laughter in the garden, echoed ecstasy
> Not lost, but requiring, pointing to the agony
> Of death and birth.
>
> (EC, III)

Eliot regathers images from his other poems, images that are themselves the creations of memory. The "ecstasy" is "echoed . . . Not lost," reverberating in time through incarnations requiring difference—"death and birth." Ecstasy cannot be separated from its random appearances in time; these events compound the idea and name of ecstasy through memory's echoings. Recollections are transfigured, glorified by a carrying over into another way of being. Remembered figures traverse the gap writing opens, and arrive at new worlds where they signify in unforeseen ways. The philosophy of disillusionment fares forward by the reillusionment repetition organizes, forward to the "wild thyme," after all "unseen," toward an unknown time that treasures those feelings by allowing them to repeat in other ways. Those times return as their own nonidentical reconstructions, recognized belatedly, composing the memorial intersection of another "present" without "secure foothold."

From the archive of history, representation conjures its images, though what they mean when they surface will exceed what they have been and whatever the writer may have intended.

> And of course only a part of an author's imagery comes from his reading. It comes from the whole of his sensitive life since early childhood. Why, for all of us, out of all that we have heard, seen, felt, in a lifetime, do certain images recur, charged with emotion, rather than others? The song of one bird, the leap of one fish, at a particular place and time, the scent of one flower, an old woman on a German mountain path, six ruffians seen through an open window playing cards at night at a small French railway junction where there was a water-mill: such memories may have symbolic value, but of what we cannot tell, for they come to represent the depths of feeling into which we cannot peer. We might just as well ask why, when we try to recall visually some period in the past, we find in our memory just the few meagre arbitrarily chosen set of snapshots that we do find there, the faded souvenirs of passionate moments. (UPUC, 148)

Eliot's poetic imagery divides itself between emotionally charged scenes and faded souvenirs. When "Midnight shakes the memory" in "Rhapsody on a Windy Night," the reminiscences that come are sunless, noxious, and mundane. The conspicuous literary allusions of *The Waste Land* are likewise souvenirs, in contrast to the hyacinth girl's appearance and the boat "beating obedient / To controlling hands." By this juxtaposition of archaeologized "snapshots" and "passionate moments," the scholastic poet transfuses his souvenirs of both kinds. What Freud called the repetition compulsion structures these remembrances, "for they come to represent the depths of feeling into which we cannot peer." This depth out of which writing and memory spring recurs frequently in Eliot's poetry and criticism. The notion of the faded souvenir follows that of Shelley's "fading coal," cited some fifty pages before the meditation on memory. Shelley's portrait of inspiration laments the poverty of belated representation whose strength of "symbolic value" is inseparable from its estrangement and obscurity. The snapshot tries for recollective verisimilitude for the past recaptured, and is thus doomed to lose it. Involuntary memories, however, repeat because they are already interpretations and not the thing itself. As symbols they recur when a structure of understanding responds once again to situations it may represent. Whether by metaphor or metonymy, these symbols stand for moments when experience and interpretation seem gathered in a single logos. This emotional imagination, however, acts only passively in Eliot's formula. Daemonic possession victimizes it, as if the forces of the unconscious or the past dramatize a mystery play through the instrument of the poet and poem. Thus, Freud might revise "we cannot peer" to "we refuse to peer," and note the exorcism within Eliot's poetics. The *Quartets* begin to peer into the darkness of unknowing, repeating the images of the unrepresentable for the symbolic, transfiguring effect they may have on the ontology of passionate moments. Paradoxically, it is only when Eliot ceases to judge such moments in terms of their sufficiency as origins that they become fully available as poetic resources.

In the characteristic manner of the *Quartets*, the images of "echoed ecstasy" are immediately followed by a quizzical discourse on method.

> You say I am repeating
> Something I have said before. I shall say it again.
> Shall I say it again? In order to arrive there,
> To arrive where you are, to get from where you are not,
>   You must go by a way wherein there is no ecstasy.
> In order to arrive at what you do not know
>   You must go by a way which is the way of ignorance.
> In order to possess what you do not possess
>   You must go by the way of dispossession.
> In order to arrive at what you are not
>   You must go through the way in which you are not.
> And what you do not know is the only thing you know
> And what you own is what you do not own
> And where you are is where you are not.
>
> (EC, III)

In subtle shifts Eliot repeats the maxims, and even the typography, of a passage from Saint John of the Cross.[5] Saint John divides the approaches to pleasure, possession, knowledge, and being between two stages—the negation of desire and the action of negation. The first characterizes the askesis of *Ash Wednesday*: "Teach us to sit still. . . . And let my cry come unto Thee." The second, the action of negation, is what Eliot here rephrases. But whereas Saint John's dictums are the recognizable paradoxes of mysticism, Eliot's are multiplicative, turning negative theology into rhetorical dissemination. His sentences practice the negative way of repetition. Each word and phrase differs from itself in each of its incarnations. Doubled, not at home in itself, the Word become words enacts the intimacy of repetition and language.

---

5 Saint John's passage is quoted in Helen Gardner, *The Composition of "Four Quartets"* (New York, 1978), 107. It is from *Ascent of Mount Carmel*, I, xiii.

· So the first lines of the passage are more than clumsy, defensive posturing. They are form and content joined in mocking illustration of the theme's quandaries, and the "I" is Eliot, Saint John, and a host of precursors. Identities stumble in darkness. "There . . . where you are," may be the present unconsciousness of the fact of alienation, turning "where you are not" into a description of the state of such estrangement and the journey into a realization of ignorance. Or "there . . . where you are," may be Being itself (where you Are), that place of real existence "where you are not" now living, a beatitude toward which the journey ascends. Language prevaricates at the crossroads of being and nothingness, and that intersection is its home. The "way wherein there is no ecstasy" is likewise a forked path, either the renunciation of complacent satisfactions or the *via negativa* of high passion. *Ecstasy* is the key confounding term of the meditation, for it echoes in itself antithetical senses, upsetting as words will do the principles of identity and noncontradiction. *Ecstasy* means both consummate union and displacement, being together and being beside one's self. Thus, if the *via* is *negativa*,—selfdoubling and exile—then it *is* a way of ecstasy. Bringing out the double play of all the terms and phrases of the meditation, ecstasy is itself ecstatic, beside itself in contradictions of bliss and madness. The former ecstasies of "streams . . . lightning . . . thyme . . . strawberry . . . the garden" are renounced, "no ecstasy." Yet, in their echoic repetition they are beside themselves again, ecstatic not in the past but in a present revision that makes them symbols of the future.

The "way wherein there is no ecstasy" can be the way wherein there is no division, no being beside one's self, though that is to be absent from "where you are." And since "where you are is where you are not," all being is ecstasy, always beside itself, and One with its passion for the Other. Similar exacerbating analyses can be performed on the rest of the passage with the same maddening results. It is a dizzying demonstration of how being and language, "are" and "there," and "you" and "I" function always within recollection and repetition, always taking place by replacement. In this way the poet arrives dispossessed of the proper things and ignorant of knowledge, owning his unknowing and being his own undoing. In a parallel fashion the poem undoes itself in its own ecstasy. Ecstatic writing dismembers full recollection, expiates the past in the endless humiliation of always repeating it errantly. What is recalled, the original moment of ecstasy, was itself double at the origin, originating and original precisely because it was beside itself and was the product of another time.

Writing and its subject live in ecstasy's hospital, where the critical condition is both transgressive and recuperative. It is a "wounded surgeon" who "plies the steel," the self-mutilated poet of ecstasies who wields the stylus of the artistic operation "That questions the distempered part." The "healer's art" is one of "sharp compassion," a cutting disruption of distempered identities: "Our only health is the disease . . . to be restored, our sickness must grow worse." Salubrious diseases and painful surgeries question the easiness of static sameness, distempering complacent wisdoms, though here Eliot shows how tempted he remains by negative theology. "East Coker" ends interrogating the poet's achievements, too, during "l'entre deux guerres," after which he takes his leave, as Harry had, of home. This time, however, the riddles of origin stay irresolute, and the sea of exploration replaces the desert of expiation as America looms on the ecstatic horizon. Eliot retraces the wayfaring of his forebears. Their journey is paralleled by a philosophical resolution to abandon nostalgia and to embrace the potentials of exile in the revisionary new world.

> Home is where one starts from. As we grow older
> The world becomes stranger, the pattern more complicated
> Of dead and living. Not the intense moment
> Isolated, with no before and after,
> But a lifetime burning in every moment
> And not the lifetime of one man only
> But of old stones that cannot be deciphered.
>
> (EC, V)

These old stones in the East Coker churchyard are the weathered elegies of the past, "marking the graves," as Helen Gardner remarks, "of those who may have been his long-dead and forgotten ancestors."[6] The names of the dead fade beyond decoding, the illegible script telling the limits of recovery. The still point of the ecstatic moment in "Burnt Norton" reappears here qualified with a "Not." The time "Stretching before and after" that once felt ridiculous now demands its justice, a thinking of history "burning in every moment." Here Eliot tropes against his own feelings in "The Burial of the Dead," in which sensations of belatedness, impotence, and resurrectional longing were the inevitable by-products of conceiving life as a meaningless sea of time that drowns sublime moments of timeless identity. Now the "pattern more complicated / Of dead and living" cannot be thought of as a series of isolated presences. Moments of presence are woven in the fabrications of a general economy of memorial reinscription, every moment an intersection of personal and historical texts. The "before and after" make possible the moment that knows itself in intensely trying to decipher them.

6 Gardner, *The Composition of "Four Quartets,"* 42.

The illegibility of origins is not the same as the disclosure of "absence rather than presence at the center of the turning world." The center of this world of homelands, the graveyard, still produces a text to be glossed, as the waste land had bred its lilacs from the corpora of fathers. What really disturbs and puzzles is not absence, but partial vision—the lingering presence of the marks of others, suggesting significance. From the start Eliot had read death as other than absence, felt its substantial impact, and known its inheritance. Simple absence would have been a relief to the modernist mind, for it would clear the poetic ground of the rubble of the ancestors. One could then really make it new without anxiety, erasing the reference of "it" to the texts of the past. Poetry would then be completely visionary, not revisionary. We vulgarize Derrida if we imply that the disclosure of absence is the business of deconstruction, for in "absence" resides the powerful trace of the "presence" used to think it. Deconstruction cautions against the shuffling of such easy dualisms; Eliot's poetry explores the horizons of such antinomies, for which ghosts and the dead are the aptest metaphors (though pushed to their limit they endanger the logic of identity upon which metaphor is founded). The impossibility of decipherment turns on the visible/invisible trace of the other in the text, preventing its absolute control of itself or the absolute control of it in a single interpretation. Reading becomes the exploration of the work of such traces, their effects in the worlds of new writers, and the kind of intertextuality of self and poem this process creates. "East Coker" proceeds through just such readings of the ancestral dead, starting with the effort to return home and ending with the necessity of leave-taking.

Striking the note he was learning from Yeats, gathering the images of that sea that once held so many drowned bodies, Eliot closes this time aboard ship.

> Old men ought to be explorers
> Here or there does not matter
> We must be still and still moving
> Into another intensity
> For a further union, a deeper communion
> Through the dark cold and the empty desolation,
> The wave cry, the wind cry, the vast waters
> Of the petrel and the porpoise. In my end is my beginning.

(EC, V)

This beginning does not circle back to the poem's opening. The reversal of order breaks the circle through repetition, as this beginning heads for open waters, uncharted seas, and America. Gardner's edition of the manuscript shows a canceled line here reading "The mind must venture / where it has not been," an injunction perhaps too reminiscent of Tennyson's *Ulysses*. "Beginning" now connotes navigation of the indecipherable, whereas at the start of "East Coker" it signaled a fall into determinism and the mechanical repetition of the Same. In "the dark cold and the empty desolation" of what has estranged itself sounds the energetic cries of the world repeating itself in variations. Human voices had wakened Prufrock to drowning; these cries echo the sailor's ecstasy in discovering the beginnings that repeat around the course of every land's end. At the "end," of this poem, comes the "beginning," the voyage of the Eliot family to the New World. This ending marks the beginning of the next poem, the poem of America, "The Dry Salvages."

Critics continue to disagree over the quality of this quartet, with some citing its first dozen lines as especially embarrassing.[7] In these lines the return to Saint Louis and the Mississippi River does not quicken with emotion. The flatness of phrase goes along with the obvious didacticism in the forgetting of the "strong brown god" by the "worshippers of the machine." This unconvincing projection of theological anthropology and social criticism turns memory into an ill-disguised sermon, losing all genuine detail of place in a moralizing portrait etched in pedestrian abstractions. We do not feel that these general symbols and universals have been produced by an attentive transformation of a particular life. Instead they continue to try to restrain and fix that life in a formulated phrase. "In the passages of discourse and opinion," writes Graham Hough, "there is a steady depreciation of the natural life—yet it is only by hints and glimpses, momentary transfigurations of the natural life, that the more-than-natural illuminations are attained. These moments have nothing specifically Christian in their content, perhaps nothing specifically religious, in a traditional sense."[8] Eliot's epiphanies occur through the imagination's work in memory and representation, a process for which the Incarnation is a grand trope that indicates and disguises the specifically Romantic, lyric, American, and autobiographical content of Eliot's illuminations. Only when memory focuses on the specific sensual elements recalling the stages of an individual's natural history does the poetry revive.

> His rhythm was present in the nursery bedroom,
> In the rank ailanthus of the April dooryard,
> In the smell of grapes on the autumn table,
> And the evening circle in the winter gaslight.

7 For representative voices in the controversy see the essays by R. W. Flint, Helen Garnder, Donald Davie, Hugh Kenner, C. K. Stead, and Denis Donoghue collected in Bernard Bergonzi (ed.), *"Four Quartets": A Casebook* (London, 1969).

8 Graham Hough, "Vision and Doctrine in *Four Quartets*," *Critical Quarterly*, XV (Summer, 1973), 127.

Examining Eliot's revisions of these lines, Gardner notes that the substitution of "rank ailanthus" for "efflorescence" and of "dooryard" for "suburb" or "backyard" connected the passage to childhood memories, gave it an American flavor, and offered another echo of Whitman. "The Dry Salvages" falters as it seeks a voice for the always present influence of this past life, trying first to displace its own repression onto the forgetful "worshippers of the machine," and then, as if perfume from a dress made him so digress, the poet drops his defensive, prophetic pose to give fuller rein to the images that come from below. The momentum continues into the following reminiscent meditations on the New England coast, some of the finest passages in all his poetry. They make the "hints of earlier and other creation" both theme and method in measuring the words out of the sea of time.

The sea of "The Dry Salvages" resembles a churning natural museum or uncataloged nautical library: "It tosses up our losses, the torn seine, / The shattered lobsterpot, the broken oar / And the gear of foreign dead men." No system of classification prevails here, for "The sea is the land's edge also," the threshold where oppositions reach, penetrate, wear down, and leave their traces on each other. The ruins of other times come ashore; the shore yields its ruin to the sea. This sea, like *The Waste Land*, "has many voices, / Many gods and many voices. . . . different voices / Often together heard." This sea recollects the simultaneous orders of literature and history, but now tumultuously, as if in a storm. The sea's ever-breaking surfaces and shoreline poundings send up an ominous cacophony of conflicting voices, greeting the uneasy sailor who rounds "homewards." The voices "whine in the rigging," sounding "the wailing warning from the approaching headland." Eliot repeats the Pilgrims' arrival in New England, remembers his boyhood sailings off Gloucester, and adds to them his sense of the urgency of their explorations' dangers. Charting new worlds can be a fatal enterprise, as the sea's tossed-up losses show. The "approaching headland" of a new historical or poetic world resounds with the voices of foreign dead men who have come before. Ghosts haunt new beginnings: Eliot and his ancestors each wander into the other's explorations, figuring fatality in the calculations of discovery. But in replaying this voyage Eliot affirms the risk, and his voice becomes that of the American genius loci.

Beneath the tempest the "ground swell" shifts in its dark rhythms, "Measures time not our time," clangs a bell that rings the symbolic value of depths into which we cannot peer. The indecipherable origin ebbs and flows at its own rate, not in the ratios of any human reason "calculating the future, / Trying to unweave, unwind, unravel / And piece together the past and the future." The bell tolls the disparity between the timely orders of the represented surface and the untimely ringing of invisible currents. The reminiscence this bell brings is of dead men's voices, like the bells in *The Waste Land*, but now it also rings for the unnamed sailors of beginnings, paying affectionate tribute, as Whitman gave Lincoln's coffin a "sprig of lilac" in contrapuntal answer to "the tolling tolling bells' perpetual clang."[9] Death is the God who receives the prayer in the following section. It ensures the temporal humiliation that guarantees that "There is no end, but addition" to "the drifting wreckage" of creations. Though old men are to be explorers, they come late to the realization, "In a drifting boat with a slow leakage," resenting "failing powers." Eliot drifts in Shelley's bark, thinking of Yeats. One sails to other waste lands, not to Byzantium.

> Where is the end of them, the fishermen sailing
> Into the wind's tail, where the fog cowers?
> We cannot think of a time that is oceanless
> Or of an ocean not littered with wastage
> Or of a future that is not liable
> Like the past, to have no destination.
>
> We have to think of them as forever bailing,
> Setting and hauling, while the North East lowers
> Over shallow banks unchanging and erosionless
> Or drawing their money, drying sails at dockage;
> Not as making a trip that will be unpayable
> For a haul that will not bear examination.

(DS, II)

"Forever bailing," the poet endures time, lets go the standard of wholeness, full repayment, or perfect retrieval from the depths.

The voice and tutelary spirit tossed to the surface here is the Whitman of the "Sea-Drift" poems.

> As I list to the dirge, the voices of men and women wreck'd,
> As I inhale the impalpable breezes that set in upon me,
> As the ocean so mysterious rolls toward me closer and closer,
> I too but signify at the utmost a little wash'd up drift,
> A few sands and dead leaves to gather,
> Gather, and merge myself as part of the sands and drift.

"As I Ebb'd with the Ocean of Life" submerges the poet's identity in endless driftings of signification. It pictures poetry as "Tufts of straw, sands, fragments, / Buoy'd hither from many moods, one contradicting another, / From

9 A. D. Moody notes this echo in discussing Eliot's "reconciliation with Whitman and America" in his *Thomas Stearns Eliot: Poet* (London, 1979), 223–24.

the storm, the long calm, the darkness, the swell." This is the poetics that the author of *The Waste Land* enacts in resistance and that the author of "The Dry Salvages" recollects and repeats. The sea's "Annunciation" of "Death its God" enunciates further the transumption of "Out of the Cradle Endlessly Rocking" and its sea chant of death. Eliot takes the place of Whitman's "man, yet by these tears a little boy again," identifying his reminiscence with Whitman's, making Whitman the mockingbird daemon whose song aroused "the fire, the sweet hell within, / The unknown want, the destiny of me." A retrospection introjects death and projects the figure of boyhood, earliness, and original creation. "My own songs awaked from that hour," writes Whitman in response to the "delicious word death." Eliot's recollection of Whitman's words likewise restores his youth, and his readings of Whitman, in a different drift.

The pattern of the past "ceases to be a mere sequence— / Or even development," two historiographical models for "disowning the past." Possession of the past arrives by way of shipwreck, dispossession. "The moments of happiness," the "sudden illumination" of an emotionally charged recollection, undergo a sea change when interpretation and repetition combine.

> We had the experience but missed the meaning,
> And approach to the meaning restores the experience
> In a different form, beyond any meaning
> We can assign to happiness.
>
> (DS, III)

Thirty-five years before, Eliot had put this realization in the language of philosophy: "In the same way in our theory of knowledge, when we leave the moment of immediate experience, we are forced to present our account either as the history of mind in its environment, or as the history of the world as it appears to mind. . . . The feeling which is an object is feeling shrunk and impoverished, though in a sense expanded and developed as well: shrunk because it is now the object of consciousness, narrower instead of wider than consciousness; expanded because in becoming an object it has developed relations which lead it beyond itself" (KE, 22–23). The earlier account accentuates the estrangement of man from world in the unrepresentability of immediate experience, taking some consolation in the object's expanded relations. In "The Dry Salvages," the happiness of immediate experience is always something assigned, a sign that something is always missing and that meaning supplements the presence of events to transfigure them beyond themselves.

The surprise that awaits an approach to the meaning parallels the surprise that awaits the voyager to the approaching headland of the New World. Eliot's early unhappiness with the American paradox of historical burdens and natural possibilities took him back across the sea to England, to a romance with the poetics and politics of restoration. Reversing his course in the thirties, he restores his American experience to his life. No longer asking it to bring happiness, he reads America as the state of exploration, a young land where the men of old are inspired to new creations. This homeward approach sails through an exile in the old, recharts the ancestral isles, and rediscovers the first home as metaphor of perpetual pilgrimage. Home restored becomes home-as-homelessness, a being at home in the double land of ecstasy, always at sea between new worlds and old. In the words of Heidegger:

> All the poems of the poet who has entered into his poethood are poems of homecoming. . . .
> Homecoming is the return into the proximity of the source.
> But such a return is only possible for one who has previously, and perhaps for a long time now, borne on his shoulders as the wanderer the burden of the voyage, and has gone over into the source, so that he could there experience what the nature of the Sought-For might be, and then be able to come back more experienced, as the Seeker. . . . But now if homecoming means becoming at home in proximity to the source, then must not the return home consist chiefly, and perhaps for a long time, in getting to know this mystery. . . . Proximity to the source is a proximity which reserves something. It withholds the Most Joyous. It keeps it and stores it away for the Comers. . . . The original essence of joy is the process of becoming at home in the proximity to the source. . . . The poet comes into this proximity, in the act of telling of the mystery of the proximity to the Near. . . . So it is that, since care must be taken to guard the self-reserving proximity to the most Joyous, care enters into the Joyous. . . .
> But because the word, once it has been spoken, slips out of the protection of the care-worn poet, he cannot easily hold fast in all its truth to the spoken knowledge of the reserved discovery and of the reserving proximity. Therefore the poet turns to the others, so that their remembrance may help towards an understanding of the poetic word, with the result that in the process of understanding each may have a homecoming in the manner appropriate for him.[10]

---

10 Martin Heidegger, "Remembrance of the Poet," in Heidegger, *Existence and Being* (South Bend, Ind., 1949), 233, 258–62, 269.

CHAPTER 14

GHOSTS AND ROSES

Follow the feet
Of the walker, the water-thrush. Follow the flight
Of the dancing arrow, the purple martin. Greet
In silence the bullhat. All are delectable. Sweet sweet sweet
But resign this land at the end, resign it
To its true owner, the tough one, the sea-gull.
The palaver is finished.

"Cape Ann"

In part 5 of "The Dry Salvages" the seas and sailors drop away. The poet begins his turn toward exploration of another approach to ecstasy, one that will culminate in the "double part" he assumes when he meets the ghost in "Little Gidding." As "The Dry Salvages" closes, the chaos of interpretative methods ("these are usual / Pastimes and drugs") motivates the recurrent hope of order: "But to apprehend / The point of intersection of the timeless / With time, is an occupation for the saint." Thus, "For most of us, there is only the unattended / Moment, the moment in and out of time," the again repeated moment "lost in a shaft of sunlight, / The wild thyme unseen, or the winter lightning." These new repetitions are now "hints and guesses" pointing to the Christian philosophy of a divine repetition: "The hint half-guessed, the gift half understood, is Incarnation." The Incarnation is God's strange repetition in time, as Christ figures the archetype of the revisionist. He is the ideal *figura* of which personal repetitions are prefigurations, as they seek the Spirit of the moment in representative reembodiments.

One poetic "saint" who glimpsed this mystery is Dante, whose *Paradiso* concludes with puzzlement at "our image" in the divine Light and with a reconciliation among the stars: "I wished to see how the image conformed to the circle and how it has its place therein; but my own wings were not sufficient for that, save that my mind was smitten by a flash wherein its wish came to it. Here power failed the lofty phantasy; but already my desire and my will were revolved, like a wheel that is evenly moved, by the Love which moves the sun and the other stars" (*Paradiso*, canto 33). By a fiery flash of the divine,

Dante receives the mystery, but cannot record it, for his receptive faculty for images ("fantasia") remains human.[1] He experiences an Annunciation of the Word made flesh; yet, its representation is reserved for the Word itself, while the poet's words record the feeling of this illumination. Love is the emotion of divinity, the unrepresentable height and depth inspiring poet and universe. Dante carries away a souvenir of this passionate moment in his poetic remembrance; his vision is not of the mystery's solution, but of the revolving love of its repetition in time. Eliot alludes to this moment in Dante ("to my thinking the highest point that poetry has ever reached or ever can reach") to prepare the way for his own version of the *Paradiso* in "Little Gidding." His love for Dante's poem moves him to attempt its reincarnation. He will end his own climactic work by repeating the end of Dante's, and the approach to its meaning will in this other time alter Dante in yet another fulfillment of the mystery's promise.

Fire is the element of "Little Gidding." The refining purgatorial fire now burns with enlightenment, as the pentecostal flame and the flash of Dante. As "un fulgore" had shown the Incarnation to Dante, so Dante will be reincarnated and show himself in Eliot's poem. This meeting of the living and the dead crosses the normal categories of time and bestows meaning upon them through other patterns. "Little Gidding" transfigures the occupation of the saint, finds in its intertextuality the "intersection of the timeless / With time." This violation of temporal rules recalls the simultaneous order of literature in "Tradition and the Individual Talent" and gives a dramatic account of such an encounter between the disciple and "some dead master." Thus, when the scene is set, it is "Midwinter spring," a confusion of the regulated order imposed on phenomena and called "natural." Designations of identity are exposed as reductions of the mystery. This undoing of classifications parallels the earlier sense that "Words strain, / Crack and sometimes break, under the burden" of stamping a single identity on disparate objects by obscuring the difference that makes possible the abstraction producing the signifier. Those trained in the ways of comparative philology, such as Nietzsche and Eliot, were quick to probe the philological relativity of language.[2] Eliot assimilated this questioning of the signifier to his own systematic interrogation of language and emotion, locating the problem in the process of representation, or what he called remembrance: "In perception we intend the object; in

---

1 Charles Singleton, *Paradiso: Commentary* (Princeton, 1977), 583, 586.

2 See Friedrich Nietzsche, "On Truth and Falsity in an Ultramoral Sense," in Geoffrey Clive (ed.), *The Philosophy of Nietzsche* (New York, 1965), 503–15; and J. Hillis Miller, "Dismembering and Disremembering in Nietzsche's 'On Truth and Lies in a Nonmoral Sense,'" *Boundary 2*, IX/X (Spring/Fall, 1981), 41–54.

recollection we intend a complex which is composed of image and feeling. We do not intend to remember simply the object, but the object as we remember it. And this new object is much more *the experience* than the *past object*, for we try to remember how we felt toward the past object" (KE, 49). A word repeats conventionally, limiting meaning. Poetic repetition "unknows" words and moments in another discourse. They pass through exile into humiliation, their repetition signaling love and their remembrance incarnating the spirit that knows, or unknows, itself through them.

This interpretative process is "Suspended in time, between pole and tropic," antinomies undone by the "pentecostal fire" that "Stirs the dumb spirit" to transfigured speech of "the spring time . . . not in time's convenant. . . . Not in the scheme of generation." The exploration leads not to the eternal, for that would be only the timeless, but to the "uncertain hour before the morning" in section 2, when the "unimaginable" trods the pavement. We have come ashore, as at the end of *The Waste Land*, but these lands are in a very strange order. Their principle of conjunction is not unlike that binding the fragments and quotes at the end of the earlier poem. What is different is the absence of hysteria, the calm passion of this entrance into that that passeth understanding. The "broken king" comes again, dethroned, repeating the Fisher King and King Charles, now humbled, without hope or fear of restoration to authority. Here "at the end of the journey" knight and poet discover the errancy that disrupts the "scheme of generation," turning each word and each accomplishment into prelude and benediction.

> And what you thought you came for
> Is only a shell, a husk of meaning
> From which the purpose breaks only when it is fulfilled
> If at all. Either you had no purpose
> Or the purpose is beyond the end you figured
> And is altered in fulfilment.
>
> (LG, I)

Undoing the temporal and historical structure of figural interpretation, Eliot's fulfillments break their *figurae*, reach back and alter the purposes of signs.

The fulfillment here is not the original figure in a different, exalted form that had been prefigured: rather these fulfillments choose their past figures, empty them, and make them "only a shell, a husk of meaning." Figural interpretation had resolved the ambiguity of original and copy inherent in the etymology of *figura* by the construction of a teleological model of figural purposes. The times were reconciled by the links to the logos figural interpretation assumed; the new testaments emptied the authority of the old and inverted their priority, turning them into hints and guesses of themselves, the new texts. Although the doctrine described a movement forward from figure to fulfillment, the actual motion ran backward as the modern moment secured itself by revising the purposeful significance of the ancient.[3] The poet, then, working at this actual level, accepts the inevitable transfiguration of his authority and words by others in their interpretations, accepts the new worlds of meaning that break, "If at all," beyond the end the poet figured, constantly altering his text in new fulfillments. It would be hard to believe that Eliot was unaware of the theory of the figural and of the history of the term, especially in light of his modest education in Romance philology and his assimilation of the Christian historiographical model. In any case, the essence of the practice is contained in Augustine's *Confessions* and in Dante's *Commedia*, two of Eliot's principal inspirations. Eliot's transfigurational poetics emerge as a revision of Christian historiography and theology, English political history, the literature of remembrance and autobiography, the philosophy of belated perception, the literary criticism of historical formalism, and his own personal quest for a reconciliation with America and mutability.

Figural breaks are the eternal recurrence of "the world's end" repeating "in place and time, / Now and in England." A simple notion of the end of history would still involve "mere sequence— / Or even development." "Little Gidding" puts an end to the end of history and begins history as altered repetitions, a constant intersection.

> And what the dead had no speech for, when living,
> They can tell you, being dead: the communication
> Of the dead is tongued with fire beyond the language of the living.
>
> (LG, I)

Thus, the theoretical model is propounded and ready for application in the conjuration of a dead master speaking in fiery tongues.

> In the uncertain hour before the morning
>   Near the ending of interminable night
>   At the recurrent end of the unending
> After the dark dove with the flickering tongue
>   Had passed below the horizon of his homing
>   While the dead leaves still rattled on like tin

---

3 Erich Auerbach, "Figura," trans. Ralph Manheim, in Auerbach, *Scenes from the Drama of European Literature* (New York, 1959), 11–76. Harold Bloom applies the notion in a heretical way to poetic genealogy in *Poetry and Repression: Revisionism from Blake to Stevens* (New Haven, 1976), 87–96.

Over the asphalt where no other sound was
    Between three districts whence the smoke arose
    I met one walking, loitering and hurried
As if blown towards me like the metal leaves
    Before the urban dawn wind unresisting.
    And as I fixed upon the down-turned face
That pointed scrutiny with which we challenge
    The first-met stranger in the waning dusk
    I caught the sudden look of some dead master
Whom I had known, forgotten, half recalled
    Both one and many; in the brown baked features
    The eyes of a familiar compound ghost
Both intimate and unidentifiable.
    So I assumed a double part, and cried
    And heard another's voice cry: "What! are *you* here?"

                                         (LG, II)

Forgotten and half-recalled, intimate and unidentifiable, the familiar compound ghost characterizes the eerie temporality and mixed identities of the literary text. This meeting and conversation may be read as Eliot's condensed summary of his poetic philosophy, the last act and statement of the individual's struggle with inheritance and futurity. In "What Dante Means to Me" (1950), Eliot says, "This section of a poem—not the length of one canto of the Divine Comedy—cost me far more time and trouble than any passage of the same length that I have ever written" (CC, 129). The recently published manuscripts of the poem prove the point.

The conception was clear at the start: an "imitation" of Dante's terza rima, a reenactment of the master-disciple scenes Eliot so often cited, the compounding of Yeats with Dante, Shelley, and others, and the echo of Hamlet's ghost. But in the first draft the concluding advice given by this ghost, some twenty-four lines, treats other themes than the published text. The distance between the warden and the ghost appears greater, the alienation more severe. "I was always dead," the speaker says in one version of their meeting, "Always revived, and always something other, / And he a face changing." Recalling King Hamlet's "Remember me," the manuscript ghost's answering injunction is of a different sort.

Remember rather the essential moments
    That were the times of birth and death and change
    The agony and the solitary vigil.
Remember also fear, loathing and hate,
    The wild strawberries eaten in the garden,

> The walls of Poitiers, and the Anjou wine,
> The fresh new season's rope, the smell of varnish
>   On the clean oar, the drying of the sails,
> Such things as seem of least and most importance.
> So, as you circumscribe this dreary round,
>   Shall your life pass from you, with all you hated
>   And all you loved, the future and the past.
> United to another past, another future,
>   (After many seas and after many lands)
>   The dead and the unborn, who shall be nearer
> Than the voices and the faces that were most near.

The *Quartets* sometimes fall to flatness of cadence and sense in the pursuit of a common style. The recourse to Eliot's cherished nautical imagery suggests the importance of this section, but it comes out a pale reflection of "The Dry Salvages." This version lapses into vagueness compared to the final copy, its reconciliation seemingly unearned and complacent. Its defect, as Eliot wrote in a letter to John Hayward, was "the lack of some acute personal reminiscence."[4]

He supplies the personal touch through Yeats's influence, inspired by the late lyrics of tragic gay wisdom. Not surprisingly, the 1940 essay on Yeats focuses on influence and maturity. While writing the *Quartets*, Eliot sets down in his appreciation of Yeats the poetic principle guiding his own work, finally admitting the primacy of a "second impersonality" wherein the poet makes a general symbol of his personal experience (OPP, 299). Redefining himself through Yeats, Eliot offers in this essay his mature position on language and social change. It is important for an understanding of the *Quartets'* approach to the meaning of current, catastrophic historical experiences. Embodied in the *Quartets*, and in numerous essays of the period after 1939, this attitude culminated a debate that had begun in *The Sacred Wood*'s attack on Arnold: "Born into a world in which the doctrine of 'Art for Art's sake' was generally accepted, and living on into one in which art has been asked to be instrumental to social purposes, he held firmly to the right view which is between these, though not in any way a compromise between them, and showed that an artist, by serving his art with entire integrity, is at the same time rendering the greatest service he can to his own nation and to the whole world" (OPP, 307).

For all Yeats's importance, however, Dante still dominates the compound. Of him, Eliot says "that of the very few poets of similar stature there is none,

4 Helen Gardner, *The Composition of "Four Quartets"* (New York 1978) 170, 183, [illegible]

not even Virgil, who has been a more attentive student of the *art* of poetry, or a more scrupulous, painstaking and *conscious* practitioner of the *craft*" (CC, 132). Having already written extensively on Dante, Eliot in 1950 means "to talk informally about his influence upon myself," in particular about the philosophy behind the composition of "Little Gidding." He does so in a technical manner, like Poe's account of how he wrote "The Raven," an account the veracity of which Eliot himself doubted (CC, 29–35). So we may also suspect Eliot's retrospect. The concentration on craft turns the passage's "rending pain of re-enactment" into only a craftsman's training. This half-truth eludes admission of the pain of comparing one's own soul to those of the Yeatses and the Dantes.

Eliot spends the first pages of his last Dante essay on the theory of poetic debts, citing his own enrichment by Laforgue and Baudelaire. He reiterates his belief that the young poet should apprentice himself to minor poets, but with his usual genealogical metaphors he cautions that the older poet can learn little unless he faces "exalted . . . distant ancestors" and "great masters," as Dante faced Virgil and as Eliot tried to face Yeats and Dante and Shakespeare. Confessing his earlier anxiety of influence, Eliot now sees how the mature poet can only rise by competition with the great, who will not leave him alone anyway. Praising Shelley's "translation" of Dante in "The Triumph of Life" as better than his own, he states that "the influence of Dante, where it is really powerful, is a *cumulative* influence: that is, the older you grow, the stronger the domination becomes" (CC, 130). "Little Gidding" submits to this domination while inscribing it in the same structure of revisionary control over the precursors pioneered by Dante. This repetition lessens the threat, paying back old debts and stamping new coinages as palimpsests on the old.

Eliot has "ranged over some varieties of 'influence' in order to approach an indication, by contrast, of what Dante has meant to me" (CC, 128). In *The Waste Land*, he recounts, he intended to "establish a relationship between the medieval inferno and modern life," insinuating that to forget Dante, or any past's potential, is a sin of the modern inferno, a symptom if not a cause of its pernicious ennui. The parallel works in "Little Gidding," too, written in reaction to the repetition that was World War II: "But the method is different: here I was debarred from quoting or adapting at length—I borrowed and adapted freely only a few phrases—because I was imitating" (CC, 128). Imitation here acts like translation and transfiguration, differentiated from the shoring of archaeologized ruins. The recollection of pieces joins a larger metamorphic repetition of style, stance, and theme as Eliot identifies with the dead master. If the transumption prevails and the dead join in chorus with the living, then the poetic father does become "like an admired elder brother." In the scheme of generations the anxiety of domination forms a hierarchy of fathers and sons, disparate rival temporalities. In the scheme of poetry, "not in time's covenant," matured poets are as brothers, contemporaneous and adjacent colleagues. Imitation disciplines the poem with a high linguistic standard. The poem undergoes askesis, metering the transfusion from other authors. As Eliot said of Yeats, "The course of improvement is towards a greater and greater starkness" (OPP, 305). The same is said of Dante (CC, 129).

The common stylistic effort, tied to a theme of the "gifts reserved for age," replaces the quest for individual authority, except as it can be made to symbolize the general. Through imitation or repetition, originality exists as the compound of what Dantesque standards can produce through the contemporary poet. In this case, repetition is not death, not the sign of exhausted sensibility or the horror of meaningless recurrence. It is the shared project of poets. Repetition and imitation order history. They interpret discontinuity by an abstraction of the Same, yet remain open to the altered fulfillments wrought by desire, accident, and fate. Thus, Eliot brings Dante to bear upon the morning after an air raid, a modern moment of breakage brought to comprehension by imitation, and the resulting poem supplements what was once the meaning of the *Commedia*. Eliot's emphasis on technique implies that one sustenance he seeks in that morning is the renewed assurance that the tongues of poetic fire can match those of material destruction. The submission of the poem to an impersonal linguistic goal coincides with the effort to place an eruptive event in a consoling frame.

Seven of the first eight lines of the imitation begin with prepositional or adverbial phrases. The syntax dramatizes the key act of placement, difficult when time and seasons are suspended. As Hugh Kenner has noted, "no other *Quartet* is so explicitly located in time as this one in which time is conquered."[5] Still, the reiteration of "In . . . Near . . . At . . . After . . . While . . . Over . . . Between" speaks of a profound difficulty of location. The reader and the text meet, as do the warden and the ghost, at an uncertain intersection of poetic crossroads, turning the streets of London into a literary labyrinth. Eliot's lines are in the first person, but deceptively so, for the singular identity of this "I" is immediately denied by the reader's knowledge that his is the Dantesque "I" as well. This "I" is neither Eliot nor Dante nor any other poet, but an intertextual compound ("I was always dead, / Always revived, and always something other"), "the recognition of a temperament akin to one's own, and in another aspect the discovery of one's own form.

5 Hugh Kenner, *The Invisible Poet* (New York, 1959), 320.

These are not two things, but two aspects of the same thing" (CC, 126). And the encounter cannot be wholly located in the text, for it is with "That pointed scrutiny with which we challenge / The first-met stranger in the waning dusk" that "I caught the sudden look of some dead master." The insertion of the universalizing "we" depersonalizes the encounter, reminding us as readers that the scene is also an allegory of our own meeting with this text, that we are also the "I" and Eliot is also "some dead master." This prefiguration recalls the mix of "I" and "you" in "Song of Myself," which enables a metamorphosis of author into text, text into the fulfilled meaning of the text, meaning into the identity of the reader. Whitman's final lines are also outside time's covenant, in literature's simultaneity. Self-consciously, Whitman's poem addresses the reader across the decades, marking the text as crossroads.

> You will hardly know who I am or what I mean
> But I shall be good health to you nevertheless
> And filter and fibre your blood.

> Failing to fetch me at first keep encouraged,
> Missing me one place search another,
> I stop somewhere waiting for you.

We should also recall the time-traveling of "Crossing Brooklyn Ferry." The uncanny Whitman enters the compound, master of temporal shuttlings and shuffler of pronominal identities.

The "double part" Eliot plays does the poets in different voices. Ecstatic, he is beside himself and compounded, "still the same, / Knowing myself yet being someone other." He is "being" in the "other" as the "other" lives through him, "In concord at this intersection time / Of meeting nowhere." He speaks to himself. The dialogue that follows is the self-reflection of the present conducted through the past, reflected across time and meant to prepare the future. So compounded beyond time, this ghost, unlike Hamlet's father, does not command the son to a stultifying obedience.

> Last season's fruit is eaten
> And the fullfed beast shall kick the empty pail.
> For last year's words belong to last year's language
> And next year's words await another voice.

The ghost tacitly approves Eliot's method, rehearsing its thought and theory while forgiving them. As he is soon to acknowledge, this theory makes his own existence possible in the untimely dawn of this text. The ghost consecrates the poem's askesis, its clear-sighted submission to the ravages of time. The "fullfed beast" aptly images the cycle of poetic usurpation that Bloom has schematized and that Eliot accepts as fate. The distance between time-bound languages, here seemingly so irrevocable, closes even as it is pronounced: this is an imitation of Dante and Yeats, and it does manage to bring "last year's words" to life again in "another voice." Kenner says that "no other Voice in Eliot's repertoire articulates with such authority."[6]

But what is the nature of this authority, and by whom has it been authored? Eliot constructs his authority by a mingled borrowing of tomes and tones. We feel the ghost's authority because a poet has craftily shaped him that way: the ghost is an allegory of authority, built consciously out of the rhetoric of wisdom. This authority is a ghost, the nonpresence and nonabsence of sunlit truth, a compound whose persuasive voice depends on convention, history, and humility. Eliot had once found Yeats "perhaps a little too much the weather-worn Triton among the streams," quoting "Vacillation," a poem consciously appropriated by "Little Gidding" (ASG, 45–46). Eliot works to save his poem from the charge by taming Yeats with Dante. Eliot steals their authority and then makes it speak in his own measure, in the passage where Yeats's dancer moves in Dante's "refining fire."

The fate of ghostly authority sung, "the passage now presents no hindrance / To the spirit unappeased and peregrine / Between two worlds become much like each other." Translated from the distant shore of Hades, the ghost depends on the present and the poet for life and authority, and vice versa. Ritually murdered by beasts, his resurrection can be of use to "next year's words." Feeling the need to mute the voice of Yeats, Eliot inserts a translation of Mallarmé: "Since our concern was speech, and speech impelled us to purify the dialect of the tribe." The allusion, from "The Tomb of Edgar Poe," compounds Mallarmé, Eliot, and Poe together in the craftsman's task. Mallarmé's poem, however, bitterly protests the hostility and incomprehension that met Poe's work.

> Just as eternity transforms him at last unto Himself,
> The Poet rouses with a naked sword
> His age terrified at not having discerned
> That death was triumphant in that strange voice.[7]

It required French translation and imitation to resurrect Poe or at least to mark his grave (a story of transatlantic influence Eliot tells in "From Poe to Valéry" [CC, 27–42]). The dismal ignominy suffered by Poe and revenged by Mallarmé inspires Eliot's own funereal colloquy, his tomb of Dante, Yeats,

---

6 *Ibid.*
7 Angel Flores (ed.), *An Anthology of French Poetry from Nerval to Valéry* (Garden City, N.Y., 1958), 156.

Poe, Shelley, Mallarmé, Shakespeare, Whitman, Swift, and others. Eliot cannot assume Mallarmé's resentful tone, because he is himself a part of the compound. Yeats's voice returns to deliver the final advice on the ironic, sad "gifts reserved for age / To set a crown upon your lifetime's effort," as Mallarmé's crown for Poe becomes Eliot's Yeatsian crown of thorns.

The embarrassment Eliot feels at the Triton's weathered reflections on his aged self prompts him to divide his echo, severing the counsel of wisdom from introspection by dramatically representing it as speech to a disciple. Though the words pertain to the ghost's experience, the pronouns and tone are carefully restricted to avoid self-pity and direct attention toward the aspirant. We sense that these sufferings have been the ghost's, but his particular experience is no more than the general symbol. "First, the cold friction of expiring sense" robs the sensual and sexual of power "As body and soul begin to fall asunder." To this loss of physical powers is added "the conscious impotence of rage / At human folly, and the laceration / Of laughter at what ceases to amuse." These might be the Sweeney poems or the vitriol of *After Strange Gods*.

Such attitudes, self-centered and superior, must yield to the wisdom of humility and repetition.

> And last, the rending pain of re-enactment
>   Of all that you have done, and been; the shame
>   Of motives late revealed, and the awareness
> Of things ill done and done to others' harm
>   Which you took for exercise of virtue.
>   Then fools' approval stings, and honour stains.
> From wrong to wrong the exasperated spirit
>   Proceeds, unless restored by that refining fire
>   Where you must move in measure, like a dancer.

The rending pain of reenactment cuts through the *Four Quartets* and is their subject and technique, as the dancer from Yeats embodies the concord of form and content, of actor and action. Many motives are late revealed: the nostalgia for childhood bliss; adolescent rebellion against home's constraints; the longing for transcendent knowledge; the hope of poetic success; the trials of love; the calamities of history; the desire to restore ancestral orders; the dream of new ships, of a language that could carry exploring old men past Byzantium's glitter to a justified paradise. The "exercise of virtue," in retrospect, had also been an evasion of self-knowledge in a waste of ill-conceived opinions "done to others' harm." Eliot carries Dante's method to its logical conclusion, consigns himself to hell, purgatory, and judgment. The "refining fire" now burning with the announcements of pentecostal flames is a text and a state of the soul: it is a processing of identity through other corrective voices, an intertextual conflagration wherein "you must move in measure, like a dancer." If one reads the scene as, among other things, an interior agon between recurrent self-images, then it epitomizes what Lawrence Lipking isolates as a major purpose of *Four Quartets*: to self-consciously reread the entirety of Eliot's career in poetry, selecting and shaping its fragments into some version of that epic unity or coherent view of life that he believed distinguished great poets from mere versifiers.[8]

The poet and the man measure steps among the living and the dead, choreograph a pattern of connections, displacements, and repositionings. There are no intermissions for the dancer of endless humility, no resting on the ground or in the heavens. This dancer's pained ecstasy is performed in the theater of repetition. Knowledge of self and other comes through representation, as a reading of the dance of estrangements and homecomings, their motives, virtues, and ends. The poet begins and ends on that estranging stage: "I cannot find any alternative for either 'enchantment' or 're-enactment' which does not either lose or alter meaning. 'Re-enacting' is weak as a substantive; and I want to preserve the association of 'enact'—to take the part of oneself on a stage for oneself as the audience."[9] So goes the drama of "impersonality."

With the end of the ghost's speech, the curtain falls on this scene of instruction, while it rises on that of the encompassing poem itself. The theater that is the poem starts up; the reader in the audience watches as the section closes at dawn and reenacts in its ending the beginning of Hamlet.

> The day was breaking. In the disfigured street
> He left me, with a kind of valediction,
> And faded on the blowing of the horn.

Eliot rejected an editorial suggestion by Hayward concerning these lines on the grounds that it would "mean my losing the allusion to Hamlet's ghost," the specter he had not even mentioned in his early essay on the play. The allusion does more than just effect a neat symmetry between the all-clear siren and the crowing of the cock that dismissed Hamlet's father "like a guilty thing / Upon a fearful summons." That moment comes at the beginning of

---

8 Lawrence Lipking, *The Life of the Poet: Beginning and Ending Poetic Careers* (Chicago, 1981), 62–68, 72–76. See also M. L. Rosenthal, *Sailing into the Unknown: Yeats, Pound, and Eliot* (New York, 1978), 45–68.

9 Eliot to John Hayward, September 22, 1942, quoted in Gardner, *The Composition of "Four Quartets,"* 194.

the tragedy, this at the end. The conflation and inversion help to situate this part of the poem as a kind of prologue to what is possible. It holds open the possibility of reversing the tragic course of Shakespeare's play, in which the son is doomed by the return of the dead and the callousness of the living. The horn comes after the destructive night, leaving us in a yet "uncertain hour" to face the days this colloquy has prepared for. The play, the reenactment of these words, is left in the audience-reader's hands. The street has been "disfigured" as well as transfigured. The puns on the former term include ruination, depopulation, and the confusion of destruction. But on this literary street, disfiguration also means the compounding of various poetic "figures" into this "dead master." Language has disfigured experience and made a strange place accessible. Figures are "breaking," sounding a farewell to past identities.

There is "a kind of valediction" at the end of certain speech, a diction of breakings and dawnings that also bids a reverent good-bye to what it disfigures. This valediction forbids mourning, for this morning sees the patterned reconciliation of double parts. The allusion to Donne's poem fits the implication of distance reserved in measurement. Donne and his lady assume their double parts: "If they be two, they are two so / As stiff twin compasses are two." The precision of Donne's conceit and the faith he has in his centering love bring him expertly home.

> And though it in the center sit,
>   Yet when the other far doth roam,
> It leans and hearkens after it,
>   And grows erect, as that comes home.
> Such wilt thou be to me, who must
>   Like th'other foot, obliquely run;
> Thy firmness makes my circle just,
>   And makes me end where I begun.

The circle, so often invoked in discussions of the *Quartets*, appears at first to manage this section of "Little Gidding." It moves from the "uncertain hour before morning" through the "intersection time" and back to the breaking of day. The firmness of the style and the ghost's poetically constructed authority make Eliot's circle "just," as it does justice to each of the many parts played by tradition and the individual talent. Where he ends, with the lessons of the past, is where he sat down to write this "imitation" of Dante. Yet, the foot of Eliot's compass is a ghost, a shadowy figure obliquely running. His ending beginning is a breaking of the circle. The blowing of the horn trumpets the fading of even a ghostly center, leaving poet and reader at the recurrent dawning of the ending. Donne's poem recollects reunion in a metaphor of circumscription; Eliot's poem repeats Donne's and breaks it into reinscriptions that can never be exactly measured.

Breaking occurs in repetition, as repetition disfigures what it represents. Thus, in the light of the eclipse, dawn breaks on the "present," and memory find its vocation.

> This is the use of memory:
> For liberation—not less of love but expanding
> Of love beyond desire, and so liberation
> From the future as well as the past.
>
> (LG, III)

Eliot goes on to reject the notion of memory as nostalgic recollection and to repudiate thinking of the future as if it were simply perpetuation or recovery.

> History may be servitude,
> History may be freedom. See, now they vanish,
> The faces and places, with the self which, as it could, loved them,
> To become renewed, transfigured, in another pattern.
>
> (LG, III)

The same interplay of recollection and repetition pertains to "history." The weight of historical inheritance lightens when "servitude" to the past becomes the "freedom" of transfiguration/disfiguration. The end of Western history, here in England and always, ceases to be a privileged, unique catastrophe. It, too, dismally repeats and must be made the occasion of a renewal sprung from disillusion. Because "history is a pattern / Of timeless moments," Eliot believes that "A people without history / Is not redeemed from time" by forgetfulness or resignation to the Same (LG, V). The timelessness of ghostly moments and their passions depends on the purpose of the historical memory. Condemned to repeat history in interpretation, humanity at least has the option of refusing to repeat it in action. Wars are revenge tragedies, directed at another whose conquest offers the delusion of purgation. Against this, Eliot counsels relinquishment, though not appeasement.

Eliot supports the war against fascism. What he questions, most pointedly in "The Idea of a Christian Society," is the "validity of a civilisation" centered on the economic imperative; a civilization deluded by the promise of recuperated investments, living as if fresh profits could erase the traces of human loss and degradation without accounting for their wastes. Eliot wondered if the combatants were dissimilar only in the degree to which they would brutalize and exploit life for political power and economic gain. Through an odd lens compounded of Marx and Christ, which often yielded strange visions, Eliot interrogated that "organization of society on the principle of private profit, as well as public destruction" reigning throughout the West, connecting the Allies and Axis in a single pattern. On this, that the root causes of the war were economic and spiritual, Pound and Eliot largely agreed. The fires of the war present an opportunity for reexamining the servitude to ruling ideologies perpetuated by corrupt desires and bad memories. Time will reduce all to vanity; freedom may be facilitated by bidding farewell to them, allowing them to vanish in the revision of humility. The war provides the "objective correlative" of the meditation that is "Little Gidding." How we are to recover from it, how its irreparable losses are to be fit into a progressive, profitable philosophical economy, poetry cannot say without disfiguring and disillusioning the partisans on every side.

Incarnating breakage, the war repeats the pattern Eliot finds in memory and literature. In fact, the poems of the *Quartets* link their subjects and levels of discourse in a general philosophical argument about the economy of waste and enrichments, in which the war is but another, if terrifying, example. In section 5 of "Little Gidding" the argument moves from the particular manifestation of the war to the general reflection on loss, value, and the aberrant economy they figure when covenants of measurement are suspended. Adjusted to the surprises at play in remembrance, the poem economically transfigures its own recollections of itself: "What we call the beginning is often the end / And to make an end is to make a beginning. / The end is where we start from." Previously we had started from "home." Home ends now; our being at home in the poem is ending. We shall soon start up from the text, go home, begin again, and find home transfigured as this text produces a different text from the one we had initially figured. The "home" we come to is a process of understanding characterized by its identification with the structure of language.

> And every phrase
> And every sentence that is right (where every word is at home,
> Taking its place to support the others,
> The word neither diffident nor ostentatious,
> An easy commerce of the old and the new,
> The common word exact without vulgarity,
> The formal word precise but not pedantic,
> The complete consort dancing together)
> Every phrase and every sentence is an end and a beginning,
> Every poem an epitaph.

(LG, V)

The ideal "commerce" set off in parentheses might be assimilated to a theology of poetic formalism or unanxious influence were it not equally asserted that every poem is "an epitaph." The poem, or any utterance, elegizes. It commemorates loss, marking the grave of that passionate moment language can only approach belatedly in a representation. And it marks its own grave, too, dies onto the page: "And any action / Is a step to the block, to the fire, down the sea's throat / Or to an illegible stone: and that is where we start." We are at home with illegible stones, in the graveyard/library of tumbled expressions, "dancing together" with the dead.

The act of writing violates the calm of supposed securities, marks the whiteness of the page and moment with a darkness into which we read. Reading starts with the illegible, and the illegible is its end. Reading repeats the act of disfiguring/transfiguring as it produces yet another pattern of language: every interpretation an epitaph. That pattern in turn appears illegible to the future that castrates, murders, loves, and resurrects it. Inscriptions, like the entombed Madeline Usher, break from their crypts with meanings beyond the figured purpose, called from their graves by their living literary lovers. Writing and reading supplement each other's destructive acts, die into each other's embrace, are each other's ghostly double, and reproduce life in their narrative. The process is memory's, too, and also conditions the formation of knowledge about identity, time, and being: "We are born with the dead." The poem will itself die and in its final stanza be born with the dying lines gathered up and returned from their previous incarnations. These last lines of the *Quartets* create an Eliotic palimpsest, its form of repetition perfectly tuned to the theme of a renewal in illegibility, an ecstatic unknowing of past versions.[10] Unceasing exploration arrives "where we started" and knows "the place for the first time" as an epitaph, thus a liberation. To know "Through the unknown, remembered gate" is to write/remember the place out of place, to be in a present place and know it as the displacement of where we have been. What was remembered was unknown, and it is known now by a repetition that occurs "When the last of earth left to discover / Is that which was the beginning." By repeating his American beginnings ("the source of the longest river / The voice of the hidden waterfall / And the children in the apple-tree"), the poet unknows them. They are severed from enchainment to past meaning or future deliverance and are made sights of rediscovery. They were

> Not known, because not looked for
> But heard, half-heard, in the stillness
> Between two waves of the sea.

10 For an elaborate analysis of Eliot's technique in *Four Quartets*, see James Olney's reading of these lines in his *Metaphors of Self: The Meaning of Autobiography* (Princeton, 1972), 260–316.

These moments, "Quick now, here, now, always—" signify the evanescent and ungraspable sensations of the moment, always flickering just before language arrives to take them home and make them known. Known, like woman to this imagination, they fall. The imagination may figure for us, remembering, the idea of a virgin present "Between two waves of the sea," like Aphrodite sprung from the breakers of past and future. In the wake of this breaking is not an absence, but the fully resounding language of ghostly compounds, voicing real beauties.

Understanding this loss and gain, readying conservation for metamorphosis into projection, the imagination, compounded of emotion and intellect, suffers a sea change to "A condition of complete simplicity / (Costing not less than everything)." Possessed by way of dispossession, the poet treasures remembered beauties as potential repetitions, recurrences exceeding the taxonomy of living and dead, same and different—and in that excess known for the first time. These categories break, in literature as in life, when the covenant of identity and abstraction is distracted, revolved as in Dante's final canto of the *Paradiso* by the loving will that explores the illegible details of passionate moments. The writing of exploration recovers by awakening/dying into the eternity of transfiguring, disillusioning dawns. An altered sense is given to Emerson's prophetic assertion at the beginning of *Nature* that "the sun shines to-day also." Night and day forever interpenetrating, the divine sun always a ghost on the horizon, losses are tossed up, and memories supplied that they may burn to light the presence of day.

> And all shall be well and
> All manner of thing shall be well
> When the tongues of flame are in-folded
> Into the crowned knot of fire
> And the fire and the rose are one.

Eliot ends reenvisioning Dante's paradisial end, recalling the ingathering of "substances and accidents and their relations" that are "bound by love in one single volume." Disfigured by Eliot, the vision incorporates an image of passionate and destructive change in the connotations now carried by flame and fire. This fire combines the actions of disintegration and revision in producing its transfigurations of the past. The flames of poetic tongues gather, laced rather than fused, in a knot that reserves their individual strands as they are tied together in a singular incendiary device. The "crowned knot of fire" stands for the torchlight that is tradition, the intersection world, the suspended timing of texts and repetitions burning to illuminate the darkness they discover at beginning and end. A dazzling metaphor, the fiery knot lights the paths of literature and consciousness, consuming the fuels of desire. So conceived and put to the torch, "the fire and the rose are one." The rose of perfection, recollection, and order is also "in-folded" in the erotic and literary fire, thus uniting the hue of natural passion with the color of the tongues of flame to form a final figure for personal and poetic history.

The rose garden is on fire. The desire for unity, consummation, bliss, the eternal recurrence of the Same, undergoes its last askesis. Polysemous, the emblem of the rose unites nature's Eros with poetry's theology in order to refine the longings and delusions of both. As a knot of fire, the rose becomes an eternal flame of enlightened disillusionment, a process of love that gains energy from its losses of identity and grows strong in the repetition of other times it heatedly ingathers. Love, as the overcoming of self-consciousness and the repetition of an ancient pattern in modern figures, renews itself just as the poem is renewed by entwining itself with its precursors. Purged of its illusions, the rose dances in the "tongues of flame" that repeat and inspire it, re-marking the measures of poetry and love.

TOM AND HUCK ON THE RIVER

*Another analogy we shall now trace, that every action admits of being outdone.
Our life is an apprenticeship to the truth that around every circle another can be
drawn; that there is no end in nature, but every end is a beginning; that there is
always another dawn risen on mid-noon, and under every deep a lower deep
opens.*

Emerson, "Circles"

The only great metaphor Eliot developed further after the *Quartets*
was that of the river. The flow of fire and that of the river join in an
image of brilliant indeterminacy and supple emotion. The river that had been
diverted through Heraclitus and Conrad runs finally back to Twain, as it had
briefly done at the beginning of "The Dry Salvages." Anglican Eliot had always enjoyed playing bad boy Huck in the guise of sly Possum. Now he
drops even that foreign mask and hops aboard the raft for the trip home.
In 1950 he writes a now notorious introduction to an English edition of
Huckleberry Finn—having read it, he claims, for the first time. An American
book at last gains admittance to Eliot's "tradition," testifying to an extraordinary outpouring of emotional response as the matured poet finds his portrait
in the errant boy: disillusioned by his father, talkative, crafty, warm-hearted,
and innocent, Huck personifies the promise and tragedy of the New World's
sons to Eliot's newly opened eyes.

Making Huck's tale his own, Eliot owns up to his American sources. After
the long years abroad he comes home in this essay to acknowledge American
fluidity and the textual philosophy it determines in its courses. The occasion
returns him to his boyhood on the Mississippi, and the essay steadily transfigures itself into a lifetime's retrospect and lesson. This self-fashioning goes
far toward explaining the "reading" of *Huckleberry Finn* in these much disputed pages. Refined in exile, Eliot rediscovers himself and his home in late,
altered fulfillments of what they early figured, discovers their purpose only
after a lifetime of dispossession and estrangement (which are purposes of the
river). Pouring himself into the figure of Huck, Eliot fondly misreads his
counterpart in a reverie of self-reenactment.

No worldly success or social satisfaction, no domestic consummation would be worthy of him; a tragic end also would reduce him to the level of those whom we pity. Huck Finn must come from nowhere and be bound for nowhere. His is not the independence of the typical or symbolic American Pioneer, but the independence of the vagabond. His existence questions the values of America as much as the values of Europe; he is as much an affront to the "pioneer spirit" as he is to "business enterprise"; he is in a state of nature as detached as the state of the saint.[1]

Literally canonized, Huck takes his place with "Ulysses, Faust, Don Quixote, Don Juan, Hamlet and other great discoveries that man has made about himself." Twain's Huck and Mississippi River are transfigured by Eliot when he suddenly capitalizes their nouns, constructing a prose-poem allegory of the "Boy" and the "River": "We come to understand the River by seeing it through the eyes of the Boy; but the Boy is also the spirit of the River." Boy and River characterize the Eliotic saint and his peregrinations through mystery toward death, leaving life along the way in eddies of meaning. The career of Huck and that of his river are made one, and one with Eliot's. Broadening the metaphors, he channels his currents of significance like tributaries to his streaming text. The River is not only Life and Death: its movements, confluences, unpredictability, threat, and promise stand for and re-enact those of writing as well. Pouring into the changeable identity of the River are its other incarnations in Eliot's thought: Tradition and Christianity. The confluence of these two with Writing and the River is apparent, for the River is a "River God, and it is the subjection of Man that gives to Man dignity. For without some kind of God, Man is not even very interesting."[2] Writing is the strange God of Eliot's essay, and of his life. The River is the Text, upon which Eliot floats and comments between frightening forays to shore. Huck is the poet of this text, his flowing speech embodying the spirit of the language river. And Huck is Eliot, too, the projected repetition of young Tom Eliot of Saint Louis, who lit out for the territories of Europe rather than suffer the civilizing strictures of his family. The River flows back now from his beginnings, as an image of the philosophy with which he has ended, as an emblem of how a text is and how the self can be. Reading, repeating, reinscribing Eliot's closing at the close of this reading, we see infolded a striking parable of a poet's life, concluded with a characteristic use of quotation that positions Eliot once again as the haunted seeker of new horizons.

1 Samuel L. Clemens, *The Adventures of Huckleberry Finn*, ed. Sculley Bradley *et al.* (2nd ed.; New York, 1977), 335.
2 *Ibid.*, 329, 333, 334.

Like Huckleberry Finn, the River itself has no beginning or end. In its beginning, it is not yet the River; in its end, it is no longer the River. What we call its headwaters is only a selection from among the innumerable sources which flow together to compose it. At what point in its course does the Mississippi become what the Mississippi *means*? It is both one and many; it is the Mississippi of this book only after its union with the Big Muddy—the Missouri; it derives some of its character from the Ohio, the Tennessee and other confluents. And at the end it merely disappears among its deltas: it is no longer there, but it is still where it was, hundreds of miles to the North. The River cannot tolerate any design, to a story which is its story, that might interfere with its dominance. Things must merely happen, here and there, to the people who live along its shore or who commit themselves to its current. And it is as impossible for Huck as for the River to have a beginning or end—a *career*. So the book has the right, the only possible concluding sentence. I do not think that any book ever written ends more certainly with the right words: "But I reckon I got to light out for the Territory ahead of the rest, because Aunt Sally she's going to adopt me and civilize me, and I can't stand it. I been there before."

INDEX

DATE DUE

MAY 1 '92			
APR 27 '93			
JUL 12 '94			
JA 05 '98			

DEMCO 38-297